Schooling, Childhood, and Bureaucracy

Schooling, Childhood, and Bureaucracy

Bureaucratizing the Child

Tony Waters

palgrave
macmillan

SCHOOLING, CHILDHOOD, AND BUREAUCRACY
copyright © Tony Waters, 2012.

All rights reserved.

First published in 2012 by
PALGRAVE MACMILLAN®
in the United States—a division of St. Martin's Press LLC,
175 Fifth Avenue, New York, NY 10010.

Where this book is distributed in the UK, Europe and the rest of the world,
this is by Palgrave Macmillan, a division of Macmillan Publishers Limited,
registered in England, company number 785998, of Houndmills,
Basingstoke, Hampshire RG21 6XS.

Palgrave Macmillan is the global academic imprint of the above companies
and has companies and representatives throughout the world.

Palgrave® and Macmillan® are registered trademarks in the United States,
the United Kingdom, Europe and other countries.

ISBN: 978–1–137–26971–3

Library of Congress Cataloging-in-Publication Data

Waters, Tony.
    Schooling, childhood, and bureaucracy : bureaucratizing the child /
Tony Waters.
        p. cm.
      ISBN 978–1–137–26971–3 (hardback)
      1. Education—Social aspects—United States. 2. Public schools—
United States. 3. Education—Aims and objectives—United States.
4. Child development—United States. 5. Bureaucracy—United States.
I. Title.

LC191.4.W38 2012
306.43′2—dc23   2012013077

A catalogue record of the book is available from the British Library.

Design by Newgen Imaging Systems (P) Ltd., Chennai, India.

First edition: October 2012

10 9 8 7 6 5 4 3 2 1

Printed in the United States of America.

Contents

Tables and Figures

Tables

Figures

Acknowledgments

Books about schooling always have their origin in our earliest memories of schools and teachers. My earliest memories go back before I started school, since my father James E. Waters was a teacher and later a principal/superintendent in small school districts in Olancha and Julian, California. My mother Virginia Benson was an occasional substitute teacher in the same schools. Both later became administrators for the California State Department of Education in Sacramento, California, and so the dinnertime talk about schools continued.

Other acknowledgments include Mrs. Skagen, my first grade teacher and my second grade teacher Mrs. Kellogg at Julian Elementary School. The principal/superintendent was my father, James E. Waters. It was there that I first became vaguely aware that graduate study and original research was possible while he was writing his EdD Dissertation.

More vivid K–12 experiences were in Sacramento, where I went to Alice Birney Elementary School (third through sixth grade), Sam Brannan Junior High School, (seventh through ninth grades) and J. F. Kennedy Senior High School (ninth through twelfth grades). I learned a lot about the reproduction of society and its hierarchies in these schools. This happened both at Brannan, where I was sent to the vice-principal's office for getting punched and beaten (twice), and at Kennedy High School, where I was briefly expelled for "defiance," when as an act of civil disobedience, I refused to purchase the prescribed green and gold uniform for physical-education class. So at Brannan, I learned that it is not always the best strategy to respond to bullying in kind, and that vice principals are not very good at sorting out the facts behind adolescent fisticuffs. At Kennedy, I learned that bureaucratic institutions really do not like to be challenged and will protect their own power even when confronted by a righteous sixteen-year-old rebel. Adolescents can be bullies, but so can school administrators seeking to protect their vision of what a school should be.

Besides these experiences, I had very positive experiences at Kennedy High School with History teacher Mr. Cozzalio, Speech and Debate teacher Miss Coulter (who became Mrs. Skelton), and Journalism/Film teacher Mr. Clazie.

Also from my high school days, I have particularly warm memories of Mrs. Gee Albietz' "Practical Politics" class, and my political work with Tim Zindel, in particular, where we had a quixotic run as the "High School Student Lobby" in Sacramento from about 1974–1976. Mrs. Albietz encouraged creativity and exploration. Other high school students participating in this effort included Anne Basye, Lisa Negri, and Jordan Budd. During this time, we managed to talk the California State Legislature and Governor Jerry Brown into dropping the requirement for physical-education attendance in California from four years to two years. We also talked them into briefly legalizing smoking areas on high school campuses, an effort assisted by Brownsville Station's raucous song "Smoking in the Boy's Room," which I highly recommend and is still available on YouTube. Alas, our successful lobbying effort was eventually eclipsed by the antismoking campaigns of the 1980s.

In terms of great teachers I have known, Ajaan Champa of Nareerat School for Girls in Phrae, Thailand really stands out. She helped me with my Thai when I was in the Peace Corps in 1980–1982, and thousands of Thai girls passing through her English classes. If you don't believe me, read Karen Connelly's memoir about being an exchange student in Phrae, *Dream of a Thousand Lives*. Everything she wrote about the wisdom of Ajaan Champa is true!

More conventional academic acknowledgments are due Professor Gertraud Koch and Nadine Hoser from Zeppelin University in Germany where I was an exchange professor in 2007–2008. This manuscript had its final origins in that year, and the theoretical bent toward Bourdieu comes from conversations with Gertraud in 2008. These conversations continued with Nadine both at that time, and later when she became a Fulbright Scholar at CSU Chico in 2009–2010.

John S. Benson, an Education Professor at Minnesota State University, Moorhead, also pops into my life at different times, and often sets my mind off in new ways when thinking about schools.

Sarah Schaale helped with the editing of the final manuscript in 2010–2011. Andrew Berzanskis has also provided editorial encouragement since this book was conceived.

I also experienced K–12 a second time via my children Christopher and Kirsten Waters at schools in California, Tanzania, Switzerland, and Germany between 1994–2010. My daughter Kirsten once lamented while living in Germany that she would rather be simply a daughter than a research assistant. Maybe she had a point, but her insights into the daily routine of German schools were textured, nuanced, and prescient. Our son Christopher also added to the international flavor this book has by somehow attending high school in the United States, Tanzania, and Switzerland,

and still graduated. He is now in graduate school in the UK, so his international education continues. Our children's education was put into context by my wife Dagmar Waters, who was trained as a teacher in Germany and later taught in both Germany and Tanzania. Together we experienced the vagaries of the American school system via our children. This book is in large part a response to our shared confusions.

This book was finished at the Department of Sociology, California State University, Chico, between 2008 and 2012, which as usual is a collegial and congenial place to teach, write, and think. Many of the theoretical points raised in this book had their origins in conversations with first Cynthia Siemsen, who shares the thrill I find in discussing esoteric points in social theory, classical, and modern. Professor of Health Service Administation Rick Narad, "Honorary Sociologist," always provides a good place to bounce ideas about the tensions between the communitarian and libertarian elements of American society which underlie this book. Practical engagement with the public schools was facilitated via Sandy Shepard and the staff of "Resources in International Studies Education," a staff development program on the Chico State campus.

Two other colleagues played an important, but maybe unwitting, role in the development of ideas in this book. Andy Dick, Bill Rich, and I spent time together in California prisons from 2008–2010 evaluating vocational-education classes. Ironically Prison classrooms highlight the high value placed on the *habitus* of learning, schooling, and teaching in American society. Musing with Andy and Bill about the contradictions involved in teaching in prison contributed much to this book. A rant by Bill one day while driving down California's Central Valley about the nature of behaviorist reasoning in the operation of prisons and the prison classroom, led to the broader assertion in this book about the role of such reasoning in the administration of schools in general.

Colleagues from the Sociology Department who deserve mention are Dan Pence, Paul Lopez, Janja Lalich, Nandi Crosby, Chunyan Song, Marianne Paiva, Laurie Wermuth, Scott McNall, and Jim Sutton. Other colleagues at Chico State from whom I've learned a lot include Steve Lewis (History), Susan Place (Geography), Lee Altier (Agriculture), Rob Burton (English), Jim Jacob (International Relations), Joel Zimbelman (Religious Studies), Hilda Hernandez (Education), and many others. Scott McNall was also provost of Chico State when this book was conceived. As Provost, he created an academic culture that also values research and writing at a state university. For this I am grateful. He continues to offer sound advice as a not-so-retired fellow sociology professor.

I would also like to acknowledge the more distant scholars on whose ideas this book is based, but who I know mainly through their writing.

Durkheim, Weber, and de Tocqueville are all liberally cited. Less cited are Rousseau, Wollstonecraft, Marx, Engels, and others of the classical tradition who wrote directly and indirectly about the influence of schooling on social life—they are still influential. Likewise in modern sociology Michael Young, Pierre Bourdieu, Annette Lareau, Fernando Rodriguez, John Meyer, Bruce Fuller, Omar Lizardo, and G. William Domhoff are occasionally cited here, though not in proportion to their influence. Their insights into social inequality influenced my thinking. Scholars from outside who contributed include James Scott, Jonathan Kozol, David Brooks, Robert Frank, Ross Dougthat, and James Q. Wilson.

Also not cited are the many students I have met in Chico, Thailand, Tanzania, Germany, and China whose thought and conversations influence my thinkings. Talking with them about their experiences has influenced this book deeply.

Friends, teachers and school administrators in the Grass Valley, California, area who contributed informally (and perhaps unknowlingly) include Geri and Dimitri Nibbs, Terrianne and Alan Dunn, Kate and Dave Morehouse, Mrs. Halvorson, Mr. Hale, Jim Nieto, and Mrs. Uppman. Vigorous discussions on Jeff Pelline's blog Sierra Foothills Report from 2009–2011 also contributed to my thinking about schools. Bloggers included (among others) Jeff Pelline, Chris Bishop, John Stoos, Greg Goodknight, Ben Emery, Steve Frisch, Kate Hancock, Kim and Barry Pruett, Michael Anderson, Douglas Keachie. We didn't always agree with each other, but usually maintained a civil tone (with an occasional nudge from Jeff).

The contribution of the educational historian Diane Ravitch is obvious from the citations in the book. The contribution of her blogging partner, Deborah Meiers is less obvious, but was also influential to me. In the early days of writing this book, I responded to her posts on the Building Bridges blog at Education Week. Her private e-mails gently nudging me, particularly about issues of educational inequality and social stratification in the United States, were appreciated.

Introduction

Authors know how books develop out of the writing process. Sometimes this process results in what was predicted in the original book proposal, and as a result, the proposal can be adapted into a foreword or preface that explains how the book started (that's the proposal part), and later developed toward its conclusion. In a general way, this book started in this fashion, too. It started with the general idea that the relationships between schooling and bureaucratic action are in tension, and this leads to an emotional tug-of-war between parents, teachers, and the public. This happens between parents who have an interest in a single child—their child—and a broader society, which has an interest in reproducing itself via the same children.

This book started as an investigation of how the bureaucratized school rationalized children and produced adults in a predictable fashion. Bureaucracies do this using rationalized techniques, even though they are working with the people for which we hold the most sentiment: children, who we like to think of as being society's most precious resource. Emerging from this is a tension between parents, emotionally engaged with how their child is raised, and teachers, who are hired in the rationalized bureaucratic labor market to instruct and *care*.

But, a second type of preface results from a book in which the author is surprised by the conclusions. This happens because the writing process itself results in unexpected conclusions not anticipated in the original proposal. This happens because writing itself sharpens thought. Prefaces are prepared for such books after the book is done and explain how unexpected conclusions were reached—usually the book proposal itself is then discarded.

This book leans toward the latter of these two extremes. The original emphasis is retained but adds a new element that emerged from the writing process, which is the addition of the social theory of the classical sociologists Emile Durkheim, who described education, and Max Weber, who described bureaucracy. This emphasis continues with a critique of "behaviorism", with a dash of the more modern school of Pierre Bourdieu, who emphasizes the importance of *habitus*, i.e. the unspoken predispositions and habits which underlie the social institutions and social hierarchy that make society possible.

I am a "classically trained sociologist," meaning that I have imbibed liberally in the sociological works of Marx, Weber, Durkheim, and others from the classical age of social science. I teach the class "Classical Social Theory" frequently, and even in classes that do not require it, I typically insist that students go back to the sociological basics that are the classics.[1]

But, I did not start this book as a "back to basics" sociological treatise. Rather I thought it would be an explanation of how emotionally grounded parents and bureaucratically hired teachers negotiate with each over how children are raised; originally I thought that such ideas were best expressed without reference to classical sociological theorists who are not well understood by line-level educational administrators or professors in education schools. But, I fear it has ended up this way, just like my other books. Thus this preface has become a statement about why I think that classical sociological concepts are important for sociology, in general, this book, in particular, and especially the field of education.

The original proposal for *Bureaucratizing the Child* began as an attempt to use sociological explanation to describe what I experienced as a child, a parent, and an educator of college-aged students. Since I myself was in high school in the 1970s, I have wondered about what was being done to me by the school system. But like most people, I did not necessarily analyze the school systems I was embedded in by stepping back from the institution, and then looking at it in order to evaluate its larger role in shaping the large amorphous phenomenon known as society.

Rather in trying to figure out what was wrong with the schools, I read books from the field of education that discussed how and why the schools had yet to be perfected. Such books emphasized policies and practices, which, if adopted (or defeated), the authors believed would make for a better school system. Thus I read books about the necessity of testing, school management, how adolescent personality is shaped, how schooling creates/blocks economic opportunity and how schools, deal with racism and segregation. I read about child development, how curriculum was designed, along with many other subjects. None of them wrote about the sociological classics of Marx, Weber, or Durkheim. They did not return to basics, so I assumed that I would not need to do so as well, even though my focus on "bureaucracy" did imply at least a tip of the hat to Max Weber.[2]

Taking for granted the nature, desirability, and power of education is common in the literature emerging from the education schools and teacher programs, and even in the sociology of education. Thus, there are books, studies, reports, and articles referring to the successes and failures of different curricula, equal opportunity, racial discrimination, teaching techniques, etc. Such books and articles are typically rooted in psychology, political science, economics, or sociology. The sociological books about inequality and race in the schools rely on the writings of people like James Coleman (1966), Diane Ravitch, (2010) Linda Darling-Hammond (2010), Thomas Espenshade and Alexandria Radford (2009) and others, who developed data explaining the persistence of racial discrimination in the schools, why America's schools have lower test scores than other countries, the value of cultural capital in preserving elite advantages, the relationship between income and education, and other factors reflecting social anxieties. Thus, from educational psychology, we get ideas about how to measure different types of intelligences, evaluations of curricula, evaluations of aggression, and so forth. From the field of education itself, we get claims about classroom-management techniques, evaluations of large schools vs. small schools, the nature of educational leadership, treatises on new testing and legal requirements, laments about school systems in crisis, arguments about the role of religion in the classroom, assertions about the relationship between democracy and education, adolescent psychology, new methods of math instruction, and new methods of reading instruction. What these typically positivistic, quantitative studies share is an assumption that there is a definable "something" that the schools should be doing, and doing better. Thus, going through the stack of books near me at the moment, I can find books that wonder about:

- Why aren't university graduation rates higher than they could be (see Bowen et al 2009)
- What is the relationship between education, technology, and income? (Goldin and Katz 2010)
- What does educational testing really tells us? (Koretz 2009)
- How do we go about learning to think like historians (or not)? (Wineburg 2001)
- What are the implications for the legal doctrine of the "best interests of the child"? (Goldstein et al 1996)
- How do you protect your junior high schooler from the cliques where there are Queen Bees and Wannabes? (Wiseman 2002)
- How did we go about learning to read and write in Colonial America (Monaghan 2007)
- What makes a good school principal? (Sergiovanni 2006)

What all these books share is a taken-for-granted idea that schools and public education are both critical to society and a good thing, but without asking the question about why that is the case. Rather the books assume that schools exist and are legitimate and appropriate to modern society. Because they assume this, the questions they ask are not broad, theoretical ones about why modern society itself needs schooling, or even more generally, why apparently modern society itself is not possible without mass schooling. Instead, they avoid seriously addressing this "what is education?" question, by burying it in platitudes about the importance of knowledge, wisdom, the nobility of the teaching profession, the centrality of the schools for promoting patriotism, democracy, science, and other skills valued by the same society. The desirability of schooling is taken for granted as a question long-ago settled by the ancestors.

And indeed, I share their enthusiasm for the modern norms for providing schooling for all, and also hope that it can be made better, more efficient, and more effective. But I still want to ask, why is it that every government in the world, as well as most of the citizenry, believe so deeply in schooling? What is it about schooling and school bureaucracies that is so elemental to modern society? And more specifically, what does this tell us about the nature of schools and society in the United States today?

And this is why in this book I return to the fundamentals of the classical sociology of Durkheim and Weber in particular, in asking why schools order modern society the way they do. The questions classical social theory asks are about the origins of modern society and educational institutions and go to the roots of who we are as a modern people, and what we will be as a people in the future. Or to borrow the prose of poet T. S. Eliot:

> As only the Catholic and the communist know, *all* education must be ultimately religious education. . . .
> Questions of education are frequently discussed as if they bore no relation to the social system in which and for which the education is carried on. This is one of the commonest reasons for the unsatisfactoriness of the answers. It is only within a particular social system that a system of education has any meaning. If education today seems to deteriorate, if it seems to become more and more chaotic and meaningless, it is primarily because we have no settled and satisfactory arrangement of society, and because we have both vague and diverse opinions about the kind of society we want. Education is a subject which cannot be discussed in a void: our questions raise other questions, social, economic, financial, political. And the bearings are on more ultimate problems even than these: to know what we want in education we must know what we want in general, we must derive our theory of education from our philosophy of life. The problem turns out to be a religious problem. (see Eliot 1950/1932, 132)

Reintroducing Classical Theory

The original proposal for this book was written *sans* classical theory, including any reference to the religious element Eliot wrote about. I thought at the time that my questions about the relationships between teachers, parents, children, and schools could be answered by analyzing schools directly rather than returning to the basics of what schooling means for modern society. And I thought that understanding how bureaucratic action structures schools would be enough to explain why schools are so "dysfunctional," as many critics from inside and outside the education establishment claim. My thought at the time was that in the process of writing about the nature of bureaucratic action in schools, I would offer a new way of understanding why modern society is so persistently unsuccessful in this task.

Instead, what I found is that at its very heart is the distinction that Emile Durkheim made in the early 1900s between the nature of education itself and pedagogy, that he sees as a separate issue and separate process. His definition of education, as with his classic definition of religion, rests on its relationship to morality:

> Education is the influence exercised by adult generations on those that are not yet ready for social life. Its object is to arouse and to develop in the child a certain number of [specific] physical, intellectual and moral states which are demanded of him by both the political society as a whole and the special milieu for which he is specifically destined. (Durkheim 1956, 71).

The advantage of this definition is that it can be applied not only to modern bureaucratic systems of schooling but traditional methods of training in premodern societies as well. Durkheim's definition acknowledges also that education is about preparation for "specific milieu" in adulthood, which by implication acknowledges the division of tasks within a society. Most importantly, it assumes that education exists in a social milieu in which the past generations are communicating with future generations about the demands that will be their very "destiny."

But over the last one hundred years since Durkheim (1956: 71) wrote, the field of education was redefined. Instead of abstract metaphysical discussions about the nature of education, what dominates is what he calls the question of pedagogy. Thus education as an academic field is focused on pedagogical issues like graduation rates, test scores, the relationship between education and technology, school management, and the range of other issues discussed in the books mentioned above. In the modern field of education, pedagogy is focused by an assumption that school management is a question of scientific management. As a result, it is believed that evidence-based understandings of learning, child psychology, and management are appropriate for school management. But few of the books described how education creates a shared social destiny by creating a connection from a past generation, to a future generation, which is at the heart of Durkheim's definition. Rather they assume the older generation will control, finance, and manage schools in a fashion that permits few surprises in how destiny is planned and shaped.

But almost by definition, destiny and the future cannot be planned as neatly as the scientific managers of our schools often pretend. And indeed, this is ultimately what much of today's education literature is ultimately about: pedagogy as a "science" that is easily rationalized and bureaucratized to create a "system." The problem as Durkheim points out, is that pedagogy is still ultimately rooted in the values and moral states demanded by political society, and not the other way around; teaching methods, curriculum, etc., always follow politics and morality. And finally, values and morals are not, by definition, scientific, no matter what direction a statistical regression equation may point.

Beginning with Durkheim

Thus, my contention is that any a discussion of the sociology of education should start with Durkheim's distinction between education and pedagogy. When this is done, the tensions inherent not only in the American education system but any education system are explained. This is because at the heart of modern schooling is the paradox that the unemotional rationalized school usurps a portion of emotional parenting from the family. And in the modern democratic world in which the state is assumed to be "of the people," it does this with a large bureaucracy staffed by people (i. e., teachers) who are paid to *care* not only on behalf of the state, but on behalf of the parents.

Of the classical sociologists, Durkheim lectured and wrote most directly about education, schools, and pedagogy. Indeed, he was a professor of education in Paris and delivered lectures to every potential teacher in France for several years in the early 1900s. But again, his lectures were not about the issues of today's education schools. They were *not* about state-written curricula, leadership, No Child Left Behind, the latest research on student achievement, reading recovery techniques, or the benefits of radical pedagogy. In fact they were not just "how to do it" lectures, but extended philosophical discourses on why, how, and where schools fit into modern society. Durkheim saw schools as the expression of what a modern society seeks as its future. Durkheim saw schools as being one of the clearest expressions of the "collective conscience" of society, and the place where the established social order sought to reproduce itself. Thus, his lectures and writings about education were extended disquisitions on the consequences of these relationships, which he claimed were inherently "functional" in the sense that the education system sorts humans into the different occupations that those in power believed were needed to reproduce the status quo. Ironically, assuming that schools are inherently functional means that they cannot be dysfunctional, no matter how prescient the critique of pedagogy may be. The implications of this assumption of functionality have been taken up most directly by Durkheim's sociological successors, such as Randall Collins and Pierre Bourdieu, both of whom wrote extensively about how modern educations systems reproduce systems of social stratification, and will be discussed below.

Weber: Bureaucracy Reemergent

The mechanism of the modern bureaucracy is what structures the transmission of morality that Durkheim, Bourdieu, and Collins describe emerging from national schooling systems. And because national school systems exist in the modern state, they necessarily are *bureaucratic*, a term more often used today as an epithet, rather than the analytical theory first proposed by Max Weber and elaborated upon by modern social scientists like James Q. Wilson (1991).

Weber (1947: 196–244) never made excuses for the nature of bureaucracy—he found it to be unsentimental, arbitrary, rule-bound, inhuman, and abusive of power. Indeed, the rule-books, impersonal officialdom, calculation of advantage, and hierarchy at the heart of bureaucratic action repulsed him. Having acknowledged that, though, Weber still found bureaucracies to be the best method known for organizing complex human activities, if for no other reason, because the alternatives are even worse. After all the alternative to hiring a bureaucratic professionalized staff, and creating bureaucratic rule books and law, is the whimsical rule of the absolute ruler who delegates duties to sons and retainers in unpredictable and arbitrary ways. Modern government is not possible in such a system, nor are modern schools. For that matter, modern factories with their complex division of labor are also not possible either. Bureaucratic order is necessary for modern life, including the schools.

But for mass public schools, bureaucracy presents a problem, as is described later in this book. The problem is that unsentimental specialists—bureaucrats—are hired in the labor market to transfer the hopes and dreams of the older generation to the younger one. Hopes and dreams, though, are inherently sentimental actions and fit poorly with rationalized bureaucratic procedure. Bureaucratic officials—also known as teachers—are thus presented with a dilemma. How are they to undertake the sentimental task Durkheim described, i. e., to "arouse and to develop in the child a certain number of [specific] physical, intellectual and moral states", when they are really just bureaucratic figures hired in the unsentimental labor market?

The solution to school administration is typically to break the task into a series of incentives and sanctions designed to elicit desired responses by using the behavioristic assumptions behind incentives and sanctions. Such carrots and sticks are, of course, the type of simplifications that bureaucracies and modern management do best. The result is that everywhere the product of schools is defined as it would be in factory, in terms of inputs and products. Personnel—teachers—in turn are managed in the same fashion.

The use of sanctions and incentives to induce compliance is of course an old phenomenon, described perhaps best by the early twentieth-century behaviorists who explained how mammals respond to needs and fears. This is of course a system that fits well with the simplifications needed by the modern bureaucracy. Thus even though academic psychologists have long discarded such explanations as overly simplistic, and reductionist, behaviorists continues to dominate bureaucratic management for the very reason that they are useful simplifications. But while simplistic and reductionist explanations may frustrate modern psychologist, they are exactly the quality that makes modern administration possible.

Optimists and Pessimists: School Bureaucracies and the Social Construction of Society

The result of these tensions is that schooling is always controversial, both in the cultural and economic realm. Any decline in the quality of schooling is likely, according to the popular view to lead to the imminent moral, cultural, and political demise of the republic. This conclusion is reached at the same time that other wags point out that the current generation is among the most promising ever and will surely do well with the trust passed on to them. Such contradictory views inevitably result in an argument about who is right or wrong, with evidence marshaled one way or the other.

The bottom line is that I am back to my old trick: Classical Social Theory. In the end, the reason why people like Weber and Durkheim (and at least a few of their successors like Wilson, Collins, and Bourdieu) are important is that they posed timeless questions, which are ultimately unanswerable using the tools of bureaucrats, including the tests, measures, and assessment goals of the positivistic social sciences, the econometric models of the business schools, or the psychometrics of the standardized test. None of these measures identify the political dynamics, morals, and values underlying the school system itself. They are really only what Durkheim called "pedagogy."

So ultimately schooling, with its emotional relationship between the older and younger generations, and the legitimation of a past and future, is not something that can be dissected and manipulated as statistical regression equations measuring the relationships between expenditures, salaries, curricula, test scores, parental education, and other common variables. Any book about schooling that pretends these questions can be answered authoritatively is inherently limited, because it assumes that there is a definite "finish line" (to borrow the title of a recent book, see Bowen et al 2009) that can be achieved by manipulating inputs. In education as defined by Durkheim, there is no such thing as a "finish line," or even "graduation." A race for a finish line may be a good metaphor by which to organize an educational bureaucracy and its pedagogy, but it is a poor one for writing about how the current generation of elders create the programs that create their successors in society.

To a large extent, this is why much of the existing education literature with its lack of attention to classical social theory, is dissatisfying. It assumes that schooling systems and education policies address an identifiable problem, which people in the past, present, and future will all agree is the same. But this in fact is something of a fool's errand. Every generation has provided for the education of their children. In doing this, morals, values, and culture are assumed to be, at least implicitly, predictable and changeless and will be passed on. Despite this society is never changeless despite such assumptions. In spite of it all, adults are still persistently trying to engineer a more perfect society via mass public-education bureaucracies. This fact is what I find most intereating. After all, no matter what a parental generation does with its children, those children will still create the future new social world. What other result could there be?

The "So What?" Factor

Fundamental to books about education—and other subjects—are the final recommendations. Sometimes, this is called the "so what?" factor. Meaning after reading the book, what am I supposed to do differently?

This book focuses on the paradoxes of the modern mass education system. In doing so it points out that many of the problems of the schools are inherent to modern society itself. School reform, and school change, is a constant because society always changes. Thus despite the fervor and emotion that goes into the school reform *du jour*, there will always be a demand for the next reform.

Society and its schools are about ideals, and ideals are always a search for a more perfect future. As will be identified in this book, this has happened in patterned ways during the last 150 years of school reform in the United States, and elsewhere. What is more, these patterns will be the basis for how the United States muddles through—always unsuccessfully—educational reforms of the future. More educational crises will be announced, and the schools will continue to be used to address the most intractable problems that adults see in society. That the schools should and can be used to strive for such high ideals should be no surprise. But it should also be no surprise that the highest values will not be achieved. The message of this book, then, is to not be surprised when this happens. Or, in other words, seek your highest ideals, but don't get an ulcer when they are not achieved.

Chapter 1

Bureaucratizing the Child: The Manufacture of Adults in the Modern World

This book is about two things. First, it is about the fact that modern schools everywhere take dependent, impulsive, illiterate, and stubborn five-year-old children, and create predictable, compliant, literate, and docile adults. Every modern society routinely and efficiently does this in a process lasting about 12 years. Every modern society does this even though it intrudes upon one of the most emotionally charged relationships known, that between a parent and child.

And secondly this book is about how when every modern country creates adults, they do it the same way: by creating a large bureaucracy controlled, albeit unevenly, by a central government. But despite the ubiquity of this task, citizens in every society are convinced that the education bureaucracy is inadequate and must be reformed. They do not want to make minor incremental changes; rather they call for radical reform. At all time and in all places it seems that the political powers are dissatisfied with the way schooling is done and insist that unless it is reformed and radically improved, the very nature of society is at stake. I could use many quotes to illustrate this point, but one from the conservative President George H. W. Bush, speaking in the early 1990s, is illustrative:

> Don't be content with incremental change . . . but "assume that the schools we have inherited do not exist." This was no ordinary task, said President [George H. W.] Bush; the redemption of society was at stake: "Think about every problem, every challenge we face. The solution to each starts with

education. For the sake of the future—or our children and the nation—we must transform America's schools. (Tyack and Cuban 1995, 110)

The irony of course is that President Bush's call in the 1990s is hardly unique to the 1990s. By then, educational reform was already a focus of US national politics for over a century, and the assumption that the schools "we have inherited" were inadequate and in need of radical quick reform was just as persistent. So despite these demands, radical reform was never achieved, and as the newest reformers—those of the twenty-first century—are quick to point out, the United States continues to operate schools based on what they call nineteenth century assumptions about learning, the agricultural season, and the purpose of schooling.

Blame for this presumably urgent need for school reform is placed on a variety of conditions, such as culture, families, teachers, unions, state governments, federal governments, and perhaps most commonly, "the bureaucracy," which manages the enterprise. Educational bureaucracy never seemingly delivers the reform that powerful leaders like President Bush always promise. This book is about how and why I think that this dissatisfaction with schools is a constant and something that by its very nature is idealized, and therefore something never achieved. Because I think it is a constant, I do one thing that other books do not: I do not offer "the solution" to the problem of the schools. Rather, I present public schools as modern human institutions that are everywhere needed but nowhere admired. By approaching the problem this way, I hope that those interested in the public schools, while continuing their attempts at reform, will come to recognize that there are no silver bullets, and in fact a level of dissatisfaction is inherent to a bureaucratic activity that intrudes so deeply into one of the most emotionally charged relationships in society—that between parent and child. Thus, even though I agree generally with President Bush that schools are elemental to addressing "every challenge we face," I doubt that another transformation of US schools will result in the redemption of society. So the elemental nature of the school system explains why, in every modern country, vast public bureaucracies are created to administer, regulate, and monitor the creation of adults out of the raw material parents provide, this is, children. But, it still does not explain why there is such dissatisfaction with public school bureaucracies in so many places and times. But look at the complexity of the problem provides context.

Public schools hire a teacher corps, develop a curriculum, supervise those teachers, and ultimately evaluate whether the types of adults desired were produced. Schools do this by slowly but surely introducing the child to a broader world that goes far beyond the confines of the immediate family. This introduction is done in a systematic fashion that creates an adult who then produces another child. This child, under ideal circumstances, repeats the process recreating a status quo. Or as Emile Durkheim (1956, 71) said at the turn of the twentieth century:

> Education is the influence exercised by adult generations on those that are not yet ready for social life. Its object is to arouse and to develop in the child a certain number of physical, intellectual and moral states which are demanded of him by both the political society as a whole and the special milieu for which he is specifically destined.

Durkheim's is not the radical call for action that President George H. W. Bush called for in 1990, but a conservative definition that emphasizes the timelessness of education as the means by which elders exert their influence in a way that will create the ideal future society that the elders dream of. This is a moral and emotional task. The bureaucracies humans create to educate children are by their nature unemotional and rational, even though the ties of humans to each other and their children are *not* rational and rooted in what Durkheim calls morality. In effect, the vast public education bureaucracies—Durkheim's political society—facilitates what movies like *The Lion King* call the "circle of life."

Kitschy movies aside, the ubiquity of vast public bureaucracies focused on the raising and training of children raises three questions, which are rarely asked. First, why is it that virtually every country invests so much in such a system rather than leaving education to parents? Second, why do most modern parents readily surrender this most emotion-laden relationship to a soulless, impersonal, and bureaucratic arm of the state? And finally, and perhaps more to the point, how has this system, despite so much dissatisfaction, nevertheless become routinely accepted and taken for granted?

My thesis is that the function of bureaucratized public schools as pseudo-parents is so taken for granted that it is part of the "high modern ideology" justifying today's complex world James Scott (1999) described. Education is part of this ideology in the same way that individual rights, egalitarianism, freedom, free markets, and self-determination are, and needs to be analyzed in the same fashion. This book provides a look at mass public education by evaluating the implications of this ideological commitment. I do this by evaluating the process by which the state uses rational bureaucracies to intrude deeply into the socialization of children via universal public school systems. My primary example is the United States, but I think that the basic paradoxes underlying what is described here could be found in any other modern country.

Schools as Factories

In the 1800s, corporate bureaucracy was developed as the ideal means to turn bales of cotton, linen, and wool into garments. The factory did this by breaking the many tasks involved in the growing of fiber, spinning of thread, weaving of cloth, cutting of cloth, sewing of garments, transport of finished clothing, and finally, the marketing of fashion into hundreds of separate tasks. Some of these tasks were done by humans, but as time passed, more and more of them were done by labor-saving machines, which because they are not human, are easier to manage than the workers they replaced. These tasks in turn were coordinated by a global marketplace, in which shareholders and their corporate bureaucracies produced profits for investors. The institution created to organize the corporations was the large, impersonal corporate bureaucracy in which tasks are divided up, hierarchies created, and rules developed to ensure that reason and science maximize production and profits. Such a bureaucracy of course abhors emotional human qualities that are unpredictable and unsuited to scientific bureaucratic management and the production of clothing. The bureaucracy in turn is held accountable by shareholders who assiduously watch the bottom line of financial profits.

Also in the late nineteenth century, the other organizer of complex tasks, the government, quickly adapted the bureaucratic model to organize its duties, such as the processing of legal cases, administration of foreign affairs, development of national defense, and organization of the emerging welfare state. They used the same organizational principle, i. e., the bureaucracy, even though there is really no easy way to calculate a "bottom line" for many such tasks. Indeed, instead of profits, the bottom line for public bureaucracies are in fact *feelings* about the nature of hope, safety, security, relationships, and justice. Nevertheless, despite the focus on tasks that are not easily rationalized as profitable, these bureaucracies still took advantage of reason and science to organize their tasks, while abhorring the unpredictability of human interaction and emotion to structure what they did.

In this context, the government's biggest peacetime task, the mass education of society's children, emerged as a bureaucratic duty, just like the manufacture and marketing of cloth. In the United States, this happened between about 1890 and 1920 as business leaders and professional educational psychologists took an interest in schooling as a way to create a new army of disciplined industrial workers (see Cuban 2005). But in the case of the schools (as well as other government bureaucracies), this created an inherent paradox. The paradox is that a large hierarchical and inhuman bureaucracy, designed with reason and science, intruded into the sentimental and emotional relationship between a parent and child. Unpredictable human interaction is inherent to the operation of schools in ways that it is not in, say, a tire factory.

As in corporate bureaucracies, sentiment and emotion were pushed aside in the new schools serving the masses of urban children in particular. This was particularly the case for the early twentieth century people financing a new system of mass education and the educational psychologists interested in developing curriculum consistent with their scientifically derived understandings which were so successful in modern factories. In this context, by the 1920 schools were asked to generate test scores and other statistical measures of how they were doing; it was assumed that just as the corporate bureaucracy must point to profits, and other government bureaucracies report success, so should schools point to test scores. Such evaluations drew on their cousins in the private sector because, after all, schools are bureaucratic factories: It is just that the inputs (uneducated children) and products (educated adults) are different. All they had to ignore were the feelings parents, teachers, and society indeed have for their children.

Because the schools are a bureaucracy, the rationalization of inputs and outputs is seemingly straightforward. You put in cash and children, and after 12–13 years society receives fully formed tax-paying adults in exchange. Of course it is not that easy because children—and adults— are not just a product like a bolt of cloth produced during the Industrial Revolution, but are, well, children. And children typically have parents, and indeed often themselves eventually become parents. And most importantly, the parent-child relationship is one of the most inherently emotional. Thus by definition, such a relationship is difficult to manage in a scientific, rational, and unemotional fashion. Nevertheless, the public school bureaucracies at least pretend otherwise by emphasizing both the "whole child," while emphasizing that they are at the same time the simplified bureaucratic category "learner."

Despite the differences between children and bolts of cloth, just like consumers, legislators and taxpayers insist on a "return" on *their* investment in public education tax dollars. Thus, programs, curricula, teachers, principals, testing regimes, and so on, are compared on the basis of cost and efficiency. The evaluative language of education as a result reflects that of science and business: Accountability and evidence are emphasized in assessing program effectiveness. As a result, evaluation of schools reflects the same economic reasoning that consumers use at Home Depot to compare lawn mowers.

Long-time observers of this business-like evaluation, such as Jonathan Kozol (2007,4) critique this approach:

> State accountability requirements correlated closely with the needs and wishes of the corporate community, increasingly control the ethos and the aims of education that are offered to the students at . . . schools . . . even though the best of teachers are not merely the technicians of proficiency; they are also ministers of innocence, practitioners of tender expectations.

What Kozol is in effect doing is pointing out the paradox: Even though public school teachers are employees of a massive rationalized bureaucracy, which utilizes business principles to organize themselves, their task is one of tending to those people—i. e., children—who are by definition "innocent."

Children as Raw Material

Children are the peculiar raw material which schools put on their production line. When they arrive at five years old, they are typically illiterate, innumerate, cannot locate themselves in the national order, and believe in the tooth fairy. As one teacher also noted, they are "leaky" in the sense that they excrete various bodily fluids unexpectedly during the day (Kozol 2007, 84). Thirteen years later, virtually all are literate, some can do calculus, and others volunteer to preserve an abstract national order in the military. The few who believe in the tooth fairy are likely to justify their faith with the philosophical reference to Western traditions, and few of them ever leak tears, at least in public. Most importantly, perhaps, as a group, they have come to docilely accept that the moral order is good, and that they too, will reproduce it, completing again that kitschy circle of life described by both Durkheim and *The Lion King*. Such is a mark of a successful school bureaucracy.

However, keep in mind what the schools started with. The characteristics of the five- and six-year-old child, whom they receive, are the opposite of what the modern employer, university, or nation wants of citizens or adults. Child-development specialists describe the five year olds who schools accept as raw material in terms of psychological and social qualities: Their attention spans are short, eye-hand coordination clumsy, and vocabularies limited. They are likely to break into song spontaneously and cry inappropriately. Their primary social relationships are with their family, and they do not have a concept of belonging to larger social groups, like the nation, company, or work group. Because they are impulsive, they do not know how to wait in line. They lose their temper easily, and are focused on immediate needs and goals. Many cannot tie their own shoes, button their own shirts, or learn when to wipe their noses. Nor can they organize daily tasks without immediate and sustained supervision. This is the raw material that the public schools take and put through that 12- to 13-year process. At the end, the schools produce someone who retail stores and restaurants seek to put behind cash registers to patiently conduct tedious transactions for an eight-hour shift. Factories of course seek them out to operate the modern complex machinery of assembly lines. Universities and colleges are ready to train them further, and militaries are ready to recruit them.

Perhaps the most surprising thing is that this process of creating adults, which is inherited from nineteenth-century factories, somehow works. After all, the military, universities, and employers all routinely demand a high school diploma as the basic indicator of adult competency. They even demand this qualification before all others.

Bureaucratic Schools: Behaviorism and Bureaucratic Management

Despite the inherent complexity of public education, the mechanism for creating, or rather re-creating, society has all the marks of that modern business-based bureaucracy first created in industrial England and described by Max Weber (1947, 196–244) in his classic essay "Bureaucracy." Bureaucracies, Weber emphasizes, are large impersonal institutions designed to accomplish a complex task. They do this in a way that is "rationalized," and therefore impersonal. In seeking to rationalize their tasks, Weber writes that bureaucracies become efficient by creating and following written rulebooks, procedures, laws, and so forth, which inherently simplify the real world. They measure success by calculating profits and seek to do so in a predictable fashion. In doing this, bureaucracies seek to control parameters that are otherwise unpredictable and uncontrollable. Ingredients and procedures that do not fit this model are simply discarded. The impersonal bureaucracy ruthlessly eliminates actions that are contrary to its interests.

School bureaucracies do this while creating adults who undertake a defined series of tasks, which any number of interchangeable persons can do competently. On the school's assembly line, the state, teachers, businesses, parents, and others in position of authority define what the product will become. In this respect, they are similar to employees in global corporations, or even drill sergeants, creating and delivering a new product (Kozol 2007, 4). In doing so, simplification occurs to the product on the assembly line of the school. But doing this assumes away childhood with all the idiosyncrasies that often delight us as parents and grandparents.

The school bureaucracy creates a curriculum to control the manufacture of adults in a fashion that is efficient, predictable, and calculable (Ritzer 2008). In doing this, the bureaucracy monitors carefully the efficient utilization of its financial resources, as well as the quality of its manufacturing process. How much money is spent to successfully produce an adult, and what is the acceptable level of spoilage in the process? Measures of bureaucratic success are taken at every step. Seat time is counted, and testing begins early and often. Success at preventing drug use is calculated, and juvenile delinquency rates monitored and correlated with specific programs. Surveys are distributed to calculate the success of safe sex (or no sex) programs. Political points are scored when graduation rates are rising. The quality of adults created successfully is monitored through graduation rates and acceptances at Ivy League colleges. Industrial wastage is calculated in terms of drop-out rates, teen pregnancy, drug-abuse rates, and incarceration rates.

Such formulae for economic efficiency fit particularly well with behavioristic theories emphasizing incentives and penalties in gaining compliance. Thus, school administrators focus on the role of carrots and sticks in structuring school curriculum. The implicit idea is that the social contract is a giant system of incentives and penalties, in which good behavior is rewarded, and bad behavior penalized by a testing regime, economic system, and vice principal in charge of discipline. B. F. Skinner and Ivan Pavlov were perhaps the most well-known proponents of this view, which made the point that learning is the result of conditioning using a system of incentives and disincentives.

Admittedly, behaviorist approaches to child development have long since been eclipsed by cognitive and developmental psychology, among other academic approaches. Indeed, today within academic psychology, such approaches are viewed as simplifications of more complex processes that are mediated by developmental imperatives, patterns of cognition, and so forth. However, a simplistic behaviorist view of childhood still fits well with the rules, hierarchies, and efficiencies demanded by what the French sociologist Pierre Bordieu called the *habitus*, the often unspoken predispositions and habits that make institutions possible. This is most obvious in the management of private corporate bureaucracies, where the manipulation of pay incentives, rewards of status enhancements, and threats of punishment are routinely used by rule-keeping human resources departments to manage large, diverse workforces. This happens irrespective of the fact that behaviorism is routinely dismissed as "old hat" by the discipline of psychology. The fact of the matter is that behaviorist principles still provide factory owners and managers with blunt but effective tools to induce the type of compliant coordinated action needed from their workforces.

A *habitus* of behaviorism is used in school bureaucracies, too. Despite the decades of findings about child development, schools are still large bureaucratic institutions seeking to regulate and condition children in predictable ways. Not surprising, their bureaucracies are structured by systems in which incentives and punishments are used to seek compliance and develop habits. Testing regimes, hiring and promotion regimes, grading, detention policies, and so forth all assume that individuals are sensitive to incentives and punishments, as indeed they are, at least in the short run. In a place like the United States, steeped as it is in the principles of the capitalist marketplace, such an ideology meshes well with the dominant economic ideology of capitalism, irrespective of what modern psychologists may have found.

Still there are paradoxes in using a model of production for schools rooted in the creation of textiles and inanimate widgets. Most basically, unlike cloth, the object on the production line of public schools is not inanimate; likewise humans, in general, and children, in particular, are more unpredictable than the engine-powered looms of the Industrial Revolution. Such unpredictability is abhorred in any rationalized bureaucracy, even to an extent that education bureaucrats try to wish it away, by claiming that they can produce a specific product, be it test scores, workers, good behavior, or the host of other disembodied characteristics at the forefront of debates about schooling.

Complicating matters more, is the fact that schools do not have total control of the nurturing process. As teacher advocates are always quick to note, parents and others have their children for more hours than the schools do. Despite the ubiquity of the schooling, responsibility is still shared primarily with parents who often have an intensely personal, emotional, and unpredictable investment in the same children the school bureaucracies simplifies as "learners" and monitors through the prism of test scores. It's as if the people who tapped the rubber trees were allowed to take home the half-finished tires each evening to tweak the product and evaluate the quality of the manufacturing process.

As I wrote above, the biggest paradox is still that humans are not strictly speaking a product of society like tires. Rather they *are* society, and they have an *emotional* interest in their role in society. This remains the case despite the fact that cold, calculable bureaucracies resist all such emotional and irrational considerations.

Formal and Hidden Curricula

Schools are part of the reproduction of society in both formal and informal ways. The formal ways are apparent to anyone who has ever paid attention to a congressional debate about education or meetings of a school board. The formal curriculum is specified in curriculum frameworks, published in textbooks, embedded in graduation requirements, examined on standardized tests, and described in school mission statements. In the modern capitalist United States, it typically includes reading, writing, mathematics, and other skills, which are widely acknowledged to be important in the workforce. In deference to parents, and reflecting American beliefs about the equality of opportunity, there are also statements that the school will help *every* student realize a vaguely described potential in a future job market and that no child will be left behind in this process.

This explicit formal curriculum reflects ideals about the role of education in serving the economy and preserving equality of opportunity. But there is also an implied or hidden curriculum, which is rooted in the need of society to recreate that status quo (Bourdieu and Passeron 1977/1990). An important consequence of such hidden curriculum is that students are tracked toward different roles in the work force, typically based on the social class they are born to. The American assignment of children to schools based on residence is the most important guarantor of this—neighborhoods reflect socioeconomic status, and so, as a result, do their schools. Until the 1960s tracking was also done explicitly and on the basis of race. As a result, working class and African American students were routinely tracked into vocational-education programs.

With internal tracks for the assignment of students to particular classes, by extension tracking becomes a self-fulfilling prophecy. Such tracking emerges in a social world that uses schools to notionally recreate the morals of society, including its hierarchies and inequalities, factors that both Bourdieu and Passeron (1977/1990) and Collins (1971) describe as latent functions of schools. For example, when schools for working-class and minority students provide vocational tracks they do so at the expense of college-preparatory tracks. By the same token, when schools for upper- and upper-middle-class students cut vocational courses and add college preparatory Advanced Placement and International Baccalaureate programs, students are steered away from vocational education. Since in the United States, there is economic segregation by neighborhood, and school assignment is by residence, schools tend to reflect the characteristics of the neighborhood with respect to variables like economics, ethnicity, and social class. Note that this tracking is not by explicit policy—to do so would be to defy explicitly egalitarian ideals. Rather it is done in the name of preserving neighborhood integrity, or other institutions, which emerge from the overarching class system. The result is that the socioeconomic inequalities between schools become implicit and hidden—a consequence of the engrained habits, dispositions, and accepted social networks.

Formal and Informal Curriculum: Social Stratification, *Habitus*, and Schooling in Modern America

In complex societies like the United States, there are different roles for adults to play, both in the labor market and as citizens. As many social scientific studies have shown, these roles are made available to individuals in fashions that reflect preexisting stratification system, among which are social class, ethnicity, gender, and race. These preexisting roles reflect the legitimacy assumed for the preexisting system, and its need to re-create and legitimate its own hierarchies and values. School systems are among the most important institutions needed to perpetuate the habits, disposition, and legitimacy that permit this to happen in an orderly and peaceful fashion, a process Pierre Bourdieu (and others) describe as *habitus*. The consequence is that individuals, sensitive to the nuances of their own social world, are uncomfortable with those above them and dismissive of that below them. As a result, such class-based activities form the basis for the cultures of both social class and status groups. Such an approach creates an understanding of inequality and the attitudes that justify a system of inequality. For this reason, people like sociologist Annette Lareau (2003, 276) find this approach much more appealing than more general "culture of poverty models," which blame inequality on the putative values of the poor, which are simply described as being dysfunctional relative to those of a particular elite.

Habitus is ultimately what the contrast between the explicit and hidden curriculum of the schools is all about. At the explicit level, it is about creating the habits described in textbooks—and school mission statements. Typically it is assumed that a population sharing literacy conventions, spelling conventions, ways of looking at numbers, understanding about the history of "us" and "them," geographical facts, citizenship, approaches to science, and the range of other beliefs that make up society is a good thing. As a result the explicit *habitus* of the classroom is evaluated by large bureaucracies using standardized tests like the SAT, Stanford-Benet I. Q. test, Trends in International Mathematics and Science (TIMMS) exams, various achievement tests, and so forth. Students who master the *habitus* with high levels of proficiency are rewarded. Those who have lower levels are ignored or even penalized. Those who do well take the values of this system for granted, admire those who also do well and are dismissive of those who do poorly. In other words it encourages what is known in popular language is a system of "kiss up/kick down." But ultimately, such tests, rooted in elaborate psychometrics though they may be, can only reflect the *habitus* of a particular culture—however that particular culture defines its own values.

But differential socialization is ultimately what makes modern society with its elaborate "division of labor" and its hierarchies possible. What does an understanding of the education system imply? What is advantaged, and what is disadvantaged? This can be discussed by evaluating the measurement instruments, curricula, and other artifacts of the bureaucratic system reveal underlying values and morals. For example, in the case of the SAT, it is primarily about English reading vocabulary, English writing conventions, and mastery of algebra and geometry problems that are valued above all else. Most other potential *habitus* are not measured and are in fact ignored. Among the most obvious of potential subjects ignored are mastery of any language except American English, British writing conventions, trigonometry problems, natural sciences, theology, artistic conventions, music appreciation, sociology, geology, mastery of popular-culture trivia, philosophy, ethics, and other subjects. In other words, the hidden curriculum favors English, math, etc., at the expense of other plausible skills. More importantly, it privileges the ideologies of democracy and capitalism, which underlie modern American society.

Bourdieu points out that the capacity and power to privilege one type of *habitus* over another is inherently a prerogative of political power. Someone holds power to determine what will be emphasized and legitimated at school, and what will not. Not surprising, the curriculum identified as important emphasizes that which has made themselves successful. These become the cultural "taken-for-granteds" reflecting shared norms. Such shared norms vary from country to country and from school system to school system as is briefly discussed in chapter 10. This hidden curriculum is why Americans become Americans, Finns become Finns, middle class become middle class, etc.

A good example of how implicit and embedded in cultural taken-for-granteds spread through a culture is found in Annette Lareau's (2003) study of child rearing and schooling *Unequal Childhoods*. She demonstrated the persistence of such hidden curricula is not only the consequence of decisions by schools but interacts very much with the manner in which families from different social classes raise their children in Pennsylvania. She studied two types of families, one that was working class and engaged in "natural growth," and the other that was upper-middle class and focused on a style of child rearing she called "concerted cultivation."

First there were families who engaged in the "concerted cultivation" of their children by speaking with them frequently, engaging them in organized activities (often sports and music) early and often, and engaging frequently with teachers. Lareau contrasted this to a more "natural growth" style of child rearing that emphasized informal play groups, unstructured time, and less direct interaction with adults. Concerted cultivation children, Lareau writes, tend to be from families that had college degrees, were upper-middle class, attended schools focused on formal academics, etc. Teachers in the United States are by definition members of this status group that includes the approximately 30 percent of adults holding Bachelor's degrees. Lareau writes that children from such families have larger vocabularies by the time they began school (a skill measured on standardized tests but a more stressful upbringing. They also learn about the culturally appropriate ways to make demands of institutions—in short they are habituated to accept the power of the upper-middle class and are and upper-middle-class adults.

The parents of children from "natural growth" families, on the other hand, tend to come from families that did not have college degrees (i. e., about 70 percent of all adults in the United States), and had less stressful upbringings in which unplanned activities and small friendship cliques were important. Interactions with adults were fewer, and these families and their children were more likely to accept without question the decisions of teachers, principals, and others in powerful roles, even if it was not in their own interest, or violated explicit rules. Children from such "natural growth" families did have ambitions to attend college consistent with the values of those above them in the social hierarchy, but often were not pushed into the courses that would qualify them for college study. The end result was that these children tended not to start college, and even if they did, they did not in the long run finish. This was not due simply to innate ability, quality of available schooling, or diligence. Rather it is due to the different patterns of interaction that reproduce preexisting systems of social stratification, i. e., *habitus*, the implicit but "hidden" part of the school curriculum.

Egalitarianism, Individualism, and Utilitarianism: The Origins of American *Habitus*

Alexis De Tocqueville (1836/1990) wrote his classic *Democracy in America* in the 1830s emphasizing the contradictory role that three ideas play in American culture and, by extension, American *habitus*:

1) egalitarianism
2) individualism
3) utilitarianism

The culture de Tocqueville described of course had not yet invented the continent-straddling school system that socializes children today. But his description of American society did describe persistent values, and he also described the vocabulary that reformers still use to frame arguments about school reform even today. Central to this vocabulary is dogma about the pragmatic utility of education for individual and society, and the role that schooling plays in guaranteeing equality of opportunity.

Such terms as egalitarianism and individualism are of course vague. Nevertheless, they are significant. As de Tocqueville noticed in the 1830s, such values do underlie the US culture and its institutions. In the United States this combination of individualism, egalitarianism, and pragmatic utilitarianism has resulted in a distinctive morality with respect to education.

The contradictions created by such practices emerge in the design of American schools in many ways, such as the comprehensive high school for children of all abilities until age 18. This happens even as stratification by individual ability in grades 7–12 via advanced classes is established, at the same time tracks for vocational education are marginalized. It is this context that gave birth to the "Individualized Education Plans" of the Americans with Disabilities Act. Curriculum itself was pragmatically tied to what "needs to be known" at the succeeding level, or in the workplace while vague goals like "critical thinking" are simultaneously pursued. Such conundrums continue to drive American policy 150 years after de Tocqueville wrote about them. Thus policymakers simultaneously seek to generate equal access, develop every child's unique abilities, while ensuring that policies are useful in the job market. In short, the result is a bundle of contradictions, as policy makers seek to reconcile what are in fact competing values.

For policymakers in the United States, it is not surprising that such tracking by academic ability at early ages is associated with long-term racial and ethnic inequality in employment markets. Hyperindividualism meanwhile created an unusual nationwide achievement standards demanded by the federal government to ensure that "no child is left behind." The strong sense of individualism is in fact particularly salient in the context of a broader utilitarianism, which is, by de Tocqueville's reasoning, a key part of the American *habitus*.

The *habitus* of American utilitarianism, egalitarianism, and individualism is persistent across time in American education and has implications for how students lead their future lives as members of professions, social classes, and ethnic groups. One influential early twentieth century reformer, Ellwood Cubberley expressed this utilitarian ethic in 1916 even more bluntly than today's reformers:

> Our schools are, in a sense, factories in which the raw projects (children) are to be shaped and fashioned into products to meet the various demands

of life. The specifications for manufacturing come from the demands of twentieth-century civilization, and it is the business of the school to build its pupils according to the specifications laid down . . .

Elsewhere, Cubberley went on to add the obvious policy implications:

> We should give up the exceedingly democratic idea that all are equal and that our society is devoid of classes. The employee tends to remain an employee; the wage earner tends to remain a wage earner. (Quoted in Cuban 2004, 1)

No matter how distasteful this sentiment sounds in 2012, what Cubberley is doing is simply highlighting the contradictions in an American *habitus,* which policymakers continue to wrestle with almost one hundred years later.

Past, Present, and Future Adults as Products

Despite the fact that bureaucratic structure is inherent to schools, mass public education deals with two important qualities that other public bureaucracies do not. First the product created—adults—is self-reflective. This means that the factory's product can turn around and evaluate how well the factory did, whether as future parents, voters, employers, or citizens. Second, the school inherently inserts itself into the emotionally charged, parent-child relationship. Both conditions ultimately defeat the point of using the scientifically rational process assumed by any bureaucratic organization.

No matter how much they may wish, what this means is that ultimately, the product of the schools is not simply rationalized test scores and crime rates, despite what rules, laws, budgets, and politicians may assert. Rather schools produce emotional and self-reflective adults who themselves create a future society. Inevitably, this creates a peculiar dynamic in which society reflects on its past, while also creating the parameters for a hoped-for future. Imagine if those like automobile tires, which were shaped and molded by a factory, were able to then turn around, critique the factory, berate the factory owner, and then redesign the tire-making equipment? Because they are self-reflective, each generation of tires would have a self-serving bias—a belief that their generation of tires is special—and that they can create a new generation of tires even better than what their parents created.

But with children the product is even more complicated than self-reflective tires. After all the raw material is not rubber but *children,* in which old habits are reproduced at the same time as a new and different future is created. Schools may be designed on a bureaucratic model borrowed from factories, but again the product is embedded in emotions—qualities rational bureaucracies abhor. The result of course is the constant demand for education reform and dissatisfaction with schools.

Teachers in the Middle, and Why We Are Always Unhappy with the Schools

There is a nice Latin legal term to describe what the schools do as *in loco parentis*, in place of the parent. Legally and socially, the schools act in the place of the parent and presumably in the best interest of the child. But this ultimately is only a convenient legal fiction, since a bureaucracy never feels the same emotional attachment to a child that a parent does. The parent-child relationship is an *emotional* one, and while no matter how much a bureaucratic school system claims otherwise, the relationship between a teacher hired in the labor market and a child sent to the school by the parent is not. Likewise, no matter how efficient they may claim to be, schools cannot produce a calculable bottom line or value per dollar invested. They may improve the ubiquitous test scores, but the real return—a satisfied parent, a pleased public, and a decent future is always elusive and never rationalized.

Teachers, hired in the impersonal labor market, balance on the edge of this paradox more than most of us. Trained and hired for a specific bureaucratic task, they are assigned the general job of creating a responsible adult using prescribed bureaucratic rule books and curricula. In the political realm they are often held accountable to this idealized standard; but that idealized standard hides behind the hidden curriculum described above. The hidden curriculum of the schools ultimately has embedded in it a hidden job description for teachers that requires them to not only be a disinterested bureaucrat but also be an adult who—*in loco parentis*—bonds emotionally with each child. Ultimately such social bonds imply emotional attachments between teacher and students, products that cannot be readily measured. This is important too, because as with parents, schools are not about creating widgets or tires, or even test scores, but creating people and their future society, which is by definition unpredictable, immeasurable, and embedded in moral definitions of what is right and good. This paradox rests in the dissonance between the explicit goals of the school and its implied goals. Where this dissonance is ignored and unacknowledged, there is likely to be dissatisfaction.

I will admit that this does not answer the question of every administrator, parent, or citizen frustrated with school reform, wanting to know "what can be done?" or even the "so what?" question such a paradox raises. Indeed, there are really only two logical ways to work outside this paradox, both of them unsatisfactory. First, don't use bureaucracies to raise your children but invent another system that will not endanger their health and welfare even more. The second is to simply stop loving and caring for your children as individuals and accept that the bureaucratic school system produces a product, and not human being. Both have been tried and both found incompatible with a decent mass society.

For example, homeschooling is in effect a school created outside the bureaucracy, at least with respect to the "hiring" of a teacher who is usually also the mother. Homeschools can occasionally be extraordinarily effective when a parent does it for their own children to whom they are emotionally attached. But the opportunity costs to the individual parent are great, and all the efficiencies of the bureaucratic organization are lost; most modern parents do not have the inclination to take on a full-time teaching job at no pay, even for their own children, much less other people's children. On a more general level, semiprivatized charter schools also meet this criteria, but as with homeschools, they are schools that only give the illusion of liberation from heavy-handed bureaucrats, and old-time faculty, but do so by shrinking from the demand of the larger system to educate *all* children equally (see Kozol 2007, 38).

This though is not a new observation. For example, demonstration schools, the earliest of which was created by John Dewey at the University of Chicago in 1899, are often associated with universities are boutique schools as well. In other words, the product of a school system that is not bureaucratized may be decent for a small number of children—estimates of those enrolled in such schools in the United States are typically about 1–2 percent. But despite heroic efforts to increase their use for mass reproduction for the general school population has been unsuccessful despite decades of trying.

As for the second alternative, simply acquiescing to the overall power of the bureaucracy, and in effect admitting children are the responsibility of the state, also has been tried. Indeed, in the twentieth century, the state took control of childrearing in a variety of authoritarian and totalitarian societies such as Germany under Hitler's National Socialists, and Soviet Union and Mao's China under the Communists. Such efforts often end catastrophically. In short, while such systems can be implemented for the masses, they risk basic human decency. Even in the less authoritarian societies of the freer west, such methods are also occasionally used in juvenile correctional institutions, orphanages, and even some foster-care systems.

Such institutions are expensive and have proved to be poor substitutes for an emotionally engaged parent.

Parents, with all their flaws and emotions, are still preferable to the state; schools themselves even with the power and efficiency of the modern state still need parents to parent, just as the vast majority of parents need mass public schools to educate.

While I hope this introduction highlights the reasons why mass public education is always a politically trying and emotionally perilous endeavor, I have not yet answered the two questions I asked earlier. Why do so many governments everywhere accept responsibility for such a complicated and perilous endeavor, and why do parents everywhere seek to surrender their children to a soulless bureaucracy? In a general way the answer is that as Durkheim wrote about education: it is because modern identity and social life are very much wrapped up in where and how schooling is done. So much is schooling wrapped up in modern society that modern life is inconceivable without it.

But more centrally, understanding the ubiquity of the paradox presented by modern-school bureaucracies is important for understanding both the practical limits of school reform on the one hand, and also the where and how of school reform on the other. The fact of the matter is that dissatisfaction with the nature of public education is not a problem to be solved but coped with. This emerges out of the relationship between the modern state and the individual family. Understanding this will I think help policymakers (and the public) identify the shape effective change can take. As will be apparent in the next chapter, these limits have been repeatedly pushed up against during previous attempts to address school reform in the United States.

Chapter 2

American Mass Public Education and the Modern World

The Paradoxes of Modern American Schools

At the heart of the discussions of how and why American schools are the paradoxes at the heart of American culture: egalitarianism, individualism, and utilitarianism. Americans hold all three values at the same time, even knowing that they are at times inconsistent with each other. And wrestling with this cultural paradox are the modern parents, business interests, and the teaching profession each seeking to control the schools. These interests in turn are the basis for persistent interest groups[1] that seek to shape the goals of schools to their interests (see Olson 1982).

First there are parents. Parenting is fundamentally different than in the past; indeed, the state now steps in to assert responsibility for a major portion of child socialization. Parents resist this, because they view their children and themselves as individuals with rights which need to be protected against the bureaucratic labyrinth schools have become.

Second there are the business interests who, because they pay for the schools with tax money, claim special rights to guide the curricular policies in the schools. Indeed, it is business that first provided the bureaucratic model used to design industrial-style school systems beginning in late nineteenth-century cities.

Then finally, there are the teachers and the teaching profession, who straddle the tension between parents committed emotionally to their child and the bureaucracy and broader society that requires that they operate the schools as a cross between a loving home, at a low cost, while also mindful of demands for equal treatment under the laws.[2]

Why Do Modern Societies All Have Systems of Mass Education?

Every society needs a way to reproduce itself, its habits, values, and morals. Education is the "social thing" by which adults through a political process assert a right to control the upbringing of not only their own children but at the same time those of other parents (see Durkheim, 1956: 62). This is of course most developed in modern mass society, which extends across nations, and even continents. In small societies this occurs in the context of unscripted face-to-face relationships emphasizing the family unit. For centuries, as long as the productive unit was small and society limited to face-to-face relationships, this was adequate. The wisdom of elders was assumed and routinely reestablished, as was learning about the seasons, family, clan, housing, and the gods. As importantly, you learn who is trustworthy and what is right and wrong (i. e. morals, in the context of daily life). Loyalty to the small group is particularly important in such societies.

But modern societies go well beyond the needs of small intimate clans and a division of labor based only on gender and age. They need to recreate society and transmit the knowledge of that society . They need to reproduce what Bourdieu described as the unspoken predispositions, that is a *habitus* that a society needs to recreate itself. It recreates itself by passing on predispositions for morality, hierarchy, loyalty, trust, respect, and sense of what is right and wrong. This internalized social system, underlies the cultural legitimacy necessary to maintain and reproduce society. The question every modern government faces is how will the *habitus* of legitimacy be created across a population, most of whom will never meet each other, but nevertheless come to recognize each other as sharing values and playing complementary roles in a vast society. In particular, who will do this when a diversity of roles emerge, which are not only patterned by age and gender but also by social class, caste, occupation, social status, skill levels, and a wide range of taken-for-granted status attributions.

Because much of the strength of modern society results from what is learned by, school systems emerge in all countries to reproduce the legitimacy of the existing social and economic order. But as in small traditional societies, it is necessary that the *habitus* and daily ways of life are internalized in a fashion that protects the status quo and also creates a society that deals effectively with unforeseeable change. But the milieu is not the family, nuclear or extended. More typically it is the nation-state, which is ultimately why every modern society needs a system of mass public education in which a scripted *habitus* is transmitted in a predictable fashion and which re-creates cultural capital in the context of a vast global marketplace. As with socialization in small clans, such education is about the transmission of older taken-for-granteds to a younger generation.

The Transgenerational Transmission of Culture via Modern Society and Bureaucracy

The habits, thoughts, and values of one generation affect the next—no human generation reinvents itself without reference to parents and the past. In modern societies, such habits are ideally written down and are explicitly fixed by powerful bureaucratic institutions in a formal school curriculum. But even in such modern societies, other such habits, which are just as powerful, are not written down, but are acted out in the day-to-day interactions between the members of national societies, which are "six degrees of separation" from each other, even in the large national societies of 300 million people like the United States or the even larger societies like the European Union and the huge societies of China and India.

The long-term effect of such natural *habitus* is perhaps no stronger than in the school system, which begins to make its mark on the brains and habits of children when they are about five years old. The habits and beliefs that are developed at such young ages come to affect the nature of the school system for 70 years or more, as individuals in their role as a citizen, parent, grandparent, teacher, or politician draw on a *habitus* that provides a template to make decisions about schools until they die. Thus what these people came to take for granted as five-year-old children affects how they see the world for many, many years and makes school into one of the most conservative institutions in society.

The Long Echo: How Nineteenth-Century Schooling Influences the Twenty-First Century

But the conservative rigidity of school policy did not simply start some 70 years ago with the first grade of today's 75-year-old grandparents. Rather it dips back even deeper into the past, since the predispositions of *habitus* carried in the heads of the grandparents and great-grandparents sitting on school boards and state legislatures today were not created in a vacuum. Today's policies are the product of the pedagogic, political, and economic interests of the school administrators of their day who in turn had a childhood *habitus* created for them some 40 or 50 years previously. Given this pattern, it is not surprising that many of the assertions made about schools in 2010 have their pedigrees in the plans, programs and predispositions created by people born in the 1870s and 1880s. A brief review of this cultural history provides a context for the changes that occurred in American education. Some of the earliest and still most useful descriptions of cultural history come from the French traveller, Alexis de Tocqueville who observed the United States in the 1830s.

De Tocqueville Describes American *Habitus*: Utilitarianism, Egalitarianism, and Individualism

Alexis De Tocqueville was one of the earliest writers to systematically assess the habits of American culture. His work in the 1830s continues to resonate today because he so astutely identified the enduring scripts of the already vast American society. Despite the many changes in technology, and the push of the country westward in the last 170 years, his observations continue to be identified with the "democratic character" of the United States, especially with respect to the most central habits he identified: utilitarianism, egalitarianism, and individualism.

Utilitarianism and Pragmatism

De Tocqueville in the 1830s marveled at the emphasis Americans placed on the "practical" as opposed to the "theoretical" sciences. He attributed this to an emphasis—not shared with Europeans—on the "methods of application" (1990, 42) rather than philosophical and theoretical approaches. He claimed this emphasis focused the American mind on "exclusively commercial habits" more so than their counterparts in Europe who, he claimed, were more likely to spend their days philosophizing about political issues rather than taking action. De Tocqueville wrote that this meant that Americans fixed their minds on economic activity, as opposed to what he called the contemplative life (1990, 37, 42–43). Such utilitarianism and pragmatism, he wrote, resulted in habits of "judging everything for yourself," avoiding doctrine, and adhering closely to observable "facts," without questioning underlying premises.

Notably, de Tocqueville pointed out that this means that the Americans are likely to defer to authority figures for conventional wisdom rather than abstract principles rooted in philosophy or even religion. In terms of business activity, a focus on the facts meant that there was less sentiment placed on relationships and a greater emphasis on data and facts, which can be counted, analyzed, and applied to a specific goal. In business, this makes for more efficient decisions focused by profits—indeed, such an approach provided the ideological justification for the emergence of capitalism, including a faith that those who are the most efficient, would reap the profits of their enterprises (see de Tocqueville 1990, 41–47).

In the case of schooling, such beliefs logically lead to a belief in testing, which is easily observable, and other presumably dispassionate measures of accountability rather than the development of abstract qualities like "citizenship."[3]

Equality and Egalitarianism

An irony de Tocqueville noted about America was that while there was a very strong belief in utilitarianism, this existed side-by-side with a belief in equality between human beings. Such love of equality, de Tocqueville pointed out, made it difficult for aristocracy to emerge. And the absence of a strong aristocracy created conditions where the pragmatic utilitarianism created was through the give and take of both democracy and the market-place; both places where birthright mattered little. This, de Tocqueville viewed enthusiastically as a positive characteristic, which would lead to an improvement in the human condition. But, he also did not hesitate to point out that the two qualities were inherently at odds with each other. Thus, on the one hand, inequality was celebrated, on the other it was despised because it led inevitably to unequal results. This paradox of course is at the heart of twenty-first-century discussions about educational policy, where pragmatic formulae to reward measurable achievement while guaranteeing equal opportunity continue to be wrestled with.

Individualism and Selfishness

De Tocqueville may have celebrated the American emphasis on utilitarianism, pragmatism, and equality, but he also pointed out that the logical consequence of this paradox was selfishness, and that "devotion [of] service to any one man becomes more rare . . . Thus not only does democracy make every man forget his ancestors, but it hides his descendants and separates his contemporaries . . . in the end to confine him entirely within the solitude of his own heart" (de Tocqueville 1990, 98).

Most descriptions of American individualism are not necessarily so gloomy; indeed, individualism is widely acknowledged to lead to an ethic of personal responsibility, which is celebrated at the modern schoolhouse door where there is often an utopian insistence that all curriculum be indi-vidualized and no individual child left behind. In fact, from a very early day, this desire for utilitarianism, egalitarianism, and individualism shaped the development of the American school system. This ultimately became the basis for how adults were to be designed, American style. The *habitus* of utilitarianism, egalitarianism, and individualism would dominate.

Egalitarianism, Pragmatism, Utilitarianism, and the Development of American Schools

This emphasis for egalitarianism, pragmatism, and utilitarianism was not the vision of the seventeenth- and eighteenth-century founders. Their vision was that a small elite of young males would then go to colleges like Harvard, Princeton, Yale, and so forth, where they would be taught classic subjects including languages (French, Latin, and Greek), theology, geometry, English literature, and so forth. Nevertheless, when de Tocqueville wrote in the 1830s, formal schooling was spreading rapidly in the United States, building on the older traditions that used literacy as a status indicator.[4] Indeed, by the 1840 census there was near universal literacy (estimated at 97 percent), among the white population, and 3.68 million children were in school, including 1.80 million girls and 1.88 million boys, which was 55 percent of the population between ages five and fifteen (see Monaghan 2005). In countless communities, "common grammar schools" were established where not only literacy but the consequences of the values de Tocqueville discussed were taught.

De Tocqueville commented about the strong attachment that Americans had to equality and schooling. It was believed in America, he wrote, that every child could benefit from the same curriculum as the elite, even those in the backwoods, a point that Mark Twain effectively satirized in his novels *Huckleberry Finn* and *Tom Sawyer*, where up-country bumpkins routinely recite Romeo and Juliet and even Cicero (in Latin, no less). Democracy and equality was celebrated in lessons on "elocution," meaning public speaking, but, schools in the 1840s were also pragmatic—they fit into the agricultural cycle.

The origins of such schools themselves were in the dispersed farming communities and not the state capitals or far-off federal government. Parents came together to establish schools that met the demands of their own community. Surprisingly given the vastness of the nineteenth-century countryside, a similar curriculum emerged. There was a practical emphasis on reading and writing, alongside programs to teach what are now regarded as the "liberal arts," especially British and American literature, patriotism, Latin, and religion. The countryside, focused on egalitarianism as they were, believed that the curriculum for farm children should mirror that of the urban-bred elite, and it did so, at least in an awkward sort of way. But, such pragmatic egalitarian approaches in rural areas belied a larger problem in urban areas. In the early nineteenth century, urban schools traditionally were affairs organized by churches to educate the poor but paid for through general taxation. With the rapid urbanization in New York after about 1840, new social problems emerged for the "street children" who were the offspring of Catholic-Irish immigrants. These children began populating the jails and were viewed as a social problem for the city government to solve (See Ravitch 1974). The staid Protestant establishment resisted funding the Catholic Church in the provision of schooling for Catholic children and, as a result, sought alternatives for the instruction of the new arrivals. Thus in the 1840s, the public schools of New York were reorganized into secular institutions, and nonsectarian schools for the indigent were established. When establishing schools, civic leaders drew heavily on the pragmatic utilitarian "civic religion" that de Tocqueville wrote about. City leaders emphasized that the investment in street-dwelling children had two benefits for the city and the emerging capitalist elite. First, the children were off the street where they were at risk for becoming thieves and criminals, who were then incarcerated in expensive publicly financed lock-ups. Second, they would be educated in a fashion that made them valuable to the many new factories.

The new public demand for mass public education (both the rural and urban varieties) was led by reformers like Horace Mann (1796–1859), who insisted that education be universal and compulsory, and publisher William McGuffey (1800–1873), whose books soon became best sellers. Both promoted virtues including honesty, truthfulness, obedience, kindness, thrift, industry, and patriotism. The literacy lessons themselves emphasized phonics and spelling rules, while the stories often described a moral dilemma rooted in the various virtues. An example is that of "meddlesome Mattie," a girl who opened her grandmother's snuff box, and broke the old woman's spectacles:

> Matilda, smarting with the pain
> And tingling still, and sore,
> Made many a promise to refrain
> From meddling evermore
>
> (see Sullivan 1994, 124–125)

Such formulaic emphases on teaching fit well with the capacity of the potential teachers. Teachers were typically young unmarried girls who themselves had done well in school, and were given teaching certificates by local school boards and/or superintendents. Unencumbered with learning theory, lessons were undertaken by rote chanting, in which the capacity to memorize facts was emphasized, policies consistent with the demands of business leaders who sought disciplined, compliant, literate, and numerate workers.

Little Rural School on the Prairie: Equality without Pragmatism in One-Room Schools

American schools have an oft romanticized origin in the rural one-room school, featured in writing like Mark Twain's *Tom Sawyer* and *Huckleberry Finn* or Laura Ingalls Wilder's *"Little House"* series about growing up on the frontier in the nineteenth century. In such representations, as well as in fact, the rural school house was a critical institution establishing equal access to a common culture. In the rural areas literacy was not yet seen as necessary for economic productivity; indeed generations of farmers had done well without schooling (Zimmerman 2009). Rather it was about American egalitarianism—the idea that any child was as good as any other. The idea was that in a nation of equals all should have similar access to the intellectual markers of refinement, regardless of birth. Instruction as a result mimicked that found in the elite schools—albeit crudely—while emphasizing recitation of memorized passages and verses that were studied at elite institutions like Harvard. Public speaking and elocution skills were also considered important for egalitarian democratic governance. Missing were the less transparent skills modeled and created in the elite schools, particularly critical thinking, composition, law, and moral philosophy.

In the rural one-room school, a teacher, who had basic literacy skills, was hired by a group of parents to impart refinement. The teacher often boarded at parents' homes. Teachers were hired locally, in a fashion that meant that school policies reflected local values, morals, and ethics rather than those of other plausible sources of authority, including a far-away central government. Teacher certification was typically done by county superintendents of education on the basis of ad hoc examinations such as that described by Laura Ingalls, when she was hired at age 15 to teach in a one-room school, or W. E. B. Dubois, who was only slightly older when he taught in rural Tennessee (see Wilder 1941, 303–307; DuBois 1903a, 46–54).

In one-room schools, children recited from the mass produced *McGuffey's Readers*, and like W. E. B. DuBois, discussed Latin poems like Cicero's *Pro Archia Poeta* (see DuBois 1903a, 49). Despite the seeming uniformity imposed by the mass-produced textbooks, schools were still local creations. The teacher was less encumbered by a distant bureaucracy than today; there was little reporting to state officials and no accountability to the federal government. Accountability was to local officials, parents, and the farmers who paid for the schools and selected the school boards. Students were likely to be of varying ages and abilities, and teachers, whether in farm or city, were given a great deal of authority to manage the classroom, and establish the curriculum, even in large "districts". As Diane Ravitch (2000, 20) points out, even in the urban Baltimore Schools of 1895, there were only two "superintendents" for 1,200 teachers.

There were 212,000 rural one-room schools in 1913, at the point when the "school district consolidation movement" began in full force. Such schools would be viewed today as alternately chaotic and authoritarian—little was standardized or bureaucratized. To emphasize the problems of these schools, Zimmerman (2009, 16) quotes from the diary of a young teacher, Eliza B:

> Eliza B. at 15 ½ years old was a teacher a teacher in a Massachusetts school in 1838 and described her 7 ½ week term as all she could take: "I wish to say the roof is all gone in one corner. You can see outside. The windows are all broken but we put paper over them. The floor is gone right under the bad roof. The fireplace does not heat except right in front of it. The wood was very wet at times as there is no woodshed. There are no conveniences for boys or girls . . . There was no blackboard, no teacher's desk, and not enough books to keep the schools seventeen students occupied . . . they tormented the young teacher. "The big boys took my bell so I could not call them in."

Nevertheless, the one-room school, in all its chaos, did produce a literate society during the nineteenth century. A consensus about curriculum also developed, particularly at the elementary level. Reading, writing, spelling, speaking, penmanship, patriotism, and moral conduct were at the center. Schools were also assumed to teach habits of honesty, industry, respect for adults, and courtesy (see Ravitch 2000, 20–22). A heavy dose of "disciplining the will" required quick, unquestioning obedience to the teacher, and school rules were typically enforced with corporal punishment. In an agrarian society, where pragmatic economic wisdom was still associated with hands-on experience, not book-learning, classic-dominated. Education in the late nineteenth-century rural context was still associated primarily with refinement and status rather than market economics and the "development of human capital."[5] Schooling was only incidentally considered to be a means to acquire better employment, or to satisfy the demands of potential employers, as it was in the city; after all, illiterate farmers could make a living too—but they could not be refined without reciting Cicero! But the nineteenth century rural schoolhouse was about equality and culture, not economic pragmatism.

Little School in the City: Pragmatism without Equality

As described above, in the early nineteenth century, schooling was established in urban New York and other cities of the eastern seaboard in the context of the church. Indeed, churches sponsored both academies for the sons of merchants in the eighteenth century and also what were called charity schools for the poor. The cities were more densely populated than the dispersed farming areas but were small by today's standards. For example New York City in 1790 had less than 50,000 people. But cities, unlike the rural areas, were large enough to become stratified by wealth, class, occupation, and ethnicity, all factors that led to greater differences in the new school systems. In particular, it meant that the wealthy merchants who were dominating city politics and wanted stability in the city, as well as a trained and docile work force, invested in school systems that promised such results. Schooling would thus have the goals of keeping out-of-control street children busy during the day, while their parents were at the factories. The school had the added bonus for the tax-paying captains of industry of training immigrant children as future factory workers.

But the urban schools were not developed with only business goals in mind; in fact, business interests entered into an alliance with the new professions of social workers and educators. During the nineteenth century, the forerunners of child psychologists and social workers emerged. Indeed, among the first urban secular schools funded by New York's business class for African American children (see Ravitch 1974). These schools were founded in the early 1800s, not by the parents of the children concerned, but by the business and church interests who wanted to provide basic educational opportunities for the children of freed slaves. These schools in turn set the pattern for the schools established for the children of the Irish Catholics who arrived after the 1830s and pushed the population of New York City to 400,000 by 1840. In the case of both the African American and Irish-immigrant children, something very different happened in the city than in the countryside: schools were financed and controlled by elites acting in the place of parents, rather than by the parents themselves. In effect, the new schools were asserting a new right, i. e., that child rearing was not simply the responsibility of the parents but a social welfare need at the heart of what the state and economy were becoming.

Thus, the rapid growth of American cities in the nineteenth century led to both a rapid expansion of urban school systems and a new belief that a strong school system was, as President George H. W. Bush was to state one hundred years later, at the heart of "everything else" that made a society strong. Schooling came to be seen as key to both a strong economy and an orderly urban society. This pragmatic and utilitarian view was of course different than that in the countryside where egalitarianism and refinement were encouraged, despite how rough rural locations were.

This pragmatic utilitarianism permitted the adoption of curricula in the city that were different than that in the vast rural areas. The business interests believed deeply that public schools were an investment that would prepare the children of immigrant workers to fill slots for moderately skilled workers and other labor needs. The urban elites may have touted the advantages of egalitarianism, but the prerogatives of wealth protected their own children from the new urban schools with their emphasis on preparation for the factory line. For their own children, though, who they saw as their successors, they continued to maintain a separate system of academies.

Business interests, combined with the emergence of professional social work, led to the first widely enforced compulsory education requirements in the late nineteenth century. This in turn presented city schools with the need to create programs for masses of children—tens of thousands were entering the schools of New York City each year. In this context, laws were established that initiated the age-graded system of school entry and progress well-known today. Children entered school as six-year-olds, because it was assumed that they had similar mental, physiological, and curricular needs. This in turn opened the door to the introduction of rules, regulations, and practices designed to make the training of children more sequential and therefore predictable.

American Schooling in 1895: The Professors and Captains of Industry of Conspire

By 1895, the United States had created a patchwork system of basic grammar schools. About 95 percent of children aged 7–13 were attending primary school at least some of the year (Ravitch 2000, 20).[6] Public schools in 1890 enrolled 13 million students in primary school classrooms, but only 220,000 were in high school; all together they accounted for 69 percent of the population ages 5–17. Schooling was still also a rural enterprise; 77 percent of these children attended schools in rural areas, then defined as areas of less than 4,000 people (Cuban 1993, 24).

While most of these schools were products of local communities, a standardized curriculum nevertheless emerged. The marketing success of *McGuffey's Readers* defined common cultural touchstones, such as Shakespeare, Dickens, Longfellow's "Paul Revere's Ride," and Marc Antony's oration in Shakespeare's *Julius Caesar* (Ravitch 2000, 20–22). McGuffey's Readers, a set of graduated textbooks designed to teach reading, were among the most influential books ever published in the United States. An estimated 120,000,000 copies were required reading for students beginning in 1836, with the result that millions of American students, even those living in the backwoods, shared a common culture, beliefs, and subconscious *habitus*. For example, President Theodore Roosevelt (1859–1920) made frequent references to "mettlesome Mattie." President Harry S. Truman (1884–1972) who presumably studied *McGuffey's Readers* as a six to ten year old in Independence, Missouri, in the 1890s, used examples provided in the books to express world views and develop policy toward education as president between 1945 and 1953. He asserted this was strategic because of both the moral tone and "soundness of the literary selections" in the *McGuffey's Readers* (Sullivan 1994:21).

So despite a lack of central government coordination, by 1895, virtually every community in the United States had a primary school of some sort, even remote African American schools where teachers like the young W. E. B. Dubois opened school for at least a brief time each year. Despite this lack of centralization, as Diane Ravitch (2000, 25) points out, the aim of these "common schools" was already clear. It was

> . . . to promote sufficient learning and self-discipline so that people in a democratic society could be good citizens, read the newspapers, get a job, make their way in an individualistic and competitive society, and contribute to their community's well-being.

Impressively, this hodgepodge school system spread across a vast country, creating a shared nationality, citizenship, and social order.

Less impressed with the insistence on shared culture and citizenship were two important elite constituencies. The first were the old colleges and universities who were expanding admissions to include not only the graduates of elite private feeder prep schools, but also a small proportion of the graduates of public high schools. They were dissatisfied with the quality of the applicants admitted from public schools, who were not well prepared for the university curriculum borrowed from older elite prep schools.

A second powerful constituency was the large capitalist firms that needed a larger army of clerks and workers who could not only read newspapers and make their way in a competitive and individualistic society but also maintain accounts, be loyal to employers, and do more complex business management tasks such as bookkeeping, surveying, and navigation

(Ravitch 2000, 25)—in other words, an ideological *habitus* of a disciplined, docile, predictable, and compliant workers able to staff hierarchically organized factories. The traditional primary school, focused on eight years of discipline, elocution, patriotism, religion, geography facts, mental math, and spelling bees, did little to create the pragmatic skills demanded by business or, for that matter, university professors seeking students capable of the abstract reasoning expected at the college level. The rapid expansion of American cities with their large immigrant populations provided a ready audience in which the professors and industrialists were to experiment. The solution was to be the American high school.

The Missing High School Rung: Industrialized Schools for Industrializing Cities

The space between the mass education at the primary level, and a relatively strong elite college system by 1900 created what Diane Ravitch calls "the missing rung of the ladder," which was high school. The virtues of the new American high schools were several. As Goldin and Katz (2010) point out, there was a consensus that the high schools should be publicly funded, open access, open to both boys and girls, and build on strong traditions of local control connecting schools to local communities. There was also to be a separation between church and state, and an academic curriculum. Unlike the mass primary education system, which emerged more spontaneously in many places to satisfy local interests, high schools served two broader applied interests—first, those of a university system that valued the classical subjects they believed led to the liberal education, and second, business interests who funded the schools through tax dollars and wanted to fill specific slots in the labor market. Both sought to shape this "missing rung of the ladder," and a competition between the two to create a new high school curriculum emerged. The tension between egalitarian insistence that "my children learn" what the elite do, and a more pragmatic view that school is primarily training for specific slots in a stratified labor market. This tension continues today (see also Bills 2004:141–178).

The universities, led by Harvard's President Charles Eliot, sought to create a high school curriculum that emphasized the "mental discipline," which created a citizen able to reason critically, observe systematically, and be disciplined in their approach to mental tasks, i. e., what late twentieth-century educators would call "critical thinking skills." Such advocates believed that it did not matter much what a student studied in high school, only that they knew how to study. In this environment, the study of modern languages, Greek, Latin, abstract mathematics, physics, and ancient history flourished.

But even as a culture emerged that associated learning and status with the classics, business demanded that skills learned in school have immediate utility in the labor market. In other words, industry demanded graduates who could be quickly employed as bookkeepers, clerks, surveyors, machinists, and factory workers. The old tension de Tocqueville described between the habits of utility, individualism, and equality reemerged. Oddly the story began in the Southeast, which was decimated by the Civil War.

Republican politicians from the North, intent on providing the recently freed slaves with the means to support themselves, financed a new string of technical schools in the Southeast, which were segregated secondary schools designed to train blacks in the manual arts and practical trades. Tuskegee Institute in Alabama, founded by Booker T. Washington, is perhaps the best-known of these institutions. The goal of such institutions was to create a docile, educated African American population ready to accept the status quo of segregation and staff the workshops of the late nineteenth-century economy. Some blacks like Washington of course implicitly accepted the "separate but equal" policies implied by this arrangement; they believed that educational opportunity that would permit them to advance economically and culturally, albeit separately. This model became important not just for the freed slaves, but for the millions of immigrants populating the new American cities.

But still there was a tension: Were American high schools to be training institutions for university professors, or the pragmatic labor needs of industry?

Utility and Knowledge: Liberal Arts Training vs. the Pragmatic Utilitarians

Harvard's Charles Eliot writing in the 1890s, was critical of this business-focused approach to education, which assumed inherent abilities and the idea that a school's primary goal was to train for economic activity. Eliot believed strongly that most if not all children could be pushed to achieve mental abilities for their own sake, whether it was in algebra, ancient Greek, or music. Appealing to American values about egalitarianism, he said there was no reason that higher level math should not be taught at lower grades than it was and that larger numbers of children could not be challenged to do so if effective teaching methods were developed. Rather than rote memorization of facts, be they in math, reading, spelling, or geography, he believed that 14-year-olds could grasp subjects like geology, algebra, geometry, physics, and so forth if their "mental power" to think, reason, and observe were developed. "The object of education," he frequently said, "was to gain mental discipline" (Ravitch 2000, 31) and, by implication, go beyond simple training for repetitive clerical tasks and factory work. He advocated for liberal education and opposed the efforts to restrict educational opportunity to only the "most capable," a category that most often corresponded with the existing elite and their children.

The actual structure for the new high schools emerged from "A Committee of Ten" chaired by the same Charles W. Eliot, who in 1890 asserted the critical nature of a liberal education for all children, an explicitly egalitarian goal. In a nod to pragmatism, the committee also asserted that a standard education in the United States should include eight years of primary school and four years of high school, establishing the twelve-year standard. But while the committee asserted that such an education was not inherently tied to older college requirements for the study of Latin or Greek, they did believe that the general disciplines of mathematics, social studies, and English were at the core. Natural science was divided into biology, chemistry, and physics at that time, and these too quickly became part of this high school core, setting the standard curriculum for the American high school for the coming century. Effectively excluded were the arts, business, foreign languages, engineering, and other plausible academic subjects. In particular Eliot and his committee believed that such an education was preferable to emphases on the rote memorization emerging from the public schools of both the urban and rural areas. And in an age of educational and social inequality, the committee optimistically asserted that *all* students could be trained in a fashion that would make them eligible for a college education.

The Committee of Ten report was issued in 1893 and quickly was criticized not only by the professors of Latin and Greek (who were slighted), but for its assumptions that all children should be trained to a high level. This criticism came from two quarters in particular. Critics like G. Stanley Hall, President of Clark University in Massachusetts, led a group that critiqued the assumption that all children could or should be provided with a curriculum that they were incapable of mastering. Hall preferred what he described as the pragmatism of the hierarchically organized European systems of education, which separated children at a young age based on ability and tracked them into different educational streams, in accordance with the capacity of each child as identified in intelligence testing.[7]

Hall's pragmatic argument focused on developing each child, as if he or she was a tool, and fit in neatly with the strong streak of American utilitarianism and the accompanying meritocratic ethic. This view also played well into the interests of America's business class, which was less concerned about thinking critically, mental discipline, and other life-long skills but simply wanted to staff factories. In this view, focus was legitimated in the context of European systems, in which about 10 percent of students were trained for management via the study of the classics (including Latin), while a larger proportion was trained for technical professions corresponding to older guild arrangements. Quite often such European programs were aligned well with a class system, which sent the children of a traditional aristocracy and the new bourgeois to academic schools where they were cultivated in what Germans called *Bildung*, while the children of farmers and workers trained for positions in the emerging industrial economy (see e. g., Bourdieu and Passeron 1977; Collins 1971). In the United States, it was aligned not only with the class system but also a racial caste system, which correlated opportunities and abilities with skin color.

In a country seeking to preserve a racial caste system which excluded blacks, Hall's pragmatic design had by the 1910s won out over the more liberal views of Harvard's Charles Eliot. Thus, high schools during a period of rapid expansion were to be meritocratic sorters of society on behalf of industry, albeit using the disciplinary categories legitimated by the Committee of Ten. The high schools were to be the place where experts assigned youth to the tracks most appropriate for their skills and background.

Utility and Knowledge: Social Engineering by Education Schools in Twentieth-Century Schools

So the early twentieth century witnessed the victory of two powerful interests in the conduct of education: education schools, which trained teachers, and business interests, focused on the nature of the industrial labor force. Diminished at least for a time, was the old "critical thinking" school that had valued highly Latin, Greek, French, and English literature whether in the schools of the elite or the rural schools of the nineteenth century.

Replacing the ideologies of egalitarianism as the movement to create high schools gained steam, were ideas focused on utility and how to achieve the goals of business elites. Education schools emerged at universities asserting that education could be a science in which the "whole child" was understood and a planned product created. Combining the new fields of Freud's psychology and Frederick Taylor's management, the new education schools claimed in the early twentieth century that they could create the worker and citizen of the future. Elemental to this was an assumption that schools could sort students into what would be needed by a future labor market.

The education schools legitimated the views of the powerful business communities of the rapidly industrializing cities that wanted to hire workers for specific tasks in factories, and as clerks and secretaries to manage the factories. Such business interests were very specific in indicating the type of product that they wanted from the schools. They wanted workers who were reliable, loyal, punctual, and had confidence in the existing social order. In their office, they wanted the same qualities and also demanded that the clerks and bookkeepers have command of higher levels of literacy and numeracy. Schools would sort and train. Utilitarianism and pragmatism won over egalitarianism and critical thinking.

Much of the movement began in the new system of professional education schools at the nation's universities and colleges. The new university-based education schools began dreaming of what the ideal American school system would look like, particularly at the rapidly growing high school level. Consistent with the enthusiasms of the day, these university-based education departments emphasized that schools should be scientifically and professionally managed, in a fashion consistent with the psychology of Freud and the management theories of Taylor.

This happened as new teachers' colleges, and university-based schools of education asserted a monopoly over the training, certification, and licensing of teacher candidates. School teachers and administrators were hired by the tens of thousands by school boards eager to establish the new high schools and engineer the precise results they believed a prosperous and glorious future demanded. By the 1920s, this though required a compromise between the often idealistic schools of education—who emphasized the role of schools and teachers as a nurturing presence in the planning of a child's development—and the lay boards of education dominated by business interests. The former emphasized the importance of the social sciences, particularly psychology, in designing effective teaching programs, while the latter emphasized that everything that was taught should be tied to some practical utility in the scientifically selected career of the child.[8]

In the early twentieth century, high schools were redesigned to establish paths that met the presumed need of each child to find a role in the economy. Thus, a single school might have a course in zoology and also a course in laundry. New testing regimens developed by university psychologists fed into this regime by emphasizing the administrative utility of assigning young children to tracks on the basis of performance on intelligence and skills tests. The testing regimes also became closely tied to teacher certification, which the universities pried away from county school superintendents. This was done in the belief that education itself was a precisely applied science (like engineering), at the heart of which was a uniform professionalism. As Ravitch (2000, 60) summarizes, there were four principles underlying this movement, which were:

- the idea that education was a science and that the methods and goals of education could be matched and measured with precision;

- the idea that the methods and goals of education are derived from the innate needs and nature of the child which in turn is described scientifically;
- the idea that the methods and goals of education can be determined by assessing the needs of the society (particularly the economy), and training specific children for those needs;
- the idea that the methods and goals of education are developed in a fashion that changes the social order in desired ways by both *freeing children's creative spirits*, while at the same time indoctrinating them *for a life in a scientifically planned society.* (emphasis added)

There are of course contradictions inherent to this approach. After all, freed creative spirits are inconsistent with scientifically planned society. Nevertheless, there was an alliance between the idealistic schools of education and the business interests from the 1910s to the 1930s, a critical period in the development of the high school. So around the country, schools of education and boards of education turned to the task of designing the future society, often at the behest of state legislatures.

High schools with the four-year-long curricula were the easiest place to develop such a program, particularly as the number of graduates soared from less than 4 percent of the population in 1900 to more than 40 percent by 1940. Using the older technical schools as a model (many of which were first designed for the emancipated but segregated freed slaves of the South), high school coursework was stratified to develop "professionals" trained in the skills needed by the labor market at that time: Bricklayers, laundresses, carpenters, housewives, metal workers, and a host of other occupations needed by the early twentieth century economy had their own high school curricula by the 1920s. As for academic subjects, the new social engineers perceived them as appropriate only for the "talented ten percent" preparing for the university and leadership. Older concepts of egalitarianism and the belief that all children could achieve, which was championed by Charles Eliot, were pushed aside in the interests of this utilitarianism, albeit in the context of the new comprehensive high school. All that was needed was buy-in from the parents of the millions of immigrant children who would be sent to the newly stratified high school system.

The Social Engineers I: Nurturing Children for the Future Economy (1920–1954)

The first alliance of "social engineers" emerging in the 1910s saw the world through the lenses of business and child psychology. They were convinced that they could engineer a school system that would both reflect the capacity of children to learn tasks useful to society and the capacity of business to predict what type of future worker was needed. This involved sharing views regarding who children were and assumed a new capacity in the business community to plan for expansion of technology and factories. Such a system also implied that the experts were in a position to test and assign children to the ideal role, such as had emerged in Europe. Such planning though was to in fact be short-lived and virtually disappear by the time the more egalitarian 1970s arrived.

The Emergence of a Two-Tiered System and the Reinforcement of Social Class

The spirits of psychologists Sigmund Freud, B. F. Skinner, management guru Frederick Taylor, and pragmatic philosopher John Dewey animated educational policy in the early twentieth century, as the new fields combined to dominate the faculties of teacher's colleges and superintendents' offices. In particular, Dewey's grouping of child psychology, experiential learning, and democratic ideals into a single philosophical approach had a profound influence on how public schools developed. Borrowing from Freud's (and others') understanding of how children experience the world developmentally, Dewey advocated exposing children to varied experiences rather than rote learning. Out of this emerged understandings that education was to be of the whole child rather than the simple acquisition of lessons learned by rote memory (Ravitch 2000, 57–61).

Educational management also established itself as a field with explicit reference to the management principles of the factory world. Thus, schooling was broken into age-graded cohorts who would be prescribed an age appropriate (and professionally developed) curricula in reading, writing, and the other prescribed subjects. From the field of social work, the school acquired the power of the "benevolent parent" under the legal doctrine of *in loco parentis* and was assumed to operate in the best interests of the child. Bureaucratic rule books were developed to monitor, observe, and correct children as they moved through the newly established system. Teachers themselves were assumed to be professionals, specifically certified as experts in the administration of the new system; even administrators were to be certified in the mechanics of the system by a rapidly expanding network of teachers colleges, housed within the nation's great universities. Buttressing such scientific decision making were psychological tests that took advantage of the latest understandings of human development; the relationship between intelligence, training, and future roles within the modern economy was assumed. Social engineers saw this as a good thing in the context of the individualistic meritocracy that was emerging.

Schooling, Pragmatism, World War I, and the Final Decline of Classical Liberal Education

America's involvement in World War I (1917–1918) gave further impetus to concerns about whether schools were producing "useful citizens" or not. In particular, army recruiters complained about the poor physical and mental conditions of men who were the children of urban immigrants (see e. g. Gould 1996, 222–234). Such government concerns about the quality of soldiers recruited were most starkly indicated by the first mass administration of psychological tests, which found that not only were the urban masses only moderately literate but that the physical condition of the draftees was compromised by poor disease, poor nutrition, and a lack of exercise. As a result, physical education and health became more important concerns for the new schools to address, in addition to concerns about the quality of instruction. The new system of both primary and high schools came to be seen as a pragmatic natural resource elemental to the military, political, and economic strength of the nation.

But immigrant parents did not necessarily see things that way. The postwar 1920s and 1930s continued to see a rapid expansion of secondary school enrollments, as educational attainment was seen as a status marker by the masses of immigrant parents living in the rapidly enlarged cities. As a result, enrollments in upper grades increased rapidly; immigrant children, who had previously left school after four or five years instruction, demanded the same twelve years that the higher status bourgeois provided their children. Economic pragmatism of the reformers still emphasized utilitarianism in curriculum development, a situation widely approved of by business interests seeking trained workers. Immigrant and poor parents at least initially, were relieved to gain access—any access—to high school for their children. In this context, vocational subjects became the focus of the new high school curriculum—courses for boys emphasized a wide range of needs, but especially agriculture, construction, mechanics, and so forth. Courses for girls emphasized home economics, typing, and child development. Mathematics also became a utilitarian subject, focused on bookkeeping, finance, and surveying rather than the more abstract algebra and geometry. But this arrangement ultimately posed a conundrum for status-conscious immigrant parents who eventually resisted efforts to sort and track their children into vocational tracks. They viewed these tracks as second rate, in spite of presumably scientific claims by professional educators about the appropriateness of such courses for their children (Ravitch 2000).

The period between World Wars I and II saw reforms to the primary school systems too, where legions of teachers credentialed in the new educational schools rather than granted teaching licenses by county superintendents of schools began to dominate. In the primary school systems, explicit theories of learning resulted in wholesale reform of reading, mathematics, social studies, and other curriculum. Rote memorization of Western classics featured in the moralistic *McGuffey's Readers* gave way to calibrated reading programs designed for "the whole child."[9] At the most basic level, this meant that classic poetry and assertions about morality gave way to "Dick, Jane, and Spot" readers that emphasized the acquisition of age-appropriate reading skills in a scientific fashion, through the development of specific skills in phonetics and repetition. The program of the past focused on reading *The Bible*, and the moralistic tales of *McGuffey's Readers* were finally gone, and replaced with the pragmatism of the modern school curriculum.

Also under attack were the hundreds of thousands of one-room schools, which were seen as inefficient and delivering a poor quality product to the labor market. This occurred particularly rapidly during the Great Depression of the 1930s, resulting in an even more rapid expansion of a high school system articulated with a particular type of primary education in which graded multiteacher schools were assumed (Zimmerman 2009). It was also a time that the "invention of the teenager" as a period in the life course between childhood and work came to be. Similar processes occurred at the high school, albeit without broad political compromises: Business interests and education schools were dominant from the beginning with a 12-year–high school diploma rapidly becoming a marker for middle-class status, as well as a gatekeeper for employers (Collins 1971). Delays in assuming full responsibilities as an adult resulted in the emergence of this new "teen culture" in association with the high schools (see Kett 1978; Hine 2000).

Thus, even as the country slipped into the economic doldrums of the 1930s, a vigorous youth culture (Kett 1978), focused by high school and teen culture, appeared in many urban areas, all in the context of an institution designed to track and sort youth into paths that would reproduce the remembered past of their parents and teachers.

Egalitarian Push Back from Parents

But in the United States, a conundrum emerged in the 1920s and 1930s, in which the values of egalitarianism and utilitarianism were at odds. Despite the meritocratic veneer asserted by psychological testing and resultant academic sorting and tracking, the egalitarian ethic de Tocqueville identified in the 1830s challenged a system that segregated blacks, immigrants, and the poor from the upper levels of the presumably meritocratic educational system. In the northern United States, immigrant children were tracked by schools dominated by business and social work interests into schools that tracked by race, gender, and social class. In the South, where separate schools for blacks were maintained and African Americans legally excluded from many occupations, segregation was much more explicit and unequal. In this context, the meritocratic apparatus of the school system was explicitly discriminatory. Arguments emerged in the 1940s and after that emphasized that what the psychological tests measured was not innate ability, but socioeconomic disadvantage.

Parents resisted the tracking and sorting system, regardless of the claim to scientific expertise of powerful business interests and university professors. Whether African American, immigrant, rural, or simply poor, parents had educational ambitions for their own children to attend universities consistent with the dominant meritocratic ideology that emerged from the middle classes. This happened particularly as a Bachelor's degree came to be seen as an important status marker for the middle class after World War II. Vocational tracks dropped in status further and became perceived as the low-status dumping grounds for the poor, minorities, immigrants, and those with academic and disciplinary problems.

The shift that began in the 1920s was most clearly challenged by the 1954 *Brown v. Board of Education* Supreme Court decision, which asserted that the Constitution guaranteed equal educational opportunities for all children despite race and that segregation. No matter how "scientific," such segregation might be by its very nature it was unequal and therefore illegal under a Constitution that guaranteed equal protection. The question though was what kind of opportunity was to be offered? In answering this question, the wants of the business community for an engineered workforce were finally eclipsed in the 1950s, and those of poor parents for equal opportunity came to dominate.

But the question was still how to reconcile the American values of egalitarianism, utilitarianism, and individualism (see e.g. Coleman 1966). Old dilemmas have a way of reasserting themselves, especially in institutions as fundamental to social life as mass public education. The time had changed, but the *habitus* of the old script did not.

The Social Engineers II: Schooling for a More Egalitarian Society (1954–1980)

The first half of the twentieth century was dominated by concerns about the utility of education, and the scientific creation of a cohesive workforce using it, however, defined. As a result, the logic of utilitarianism permeated discussions about school curriculum at mid-century. And while this logic was never completely abandoned, the second half of the century was also defined by the logic of egalitarianism, in which individual opportunity with respect to the disadvantages inherited as a result of race, poverty, and socioeconomic conditions were emphasized. This of course was not a new emphasis; previous generations of immigrants and farmers had insisted on the same rights. Both ethics—that of pragmatism and equality—reflected an American faith in the value of individual achievement. But both also highlighted the contradictions in a school system which valued equality, utilitarianism, and individual merit at the same time. This older pragmatic school system in which inequality was tolerated, and even encouraged, came under a withering critique from education scholars like Paolo Freire's (1968/1970) *Pedagogy of the Oppressed*, and Ivan Ilich's (1971) *Deschooling Society* who viewed the mass schooling as a capitalist instrument blocking the liberation of the human spirit.

Education, Opportunity, and Race

Access to educational opportunity was a focus of the Civil Rights movement because the schools were the legitimated gatekeeper for economic and socioeconomic improvement, i. e., the sorters and trackers. Because educational institutions controlled entry to the labor market and professions via certification, the problem of race and racism was laid at the school door. In the same way that schools transformed an agricultural society into a bureaucratic, industrial one, it was hoped that schooling could transform a racially segregated society into an egalitarian one.

Race like no other issue in the twentieth century exposed the dissonance between the key American ideologies of egalitarianism, utilitarianism, and individualism. The result since the 1960s in the schools was the adoption of bureaucratic formulae to desegregate, the promise of the schools was somehow that the magic of education could overcome the other sources of this inequality. Desegregation policies took for granted the utility of schooling for ordering society.[10] Policies demanded much from the schools, which became flashpoints focused on bussing for desegregation, affirmative action in college admissions, antipoverty programs, remediation programs, and so forth. Education—or at least what Durkheim called pedagogy—was seen as the way for the oppressed to match the ideals and promises the United States offered. This ideology was so strong that it soon was applied to inequalities that go beyond race.

Other Inequalities of Opportunity: Gender, Language, and Poverty

Demands for equal access to education were most prominent among African Americans, but the logic soon came to be applied to other groups: women, language minorities, and others, all of whom were routinely tracked by the educational scientists and managers of the school establishment. For example, ethics of equal access threatened programs that historically tracked girls into homemaking tracks, Mexican Americans into manual trades, and immigrant children away from college. But the logic was soon extended to other conditions, which a new generation of educational scientists believed shaped the life chances of children, especially poverty. Most importantly, new social science firmly established that poverty and home life played a major role in how well a child was served by the system. In this context, schools began to reorient themselves away from the business-friendly tracking and sorting functions and toward goals for rectifying historical wrongs.

With the growing emphasis on using the school as a tool to realize egalitarian ideals, education policies were pushed to rationalize the programs beyond the needs of African Americans to other sources of inequality. As a result, the schools in the 1960s and 1970s began to address the concerns of other groups that had been victims of group-based discrimination. Schools in this context came to be seen as responsible for a broader range of social issues besides desegregation.

Thus, by the 1960s, the public school systems created by the state were the key institution used to create adults. Children were no longer the sole responsibility/possession of parents, but a resource in which the broader society had claims, and invested on its own terms. As a result, what was demanded of schools no longer stop at literacy, numeracy, culture, or even ending racial discrimination. Rather the responsibilities of the schools were extended to a wide range of emotional issues, which social scientists were quick to point out limited the quality of adults being produced for the workforce. The range of social problems that the schools sought to address are illustrative of the central role schooling plays in the national imagination:

- control of hunger, and the provision of healthy food
- control of drugs
- safe sex
- prayer in school
- physical fitness and childhood obesity
- excesses of television
- lack of employees in science and engineering

But this also meant that by the 1970s, the academic mission of the schools was less central. This was particularly the case when it exacerbated unequal access to the meritocracy represented by a higher education. In the 1960s and 1970s as a result, high school graduation requirements became less academic (Ravitch 2000, 408–415) in order to improve graduation rates, which were strongly patterned by race and socioeconomic status. Many public colleges and universities responded by lowering formal study requirements for admission, increasing the size of incoming classes, while relying on standardized testing conducted by private companies to compensate for the varying levels of academic rigor in different high schools. This in turn created the illusion, if not actual fact, of equal opportunity.

The emphasis on equal opportunity and access eventually created a backlash in the 1980s, particularly from the business community, which claimed that high school graduates were unprepared for the workforce, and from college professors who believed students could not write, read, or do math at levels they had in the past. In effect the old coalition of the 1910s was reestablished. In part this was undoubtedly due to the rapid expansion in access that had occurred in the 1960s and 1970s. More importantly for the story of K-12, the professors blamed the high schools for lacking rigor, with relaxed graduation requirements being an obvious target.

Thus, the tension between those who saw the schools' primary function as promoting egalitarianism and those who saw it as a pragmatic way to train prospective workers, shifted again with the victory of the conservative business-friendly Ronald Reagan in the 1980 presidential election. Most importantly, Reagan appointed a National Commission on Education Reform chaired by the President of the University of California, David Pierpont Gardner, along with business and education leaders. Using dramatically emotional language, the report announced most famously that "if an unfriendly foreign power had attempted to impose on America the mediocre educational performance that exists today, we might well have viewed it as an act of war" (NCER 1983). The report announced that the intellectual capacity of the nation was at risk, and that steps must be taken to ensure that the students trained by the K–12 schools were ready for college and the workforce. In other words, the emphasis on egalitarianism was coming to an end, and a new emphasis on utilitarianism would return. Nostalgia was at the core of the *Nation at Risk Report,* (see NCER 1983 and Hayes 2004) which focused on drops in relative international rankings as the countries of a new Europe and Asia became richer and on a limited number of comparative exams in literacy and mathematics. This result was assumed to reflect an absolute decline in the quality of American curricula and blame was laid at the door of the looser academic standards (see e.g. Ravitch and Finn 1987) which emerged in the wake of the Civil Rights movement. The sunny figure of President Ronald Reagan fed upon a nostalgia for the presumed advantages of the schools of 50 or 60 years previously, during the childhoods of him and his advisors. Their memories, though, were not dominated by the battles between business, World War I–era psychometricians and The Whole Child movement, but by the remembered symbols that had survived, whether it was the Little Red Schoolhouse of the rural areas, the corporal punishment meted out by the "Board of Education," or recitation drills.

Teachers and Their Multiple Tasks: Tenure, Unionization, and Employment Protections

The increasing belief that schools were the major force for social change and the implementation of long-term government policies about equity pushed the teaching profession into a new array of responsibilities. This happened in the context of the tumult of the 1960s, which among many other changes, led to the unionization of the teaching profession by the National Education Association and American Federation of Teachers. Superintendents and principals, appointed by elected school boards (and in some cases, elected superintendents), who had had a great deal of leeway in evaluating, hiring, and firing teachers, suddenly found that well-educated teachers could legitimately assert the expertise gained in education schools as a basis for employment protection from political winds. In such a context, and given that superintendents, school boards and principals had long asserted the utility of the factory model in organizing schools, it is not so surprising that teachers began to think of their jobs in terms of factory-like labor relations. Teacher unionization was born.

But, professionalization and its advocates in university departments of education had left their mark on the teaching profession as well. Increasing control over teacher credentialing by state-level commissions meant that the pool from which school boards could hire became smaller. Candidates for teaching jobs credentialed in the past by an elected superintendent, found themselves subject to the whims of both the university-based education schools and politically selected school boards. Most importantly, many states began to require post-BA course work, which reflected the combined goals of university education departments, and the proliferating demands of legislatures and politically appointed credentialing commissions to address the social problems *du jour* with more specific training.

This increase in responsibilities along with the ferment of the 1960s was the context in which teachers unionized. After threading the hazards of the teacher credentialing process, school-district level hiring, and isolation on school campuses away from the broader political winds, teachers created a profession whose power was enhanced by union activity. The influence of the many elected positions in education also provided openings for politically active unions able to make campaign donations and sponsor candidates sympathetic to the profession. Key to this was a script that teachers, were in a unique position to protect the educational rights of children and therefore the future of society itself.

The Social Engineers III: The Blackboard, the Bottom Line, and a Conservative Revolution (1980–2010)

During the 1980s and 1990s, mythologies about the presumed pathologies of society emerged to justify the new policies. Complaints were aired about:

- high school graduates who could not read
- a new generation of juvenile delinquents described as "superpredators" intent on bringing mayhem to cities and neighborhoods
- teachers who did not teach and were protected by the teachers' unions
- administrators who could not discipline the unionized workforce
- a general decline in social morals

But of course these complaints were not new, but reflected the ongoing tension between egalitarianism, individualism, and utilitarianism. Indeed, if in fact this was the case that schools were experiencing struggles with old problems, then there must be a common underlying social force shaping the controversies. The battlelines between the interests of parents, businesses, teachers and others reemerged in a predictable pattern. This is in fact the *habitus* of the American character, which still values utilitarianism, individualism, and egalitarianism. They do so though in the context of an emotional tension as parents grudgingly but willingly release their children to be tutored by bureaucratic institutions.

Chapter 3

Bureaucratized Childhood and the Persistence of Schooling Systems: Irrationality in Rationality

Introduction

Like all other school systems, the United States' is rooted in values emerging out of a history and the dominant ideology. Among them were the habits of individualism, utilitarianism, and egalitarianism described in chapter 2. These values make for a coherent ideology in the abstract, but in bureaucratizing them, the logical conflicts between being individualistic and egalitarian, or idealistic and pragmatic at the same time inevitably present themselves. This happens as the very pragmatic bureaucratic structures needed to create a school system are developed. This chapter asks how the nature of bureaucratic organizations shapes the practical limitations for how such goals and all their inherent contradictions can be expressed.

Bureaucracies and Modern Societies

Bureaucracies are at the heart of any modern large enterprise. As the classical sociologist Max Weber noted, bureaucracies are essential for organizing modern life; they are the only human institution known capable of managing large tasks, be they the manufacture of automobiles, organization of a military, worldwide banking, enforcement of food and drug regulations, distribution of janitorial services, regulation of markets, conduct of foreign affairs, or any of the other modern specialized activities we take for granted. Bureaucracies do this by routinizing tasks, establishing hierarchies, insisting on efficiency, and endlessly quantifying the process of production. Educating children is a massive bureaucratic undertaking for every modern government, as it seeks to both create and define the good society, while also protecting an entrenched status quo.[1] To do so, the government sees like a bureaucratic state, which as Diane Ravitch (2010, 10) describes, is similar to "looking at schools and teachers and students from an altitude of 30,000 feet and seeing the students as objects to be moved around by big ideas and great plans."

In a bureaucracy, specialized tasks are divided between positions, not people. The end result is that a bureaucracy takes on a life of its own, as people become their positions, despite their individual personal qualities. "It is written therefore I can do no other regardless of my affection for you," becomes a bureaucratic watchword, meaning that personal considerations do not enter into evaluations of value, merit, and so forth. Personal details are inevitably lost when administrators examine programs. This is the case even though bureaucracies are still made up of humans who do seek personal relationships with each other. This happens despite the obvious paradox that bureaucracy is a rule book and a hierarchy, not a human being, even while the individuals mechanically enforcing (and following) the rules are normally (and obviously) very human (Weber 1947, 214–216).

But bureaucracy is still a complex and varied phenomenon, not a simple social category and especially not an epithet (Wilson 1991, 1). Different bureaucracies define tasks differently and take on characteristics of their own. This is particularly the case with public school bureaucracies whose goal is not to make a financial profit, but to create in children some vaguely described product, i. e., the adult. A range of such vaguely worded statements follows:

> The mission of Bear River High School is to provide a positive learning environment with opportunities for students to develop a *solid educational background* enabling them to become productive members of a changing society.

> The mission of Phineas Banning High School is to educate ethnically and economically diverse urban youth in *critical thinking and problem solving*, while also providing vocational and academic options to ensure a successful transition to the future as responsible adults.

> *The Sacramento City Unified School District provides all students the knowledge, skills, and educational opportunities to achieve* high academic standards *and be successful in a changing global society.*

OUR MISSION: Today and tomorrow: committed to *excellence for all.*
(Hutchinson High School, Kansas)

In Juneau we are all partners in providing each student with the skills, knowledge and attitudes to be a *contributing citizen* in a changing world.

Manhattan Hunter Science High School is a science-focused college-preparatory high school designed to give students the tools they need to achieve academic success.

(Emphases added)

In this inherent ambiguity and vagueness, teachers, managers, and executives in different schools shape and are habituated by a culture and ideology that serves the needs of the bureaucratic organization and, to borrow James Scott's term, they learn to "see like a state." Individuals, in other words, necessarily become invisible to the school bureaucracy focused on statistical abstractions. Notably this is different than business bureaucracies that, while also having their own culture (e. g., IBM likes one kind of suit, and Apple Computer prefers blue jeans) nevertheless see their task, i. e., generating profits, in sharper and less ambiguous terms.

James Q. Wilson (1991, 168–171) writes that public schools are "coping organizations," because it is inherently difficult for managers (i. e., principals), and executives (i. e., superintendents) to supervise the people (i. e., teachers) actually delivering the schools' products, be it "solid educational backgrounds," "critical thinking and problem solving," "high academic standards," "excellence for all," or "contributing citizens." These vague ideas are inherently difficult to define, much less "operationalize" into a "calculable metric," even though a responsible principal will insist that this be done. Nevertheless, as every administrator (and teacher) knows, once the classroom door closes, the administrator has little control of what learning happens or not. For that matter, neither does the teacher have much control, because they in turn are dependent on who parents send to school each morning.

To understand why this creates a difficult task for the schools, it is useful to return to the origins of bureaucratic organization, which is rooted in the nature of "rationalization." Rationalization is the process by which modern society is organized into deliberate, systematic, sober, methodical, and impersonal "jobs" to be undertaken by people with specific "skills." Rational systems are rule-driven and legalistic, and organized by the impersonal free market principles of capitalism (after Brubaker 1984, 2). In rationalizing tasks, be it the manufacture and marketing of widgets or the training of children, any rational bureaucracs always seek to control using nonhuman techniques, such as clocks, machines, procedures, and impersonal rule books. Schools are no different.

Bureaucracies, Manufacturing, and the Corporation

Bureaucracy long predates modern school systems—Egyptian Pharaohs had bureaucracies, as did Chinese Emperors who taxed far-flung farmers. But this was an old type of bureaucracy, rooted in coercion and the inheritance of position, and not the hopes and dreams of the modern marketplace. The modern form of the rationalized bureaucracy emerged only in recent years when capitalist marketplaces came to order the work, production, manufacture, and distribution of the world's goods. Rather than raw coercion, these bureaucracies sought to please and charm populations to desire consumer goods.

Adam Smith (1776) is the social scientist best known for describing why a rationally organized workshop with a reliance on wage laborers doing one task over and over was so much more efficient than the earlier forms of production. Such methods did not reward the different skills of laborers, but were run as households. In such patrimonial workshops or farms, the patriarch operated as an inefficient (but self-sufficient) unit, which focused not on market production but on feeding the household despite the demands of the marketplace. Thus on any one farm, most production is directed toward the needs of that one farmstead. There were few if any economies of scale; for example, sheep were raised, thread spun, cloth woven, and clothing sewn, all on the same farmstead by the same clan. Production occurred in the context of many other tasks that were needed to subsist, particularly the growing of food, and the raising of children. As for labor, the farmstead typically used only those born to it, married into it, or were indentured to it, rather than matching skilled job descriptions with applicant resumes like a bureaucratized human resources office does.

But when the powers of bureaucracy and the modern capitalist marketplace were combined, a new type of organization emerged. Adam Smith's (1776) classic example is a pin factory. He pointed out that when an unskilled individual attempts to make pins in the context of a home-based cottage industry, they can make only a couple of pins per day. But, when the tasks of making a pin are broken down into 18 different motions (e. g., pounding the head, attaching the head, lengthening the wire, sharpening the point, etc), given to specialists practiced at that particular task, and then organized on an assembly line, ten workers will make up to 48,000 pins in the same day! In short, he described the economies of scale in production that would drive the economy of the modern world via the rationalized impersonal free marketplace.

As Smith went on to point out, this required the presence of a large marketplace into which products could be sold for money. This in turn implied production, and the buying and selling of standardized goods by strangers whose only relationship was in the impersonal marketplace. Unlike the guildmaster and apprentice, they did not have much sentiment (positive or negative) for each other; rather they simply pursued cash profits. The advantage of this marketplace meant that everyone could specialize and become highly skilled at their particular task, and most importantly trade with other specialized factories for that which they needed. Products and even parts of products became standardized so that the vast world marketplace, could readily recognize the utility and desirability of an item. This happened particularly in textiles, as the new capitalists purchased cotton from North America and India, which was then spun and woven into cloth in Great Britain, and exported to the world. All this of course was dependent on the standardization of the money, capital, and labor, which created the product. A combination of market incentives and punishments (i. e., the assumption of psychological behaviorism) underlay the efficiencies of the marketplace.

Driving such "rationalization" was a very simple measure of success: cash profits as measured in money. The new industrialists found that as long as they watched their bottom line, their businesses generated more money than they put in. Such profits, which were easily measured by accountants, highlighted the power of the new capitalist mode of production. And more importantly, the market provided an important check on inefficient and weak economic performance. Companies, product lines, and individuals who did not help produce a profit were quickly dismissed, regardless of sentiment. This applied to the nonhuman ingredients and to the human workers as well. Indeed, this is why capitalism came to be seen as a cruel taskmaster by nineteenth century social theorists who saw the armies of workers who produced great wealth thrown out of work, and denied basic subsistence whenever the economic cycle had a hiccup.

In this context, the older sentimental modes of production in which guildmasters cared for their apprentices as individuals disappeared and was replaced by the naked logic of cold, hard cash in the labor market. In short, an old way of life, inefficient, impoverished, but emphasizing relationships, was replaced by a new one, which was productive, impersonal, and rational. More importantly, this new world had an effect on the culture and *habitus* of society, as people came to think routinely that life was shaped first by the rationalized marketplace and second by the rationalized impersonal legalisms, which shaped the new markets and described when and how trade is conducted. For just as markets require predictable supplies of inputs and demand for products, self-interested producers and consumers demand the application of rules without respect to personal relationships.

Government Bureaucracies and Schools

But, unlike a private corporation, government bureaucracies are not dependent on their existence for profits in the rationalized marketplace. They are though dependent on political legitimacy, which, in the case of democracies, is rationalized in terms of votes and proxies for votes, such as campaign contributions. This makes public bureaucracies different from the more focused private bureaucracies, as Weber recognized long ago. But they both still share the characteristic of rationality, in which depersonalization means that for schools the tasks of creating an adult are divided into discrete specialized tasks and ordered by grade level, using the same principles Adam Smith described in the pin factory.

But what is "the product" of the school if it is not financial profit? In the United States where egalitarianism, individualism, and utility are all important values, government services are often evaluated in the context of these values, not the hard-nosed profits of the private sector. And while all government agencies do have such pressures, the unique task of the schools make them a different type of institution than the post office, whose efficiency is easily measured by evaluating how fast and accurately letters are delivered. In the case of schooling and the rearing of children, this also includes coping with vague goals and emphases on equity, utility, parental rights, and child development. Despite the contradictions embedded in such goals, the *habitus* that make up culture emerges in the relationships of administrators, principals, teachers, parents, and ultimately the children they all profess to serve. The result is constant evaluation and self-evaluation via such measures as graduation rates and data designed to measure bureaucratic success. The only question remaining is a cruel one for a bureaucratic schools system that they never answer very well: the question of how to dispose of the imperfect waste products resulting from the manufacturing process?

Coping with Vague Goals

Government takes on many tasks which the private sector cannot, or will not. Some are easily defined by the bureaucracy. The postal service comes to mind (how many letters were delivered without error?), and the social security administration does too (how many monthly checks were distributed in the right amount?). Both are government bureaucracies, which lend themselves to bureaucratic metrics borrowed from the private sector. But all government bureaucracies are not like that. Among the more vague tasks are things like the conduct of foreign affairs, administration of justice, guaranteeing social welfare, enforcement of criminal laws, those regulating the economy, creating and enforcing safety regulations, and maintenance of national identity. Schooling is certainly among these tasks, as mission statements identify vague but impressive goals like a "solid educational background" or "contributing citizen" rather than the evaluative procedures like test scores, graduation rates, etc., which are used as *de facto* proxies. In other words, the "critical task" (Wilson 1991:365) of the schools are very different than a pin-making factory. Nor is it clear when these tasks are done in a more or less effective fashion, since there are no metrics, like profits or votes, to decide when a government bureaucracy has been successful.

Many government bureaucracies are what James Q. Wilson (1991: 168–171) called "coping organizations," whose mission is to deal with an ongoing issue such as management of foreign affairs or providing defense. Such coping agencies, as a result develop similar cultures and structures. The people at the "ground level," who Wilson calls "the operators," are necessarily given a great deal of discretion because of the vague nature of their task, a situation that puts their supervisors at risk because ultimately police officers, teachers, social workers, and so forth can only be imprecisely supervised as they cope with their vague tasks. As a result, an implicit exchange is made; supervisors are expected to back up their subordinates, while the subordinates avoid situations that are politically embarrassing. Except for the very highest levels, in such coping agencies, those promoted tend to come from within the organization. In the schools, this means that principals tend to have experience as teachers, and superintendents as principals. Professional loyalty is valued.

Coping agencies most famously include police departments where individual officers operate in mobile cars without direct observation by supervisors. By the very nature of their job, police officers have a great deal of discretion in how they enforce laws. Schools, in which teachers operate for the most part unobserved by supervisors are also coping agencies, and teachers most often teach without direct supervision by superiors and have a great deal of discretion in how they deal with each student. School administrators are expected to support teachers, as are their colleagues, against challenges by students and parents, just as police officers expect superiors to protect them from complaints, and give the officer the benefit of any doubt. In such coping agencies, too, "success" is only defined by what others do or not do. In the case of police officers, it is in terms of what crimes are *not* committed, and for teachers, it is quite often focused by how students assigned to them for a brief period do on an exam. Both are at best only imprecise stand-ins for the type of direct supervision you have on a normal factory line. But it is often the best that can be hoped for given the nature of the copying profession.

Emphasis on Equity

A capitalist economy is about the unequal results of economic competition. Impersonal markets are ideally allowed to determine which corporate bureaucracies will make money and who will be put out of business. Regardless of the sentimental worth of the individuals concerned. Government agencies are different, at least in theory, and seek to provide citizens with equal protection under the law. A professionalism focused on equal treatment of all clients is highly valued, and in theory at least, teachers are typically rewarded for serving both the winners and losers in academic competition.

This emphasis on equity permits schools to be at the forefront of the post *Brown v. Board of Education* civil rights revolution, which included controversy about desegregation policies such as bussing to affirmative action. But as discussed above, while education and equal rights have long been associated with schooling, this is not the only source of its legitimacy. Economic utility is, too.

Emphasis on Utility

Thus, much of the critique of modern twenty-first-century schools comes from a business community that asks what value per dollar "invested" is delivered to society by the schools? This is often framed in terms of the labor market, which is why American schools so often point to statistics indicating that the more education a worker has, the higher the lifetime earnings (see Figure 3.1).

Thus, the worth of any particular course of study is evaluated based on success in the labor market, even though any one course can only very imprecisely be correlated with on-the-job productivity months or, more commonly, years and decades after graduation; such studies were why students were tracked into laundry and other vocational programs in the 1910s and is the basis for career vocational education in the 1990s and early 2000s. An example of how the value of education is monetized follows:

> How much is higher education worth in cold hard money? A college master's degree is worth $1.3 million more in lifetime earnings than a high school diploma, according to a recent report from the U.S. Census Bureau.
>
> The report titled *"The Big Payoff: Educational Attainment and Synthetic Estimates of Work-Life Earnings"* (.pdf) reveals that over an adult's working life, high school graduates can expect, on average, to earn $1.2 million; those with a bachelor's degree, $2.1 million; and people with a master's degree, $2.5 million. (Accessed at About.com by Robert Longley, August 24, 2011). http://usgovinfo.about.com/od/moneymatters/a/edandearnings.htm

Because of the claims that schools make for the financial utility of their "product," this emphasis is perhaps stronger than in other coping bureaucracies. For example, prisons are not asked to justify themselves on the

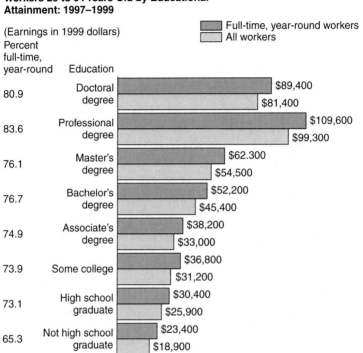

Work Experience and Average Annual Earnings of Workers 25 to 64 Years Old by Educational Attainment: 1997–1999

(Earnings in 1999 dollars)

■ Full-time, year-round workers
□ All workers

Percent full-time, year-round	Education	
80.9	Doctoral degree	$89,400 / $81,400
83.6	Professional degree	$109,600 / $99,300
76.1	Master's degree	$62.300 / $54,500
76.7	Bachelor's degree	$52,200 / $45,400
74.9	Associate's degree	$38,200 / $33,000
73.9	Some college	$36,800 / $31,200
73.1	High school graduate	$30,400 / $25,900
65.3	Not high school graduate	$23,400 / $18,900

Figure 3.1 Census Data Describing the Relationship between Employment and Earnings, 1997–1999.
Source: U.S. Census Bureau, Current Population Surveys, March 1998, 1999, and 2000.

basis of the value of justice delivered to victims. Nor do diplomats figure into their cost-benefit ratios the "value" of wars averted. But schools routinely produce such figures, even if the product is vague and money an imprecise measure at best.

The problem for schools is that despite assertions to the contrary, the product of schools is still inherently difficult to monetize because there is at best a weak relationship between what is done in any one particular classroom, and what happens in a job market months or, more likely, years later. But monetization of projected salaries, is deep in the American cultural *habitus,* because it is also about what private business, whose own bureaucracies are rooted in such marketplace calculation. Because schools are indeed bureaucracies, such practices seemingly cannot be avoided, no matter how fallacious they may be.

Emphasis on Legalistic Parental Rights

Parents are involved in the school system in a longer and more intimate fashion than in any other public bureaucracy. They bring children to teachers hired in the labor market, and routinely surrender traditional parental rights, usually willingly. Indeed, this surrender even has a legal term and doctrine associated with it. Schools act *in loco parentis* under the assumption that this is in "the best interests of the child" (Goldstein et al 1996). Ironically in exercising this responsibility, schools call on parents to remain engaged with the school. And as any parent who has ever signed the multiple beginning-of-school forms knows, they are expected to support school policies regarding discipline, study habits, teacher rights, drug policy, free lunch programs, and (my favorite) notifications regarding the application of pesticides.

But parents are not disinterested observers meekly surrendering rights. Parents themselves have typically experienced at least 13 years of education, themselves and more, as a parent. Parents assume an expertise alongside the professional teacher—an expertise acknowledged by laws encouraging parent involvement in the classroom environment. Indeed, this expertise is even assumed in the context of the legal statutes, which permit parents to intervene in the implementation of school policies regarding the delivery of curriculum and participation in school governance.

Thus, in the give-and-take process of surrendering a child to be trained by the schools, the prerogatives of both parents and teachers are jealously guarded in legalistic and emotional dances ostensibly in the best interests of the child. This sustained interaction is the most intense one parents are likely to experience on behalf of their children, even if in the end, rights are indeed surrendered, not just to the school but also the end-product who is the 18-year-old adult.

Schools and Teachers

Logically, teaching by its very nature is a profession that should be professionalized in the way the practice of law, medicine, nursing, and social work are rather than bureaucratized like the work of factory-line worker. This is because teachers are independent operators possessing particular skills that are difficult to observe and control using the rule books that organize the assembly lines of the modern global marketplace (Wilson 1988). Indeed, two of the general goals that a teacher faces are even contradictory. For example, on the one hand, teachers are asked to generate student energies to produce learning and control student energies in order to maintain order (see Wilson 1989:40; Waller 1932). On top of this, student energies, learning, and order, while complementary, are not easily measured, quantified, or supervised in a bureaucratic fashion.

Nevertheless, unlike those other professions, teaching is bureaucratized rather than professionalized. The result is elaborate involvement by local, state, and national governments attempting to control what happens in the classroom. State legislatures, school boards, and other legislative bodies respond to political pressures by promulgating more rules and regulations for entry into the classroom, requiring self-reports on teacher activities inclusion of curricula demanded by particular interest groups, and prescribing ever more elaborate testing regimes. Teachers meanwhile respond by becoming increasingly defensive in response to administrative and parent involvement in the classroom.

As James Q. Wilson writes (1989:150–153), this results in a paradox for school reformers, particularly those emerging from the outside. Reform is dependent on controlling teachers, but teachers are inherently difficult to control using available bureaucratic metrics and methods. Superintendents cannot directly observe the tasks undertaken, even assuming they can figure out what that task is. Political pressures of different constituencies multiply through institutions like parents clubs, school boards, Rotary Clubs, Chambers of Commerce, state school boards, regulations generated by state education officials, and finally federal bureaucracies attuned to issues of equal opportunity. As is well known, the result is that all reform affects only the margins, particularly if teachers do not buy in.

Bureaucracies, Institutionalized *Habitus*, and the Irrationality of Rationality

Individual teachers (and policemen) create a defensive *habitus* as a result of their peculiar relationship between the inherently political nature of their profession, the organization of the school as a factory line, and their status as a skilled profession. Among the consequences are that friendships on and off the job tend to be with other teachers, and credentialing, licensing, and certification systems emerge, which focus careers and energies on one district, often for decades, isolating them from broader professional trends. This *habitus* extends up the line, as supervisors, who are typically promoted from the ranks, are asked to "keep the back" of the teachers who work for them, particularly with respect to parent and student challenges to their authority.

A big part of the teacher's protective armor is the legalism of the rationalized rule book, including union contracts, written in anticipation of any and all contingencies. This results in "the rationality of irrationality" as enforcing the rulebook, without reference to the overall task, becomes a strategy like it is in many coping bureaucracies (See Waters 2001, 37–38; Ritzer 2008, 26–56). Examples developed below include The Rubber Room (Freedman 2007) created by New York City schools for teacher punishment, Individualized Learning Programs designed to satisfy highly valued efforts at preserving equity on behalf of vulnerable disable students, and the persistence of small school districts. Each condition results in widely told tales about what are, from a strictly utilitarian perspective, about waste and calls for further attempts to rationalize in the interest of budget efficiency. These are stories about "the irrationality in rationality" But the best example I know of the "irrationality in rationality" is not about schools but comes from another coping bureaucracy, the police force. The story is about "The King of Ruffle Bar," which is about a dog who was happily living on an island off Long Island in 1970.

> Visible only from a distance, the dog, nicknamed the King of Ruffle Bar, had sustained itself for an estimated two years, was apparently in good health, and presumably would have survived in this semi-wild state, barring accident for the rest of its natural life. However, some well-meaning soul heard about the dog and reported him to the Society for the Prevention of Cruelty to Animals, thereby setting the bureaucratic wheels in motion. Since the King could not be approached by people, a baited trap was set. According to the Times report, ". . . every day a police launch from Sheepshead Bay takes off for Ruffle Bar, the uninhabited swampy island of the dog. Every day a police helicopter hovers for a half hour or more over Ruffle Bar.". . . When questioned, representatives of the ASPCA said: "When we catch the dog we will find a happy home for it."
>
> The ASPCA became obsessed with capturing the dog. Once triggered, the ASPCA involved the police with remorseless, mindless persistence that is too terrifyingly characteristic of bureaucracies once they are activated . . . Emotionally [the police] sided with the King, even while carrying out their orders. "Why don't they leave the dog alone?" said one policeman. Another observed, "The dog is as happy as a pig in a puddle.". . .
>
> The delusional aspects have to do with the institutionalized necessity to control "everything," and the widely accepted notion that the bureaucrat knows what is best; never for a moment does he doubt the validity of the bureaucratic solution (see Hall 1976:10–11).

The King of Ruffle Bar ultimately is really a story of bureaucratized institutional *habitus*. The impersonal rule book overrode the actions of all others involved. Legalism reigned, despite the complaints of the field level operators flying the helicopters, chasing the dog, and presumably those reporting the story on television. No supervisor overruled the decision of any police officer to follow the rules. No police officer challenged the rule-book, which under normal conditions gives their job meaning and protects and defines not only their job, but their identity. This happens even as they are ordered to capture the King of Ruffle Bar.

In the same fashion there is a dance in the schoolhouse. Rules are cre-ated and mechanistically obeyed. Operators (teachers) suspend profes-sional judgment to mechanistically satisfy abstract regulations in a rule book. The stories of irrationality in the rationality are legion and heard often in teacher's lounges. Among them are complaints about the large expenditures made to accommodate special needs student in otherwise cash-strapped classrooms, the funding of politically sacred programs while class sizes rise, and so forth.

The "Rubber Room," created by the New York City schools in the 1990s and 2000s to discipline teachers, reflects the irrationality in ratio-nality well. It is a story from the nation's largest school district, which has made the rounds of not only the teachers' lounges but also leaked into the popular press in the form of articles in the New York *Times* and other pub-lications. There was even a movie *The Rubber Room* released in 2009. The Rubber Room is a nickname for the reassignment centers where, in the early 2000s, about 760 out of New York City's 80,000 teachers would be assigned to sit and do nothing. Teachers assigned were those who typically ran afoul of administrative rules, the law, or other disciplinary actions, and contested it. The rubber rooms were small rooms without access to the outside world where teachers would quietly spend the day while collecting full pay until termination cases could be brought to an arbitrator. Teachers in effect reported for work, did nothing, and at the end of the day returned home. According to a 2007 New York Times article:

> "From our perspective, it's not punitive," said Andrew Gordon, the direc-tor of employee relations at the department [of education]. "It's all about respect for the other employees" both in the rubber room itself and in other department offices on the floor, he said. Of the ban on keeping personal items, he said: "We don't want to play policeman. It turns into an adminis-trative nightmare." (Freedman 2007.)

This may make sense from the perspective of the New York City schools administration—after all on any one day, fewer than 1 percent of their teachers are undergoing administrative sanctions in the rubber room. But from the perspective of the individual teacher, the consequences are pro-fessionally and emotionally catastrophic, even though there is no financial sanction—in other words, the policy achieves its administrative goal of cheaply creating a disciplined teaching force. Administrators apparently appreciate the terror that the presence of the rubber room extends to their

80,000 teachers at a relatively low financial cost. But such policies are ultimately what the irrationality in rationality is all about. The rubber room suits administrative convenience, as the immediate needs of the bureaucracy to fulfill the demands of the rulebook come first—to deviate threatens the integrity of the overall bureaucratic structure.

The *Habitus* of Irrationality and the Search for Utility, Equity, and Bureaucratic Conformity

In such a bureaucratic context, responses to general problems are easily pushed aside to accommodate the *habitus* of entrenched interests. Perhaps my favorite is the general response to the idea of having school hours changed in order to control juvenile delinquency. It is widely understood from research that most "bad behavior" by teenagers occurs after the time that students leave school and before parents get home about 5:30 in the evening. The general proposal is to move the "latchkey" time to the morning by having schools begin class at 10:00 a. m., and have the children go home at 5:00 p. m. The idea is that fewer kids will get out of bed to commit crimes while traveling leisurely to school in the morning than would do so while returning home from school. This common-sense idea is typically dismissed by observations that it would disrupt established bus schedules, teacher contracts, etc. None of the objections question the validity of the data or the logic of the assumption. Rather the objections are to the disruptions of the established *habitus*.

Two more general examples, Individualized Learning Programs and the persistence of small, inefficient school districts, illustrate most directly the contradictions embedded in the irrationality in rationality. In the case of Individualized Learning Programs, the importance of individualism trumps economic utilitarianism. The persistence of small schools reflects a nostalgia for equity between rural and urban society; this time equity trumps economic efficiency, and the irrationality in rationality again appears, at least by the terms of the programmatic business interests funding the school programs via taxes.

Individualized Learning Programs in a Mass Institution: Equity and Bureaucracy

In the United States, individualized educational programs are a civil rights issue under the Individuals with Disabilities Education Act (IDEA). The act itself appeals to very deeply embedded conflict in the American *habitus* of individualism and egalitarianism, but a paradox emerges when utilitarianism is considered. Bureaucracies derive their efficiencies from standardization and economies of scale; they are not well-suited to the individualization of instruction or anything else.

IDEA was a successor law to earlier guarantees from the federal government that handicapped children would have access to a free and appropriate education. Passed in 1990 (and renewed in 2005), IDEA specifies 13 physical, emotional and learning disabilities, including vaguely defined disorders such as "developmental delay," Attention Deficit Hyperactivity Disorder (ADHD), emotional disorders, and so forth. In effect there are 13 exceptions that require the bureaucracy to suspend its demand for economies of scale and create an alternative. Any parent can petition to have their child covered by the act, and a successful petition in turn triggers a board meeting composed of teachers, administrators, parents, and special education specialists who develop an "Individualized Educational Plan" for the child. In essence, a bureaucratic organization is assembled to apply rules that require individualization in the context of the larger group. To satisfy the letter of the rules—another bureaucratic goal—cost is not to be a central consideration; rather all reasonable alternatives are to be accepted by the school district in order to accommodate the best interests of the child. In such a context, a savvy, emotionally engaged "helicopter parent" becomes an advocate for a particular plan and program for their only own child.

Prescriptions for eligible students can lead to very expensive "treatment" for children, particularly for those who have both a serious disability and an aggressive parent who has a grasp of the law. Thus, the irrationality in the rationality of IDEA emerges. Designed as a rational way to deal with those who fall outside the more general law, it creates new situations which are irrational, albeit in different ways. One problem—i.e., the inability to provide equal opportunity—is traded for another—i.e., the capacity to efficiently deliver uniform services. Whether one type or the other of these compromises is preferable, I will leave to the reader. Suffice it to say, though, that implicitly and explicitly, compromises in the rationality of bureaucratic goals are always made.

Small School Districts

The irrationality in rationality is perhaps no more surprising than in the protection extended routinely to the small rural school districts in the United States, many in the rural West. Schools that were funded locally in the distant past are now funded with tax money collected by state-level bureaucracies. However because such districts are small—including perhaps only a few dozen students—per-student operating costs are inevitably higher, often for programs that are academically weaker and a curriculum that is inevitably narrower because economies of scale cannot be realized. In other words, these are districts that should have long ago been consolidated into larger schools in the interests of equity, utility, and economy. But individualism and its close cousin "local control" are also important. The rural elected school board remains to protect local interests in having "their" own school and "their" teachers. Small schools with small class sizes and three to four teachers for the K–8 persist, even as other nearby schools are overcrowded. The small school districts are justified basis of the ultimate confession of irrationality: "tradition." Indeed, many states have specific funding provisions to pay for the persistence of small school districts, regardless of the fact that study after study has shown that as a group, they are more expensive and of lower quality (see e. g., Zimmerman 2009). This is often justified in the context of nostalgia for "The Little Red Schoolhouse." What is more, such schools successfully demand subsidies to compensate for the lost economies of scale:

> Compensating rural, small schools for high operating costs does require extra funding. But if small schools seem to offer environments more conducive to learning than those in large schools, then the investment makes sense. Moreover, the total cost in state finance formulas is insignificant when compared to the high cost of neglecting the needs of the 40 percent of the nation's children who attend schools in rural areas. (Verstegen 1991.)

As with the persistence of Individual Learning Programs, the small, inefficient schools reflects important *habitus* of the American culture, in this case an emotional insistence that rural children should have the same rights as urban children, despite cost. The result is the persistence of such schools, despite what rational efficiencies might otherwise be realized—there is rationality in the irrationality due to the emotional tug of local control, individual rights, and sentiment.

School Bureaucracies and Their Limitations

Individual Learning Programs rooted in equity, and small schools rooted in demands for individualism, are just two examples of the many inefficiencies introduced to the nation's schools. Ultimately what such examples illustrate is that, school bureaucracies administer a task outside the rationalized world of tests, budgets, rule-making, and planning. It is a reminder that the product of schools is irrational, emotional individuals, families, generations, and nations. Unlike businesses, schools go beyond the simple demands of economics and investment and are, as Durkheim and Bourdieu pointed out, about re-creating society itself. It is in this context that the limitations of school bureaucracies emerge, focused by the 70-year-long habitus of generational change, the emotion of parenting, the problem of self-reflectivity, and nationalism.

The 70-Year-Long *Habitus* and the Rhetoric of Nostalgia

In chapter 2, I discussed the 70-year-long *habitus* of education. This long cycle emerges because people begin their socialization into schooling as five- or six-year-olds (in the United States, anyway) and come to take the procedures they observe for granted as being the right and good way to conduct schools. As I discussed earlier, this happens in the context of teachers and administrators who themselves are influenced by institutions they attended some 40 or 50 years earlier.

A good example of how the *habitus* of such nostalgia drives policy and discussion about schools is well-illustrated by the wide circulation of the results of a survey of teachers done in 1940 and in 1990. In the survey, teachers were asked what were the top disciplinary problems in the schools. The following lists were generated (Table 3.1)

This list became an important driver of public policy in the 1980s, 1990s, and 2000s, and cited by a wide range of policy makers concerned with what they saw as the deterioration of schools, in particular, and society, in general. Among the public policy advocates explicitly citing the study were Billy Graham, Rush Limbaugh, Ross Perot, Barbara Bush, and President Clinton's Surgeon General Jocelyn Elders. By 1994, O'Neill (1994) claimed that he had collected "almost 400 examples of people quoting these lists. Their diffusion was amazing—they were surely the most

Table 3.1 Top Disciplinary Problems in Schools in 1940 and 1990

1940	1990
Talking out of turn	Drug abuse
Chewing gum	Alcohol Abuse
Making noise	Pregnancy
Running in the hall	Suicide
Cutting in line	Rape
Dress code violations	Robbery
Littering	Assault

cited educational statistic, used by private citizens, mayors and senators, and movie stars."

The list popped up in Dear Abby, Ann Landers, and all of the major news magazines. Former Education Secretary William Bennett also did a great deal to disseminate the list, scolding schools during his campaigns to promote public morality, using it in interviews, and in an article he wrote for *Reader's Digest*. The survey results resonated a great deal with what older Americans remembered about their own school experience and the world they perceived their grandchildren were experiencing in the 1990s and later. In other words, the studies resonated so deeply with the ingrained, persistent American *habitus*.

There was of course, only one problem, as O'Neill described in his 1994 article "The Invention of the Schools Discipline List," which was that no comparable surveys had ever been undertaken in 1940 or 1990. What O'Neill found was that the lists were in fact a rhetorical device crafted in 1981 by billionaire T. Cullen Davis from two different studies. The first was probably from a study of "daily disturbances" undertaken in the early 1940s. O'Neill was able to find such a reference in *Texas Teachers* magazine. As O'Neill points out, the prominence of gum chewing on the list was probably due to a 1930s campaign to restrict that habit as being unsanitary. As for the "1990" list, it actually came from the "Safe School 1977" study in which principals were simply asked whether they had reported a particular crime to authorities during the previous six months. Just how much this study really resonates is illustrated by the fact that despite O'Neill's high-profile debunking, the lists continue to be cited in articles and dissertations (see e. g., Pentasuglia-Filipek, 2008; Volokh and Snell 1998) into the twenty-first century.

The use of such "remembered past," and the long *habitus* it reflects, is perhaps nowhere more evident than in the comment section of legislative debates, blogs, and newspapers when there is an educational policy issue. Advocates frequently root their view of a particular policy in their own experiences from previous years. I follow one particular blog in particular, *Bridging Differences* by education experts Diane Ravitch and Deborah Meier. Both women are in their 70s, and very well schooled in educational history, as are a number of their commenters. Both Ravitch and Meier, and especially those commenting, draw on personal experiences as teachers, parents, and students. For example on December 1, 2009, Ravitch recalled what happened to her mother in Houston's schools of 1926:

> One of the institutions that made this country a great haven for immigrants was its public education system. After only a few years in Houston, my mother learned to speak perfect English, and she was a proud graduate of

the Houston public schools (circa 1926). Free public education helped our country to prosper. And above all, it provided almost everyone a chance to make a better life for themselves and their children.

Ravitch, Meier, and others argue this way because in the American *habitus* of pragmatism one sentence such practical experience is an effective rhetorical technique in debating policy issues; Ravitch is hardly the only American to have a mother or grandmother who in retrospect credits the schools for their success and wonders why this success cannot be repeated. As a result such stories shape political decisions, in this particular case over 80 years later. And indeed, this technique is more likely to be tried with education, something that all of us at some level experienced, as opposed to issues clouded in more esoteric expertise like engineering, medicine, or law. This is because, more so than such technical fields, rational schooling is tied to emotional parenting—and vice versa.

Parenting, Emotions, and Flunking

Parents and schools are fundamentally different social institutions. Parents are emotionally and sentimentally attached to one particular child and evaluate what a school does in that context. Schools on the other hand are bureaucratic institutions and evaluate what is done to a *group* of children, not the individual. Schools necessarily, as James Scott (1999) wrote, "See Like a State" via numbers and reports. This is why averages (or medians) on assessment tests are important for school management, and the outliers at one end or the other, or the learning disabilities or strengths of any particularly exceptional child can be ignored. In reconciling this tension, the bureaucratic face of the school, the teacher, is called on to both "see like a state" and "see like a parent." Like parents, they are responsible for making children into adults who fit into preexisting social order as workers, citizens, and even parents. But, unlike parents, children who fail to fit into these roles can be flunked by the teacher, and at least told to try another class. Parents of course do not have the privilege of flunking *their* child, and asking them to try a new parent.

The net result of this paradox is that there is a chronic tension between parents and teachers in the bureaucratic order. One of the more ironic consequences is that teachers become valued for a capacity to connect emotionally with their students, particularly in the early grades. This is despite the fact that teachers are explicitly hired in a bureaucratized labor market and undertake teaching as a source of financial income. Such commercialization of feeling, or "emotional work," is inherently a constraint on what teachers can become, as surely as it is for flight attendants and bill collectors (see Hochschild 1983), or more precisely perhaps, professional attorneys who are called upon to defend rapists (see Siemsen 2004). Teachers are told to routinely establish an emotional bond with children, which will be maintained across a school year but then shed. This relationship is among the most intimate a child will have. Or as third grade teacher Philip Done (2009, 3) writes

> We love, care, guide, and nurture. We collect baby teeth, check foreheads for fevers, and can punch the little silver dots on top of juice boxes with one swift poke of the straw. We are used to being called Mom and Dad. I wonder: Why don't we have a word that captures the essence of being a teacher—a word that encompasses the spirit of teaching? *Motherhood* and *fatherhood* are words. *Parenthood* is a word. I think *teacherhood* should be a word, too.

But, unlike the parent, every year teachers let go of this relationship, in order that a new one can be established with the next cohort of children.

Corporate Bureaucracy, School Bureaucracy

A utilitarian ethic underlies much of American business, and as discussed in chapter 2, permeates the culture. In business, there is an excitement about the efficiencies that such utilitarianism permits, particularly in the manufacture, distribution, and marketing of products. As is often pointed out this "business model" makes for efficient corporate bureaucracies in which utility is valued, and specific ingredients, parts, workers, and operations are ruthlessly evaluated for their effectiveness in a competitive marketplace. This is impersonal bureaucratic management at its best. This prompts people like Frederick Hess (2006, 1), one of the promoters of the 2001 No Child Left Behind Act, to assert grandly: "I want to talk bluntly about accountability, competition, excellence, and the public good," and to advocate the "tough love" and "entrepreneurship" learned in the private sector, as if no one else had ever thought of the problem, bluntly or otherwise.

Hess of course is not the first reformer to try their hand at inserting putative business principles into public education. There were business reformers in the early part of the twentieth century, and there have been more since the 1970s, all seeking to create the system that produces a desired result from the public schools. Some of these programs have worked and contributed to the efficient operation of central office. They have been less successful in attempting to change what happens in the classroom. One businessman turned education reformer tells this story about why such efforts inevitably fail.

The Blueberry Story: The Teacher Gives the Businessman a Lesson

"If I ran my business the way you people operate your schools, I wouldn't be in business very long!"

I stood before an auditorium filled with outraged teachers who were becoming angrier by the minute. My speech had entirely consumed their precious 90 minutes of inservice. Their initial icy glares had turned to restless agitation. You could cut the hostility with a knife.

I represented a group of business people dedicated to improving public schools. I was an executive at an ice cream company that became famous in the middle 1980s when *People Magazine* chose our blueberry as the "Best Ice Cream in America."

I was convinced of two things. First, public schools needed to change; they were archaic selecting and sorting mechanisms designed for the industrial age and out of step with the needs of our emerging "knowledge society". Second, educators were a major part of the problem: they resisted change, hunkered down in their feathered nests, protected by tenure and shielded by a bureaucratic monopoly. They needed to look to business. We knew how to produce quality. Zero defects! TQM! Continuous improvement!

In retrospect, the speech was perfectly balanced—equal parts ignorance and arrogance.

As soon as I finished, a woman's hand shot up. She appeared polite, pleasant—she was, in fact, a razor-edged, veteran, high school English teacher who had been waiting to unload.

She began quietly, "We are told, sir, that you manage a company that makes good ice cream."

I smugly replied, "Best ice cream in America, Ma'am."

"How nice," she said. "Is it rich and smooth?"

"Sixteen percent butterfat," I crowed.

"Premium ingredients?" she inquired.

"Super-premium! Nothing but triple A." I was on a roll. I never saw the next line coming.

"Mr. Vollmer," she said, leaning forward with a wicked eyebrow raised to the sky, "when you are standing on your receiving dock and you see an inferior shipment of blueberries arrive, what do you do?"

In the silence of that room, I could hear the trap snap. . . . I was dead meat, but I wasn't going to lie.

"I send them back."

"That's right!" she barked, "and we can never send back our blueberries. We take them big, small, rich, poor, gifted, exceptional, abused, frightened, confident, homeless, rude, and brilliant. We take them with ADHD, junior rheumatoid arthritis, and English as their second language. We take them all! Every one! And that, Mr. Vollmer, is why it's not a business. It's school!"

In an explosion, all 290 teachers, principals, bus drivers, aides, custodians and secretaries jumped to their feet and yelled, "Yeah! Blueberries! Blueberries!"

And so began my long transformation.

Since then, I have visited hundreds of schools. I have learned that a school is not a business. Schools are unable to control the quality of their raw material, they are dependent upon the vagaries of politics for a reliable revenue stream, and they are constantly mauled by a howling horde of disparate, competing customer groups that would send the best CEO screaming into the night.

None of this negates the need for change. We must change what, when, and how we teach to give all children maximum opportunity to thrive in a post-industrial society. But educators cannot do this alone; these changes can occur only with the understanding, trust, permission and active support of the surrounding community. For the most important thing I have learned is that schools reflect the attitudes, beliefs and health of the communities they serve, and therefore, to improve public education means more than changing our schools, it means changing America. (Vollmer 2002 used with permission)

Vollmer's anecdote well identifies the tension between schools and business bureaucracies, and indeed, the inherent differences between them. What it highlights is the fact that schools are not both a business and a school; even though both of them are bureaucratic organizations, it is still the case that, as Max Weber (and James Q. Wilson) pointed out, private and public bureaucracies by their very nature are inherently different.

Blueberry stories are used by teacher advocates focused on a demand to promote equality at the expense of "quality," and who want to explain why business should retreat from the education arena and leave the job of education to professionals (i. e., themselves). But this is not going to happen in a society in which economic utility is still a central underlying habitual value—in such a context, there will always be the temptation to apply the dominant bureaucratic paradigm, that of the private corporation, to a vast education establishment that seems to operate less efficiently. But the blueberry example does highlight the limit to how far business models can be used to develop in the American school system. In essence, it points to first the limits of bureaucratic action in school administration, as well as the nonrational behavior always found in the creation of adults out of children.

Why Business Leaders Are Always Frustrated:
The *Habitus* of Utilitarianism

Still, even though bureaucratic action remains the most effective way to deliver public education, its level of cost efficiency can never reach that of the private sector. The tasks are different, constituencies are too diffuse, goals too imprecise, and most importantly perhaps, embedded in emotion. Demands for "reform" are really a coping strategy in a bureaucracy that depends on the rhetoric of emotion to maintain political legitimacy. Administrators assert that particular goals are reached or not, depending on a predetermined moral position. But ultimately such coping is not about finishing a structure like building a dam or achieving a sales goal; the result is that business leaders are always likely to be frustrated when applying their methods, embedded as they are in incentives and sanctions, to public schooling. In the mind of American business, the step to imagining the public schools as one giant human resources department for a blueberry ice cream plant, focused on training and sorting workers for the modern work force, is a short one. But of course, as Vollmer wrote, children are not blueberries and the match between the business model and schools is imprecise at best.

This means that the goals of people applying bureaucratic business principles to schools are inevitably frustrated, as they wrestle with the irrationality in such rationality. Schools are not the same as a corporate bureaucracy making blueberry ice cream, or for that matter capturing the "King of Ruffle Bar." Nor are they simply serving business interests by training workforce-ready employees for private human-resources offices. The problem is that businesspeople in their daily lives develop a *habitus* that directs them to look at human institutions, including businesses and schools, in terms of efficiency, predictability, calculability and control; they believe as a result that their own *habitus* for running business enterprises can be transferred into the classroom. When this does not work, or there is resistance from students, parents, or teachers—it is indeed frustrating.

But if business reformers are frustrated, so are parents. They surrender their children to a bureaucracy where they are systematically pushed aside, albeit willingly, as their children are shaped to the goals of the state and its economy by technicians hired in a labor market. Improbable as it seems, for parents such alienation is indeed a desirable goal, which is why public schooling does in fact share a great deal of legitimacy in the modern world.

Teachers are of course caught in the middle of these demands and respond by isolating themselves as individuals and a profession from both the emotions that people like the third-grade teacher Philip Done quoted above, are expected to deliver, and the dry test results that they are asked to produce. Teachers are held accountable by the state for the achievements and mistakes of children they did not parent, and by parents for emotional bonds they cannot sustain. Pushed into a frustrating corner, they respond by becoming more insular and isolated from the community and parents who are purportedly their "partners."

The *Habitus* of the Educational Paradox

The *habitus* of parenting is not new—it is as old as humans. After all, as Durkheim wrote, the earliest humans created the routines necessary to reproduce society, values, and morals via their children. In premodern societies, this occurred in unscripted face-to-face interactions, and indeed, this was enough to deal with the demands of the seasons, horticultural and pastoral responsibilities and the reproduction of the rights and responsibilities of clans, castes, lineages, kingdoms, and even empires. But, it is no longer enough; new are the demands of a mass society for an even more intense division of labor capable of producing the wonders of modern civilization, and organized only by that creative institution, the bureaucracy. For this to be possible, the cultural legitimacy necessary to maintain itself through literacy, numeracy, and cultural values shared by hundreds of millions and even billions becomes necessary. This is why the modern bureaucratic school system was invented in the first place.

Paradox is when two things coexist which are logically inconsistent, but nevertheless true. What is true in this case is that everywhere, and in every country, schools seek to bureaucratize and rationalize childhood in order to separate children from their parents, and create the adults for the modern state, not just the parents. They create rationalized humans, using the same principles that modern factories use to create manufactured goods; in doing this they create the modernist dream of the perfectible human. But at the same time what is also true is that humans—be they children or adults—are not rationalizable. They are simply too unpredictable and well, human.

Chapter 4

Behaviorism, Developmentalism, and Bureaucracy: Leaky First Graders, Defiant Teenagers, Jocks, Nerds, and the Business Model

Standardizing Childhood: Normative Childhood Development

There are formal and informal curricula in schools. The formal curriculum is typically spelled out in the form of standards, goals, objectives, rules, laws, and other bureaucratic markers that Durkheim described as pedagogy. But the pedagogy also includes an implicit hidden curriculum as well. The hidden curriculum is focused on reproducing society, including the status quo with its preexisting power relations as a coherent system in which citizens generate a faith in its basic moral orientations. This includes what Bourdieu called practice and *habitus*, and it is discussed in some of the short-hand terms described in this chapter, like leaky first graders, defiant teenagers, jocks, and nerds. This hidden curriculum is not necessarily written down, but is acted out in the way the explicit curriculum explains its policies. This *habitus* is what makes its citizens feel comfortable, and how they evaluate social problems in terms of culturally embedded "taken-for-granteds."

In this chapter, I will discuss how the *habitus* of child development results from the emergence of patterned ways of relating with adults in the context of normal child development. Oddly enough, this happens in a world—the school—in which humans are isolated primarily among their own age group. Thus, even though the system of stratification is generated in isolation from adults, nevertheless, it is very much the product of the cultural *habitus* of the broader society.

Normative Child Development

The standardized school curriculum has embedded in it implicit assumptions about what a normative childhood will be. Rooted in it are moral assumptions about social development, learning capacity, and even brain development. Within this moral calculation, particular types of social relationships, learning, and brain change are regarded as age appropriate and normal, while the exceptions are defined as abnormal or even deviant. But this is always a contested realm, as the *habitus* of past identities and "group position" remembered by the powerful adults who create the schools. For this reason "child development" is always defined relative to a broader cultural standard. These are all embedded in what Durkheim called values and morality.

A useful way to ask about this is to focus on the basis for normative behavior. Where do ideas about what is normative come from? Look inside an adult, and the socialization that defined them as a child: perhaps a leaky first grader, cute third grader, cliquish middle schooler, or defiant, hedonistic teenager remain. These preexisting categories are waiting in the *habitus* of the culture to be passed on to the next generation as surely as literacy, numeracy, and patriotism.

Politicians and school administrators, not scientists, are charged with identifying what is regarded as normal child development and, by implication, what is abnormal. The consensus they develop is the basis for the planned scientific curriculum, which is age-graded so it can be adapted to the goals of the school. Ultimately it is a sociocultural assertion about what is normal, i. e., the "One Best System of Childhood" (see Fuller 2007, xi–xiii). This in turn is embedded in a school bureaucracy in various forms including calculable test scores, rationalized rules, and law.

In the rationalized United States, this resulted in typologies that tie specific ages to normative developmental skills. Underpinning this are patterned social and physiological changes, with which any curriculum—explicit or hidden—must negotiate. In turn are created cultural expectations that are embedded in the ostensibly scientific curricula, school rules, and education policies. Thus created is a paradox in how schools and childhood are administered. Bureaucracies assume predictability and constancy in human behavior, because such an assumption is well suited to bureaucratic action and is rooted in behavioristic expectations. In this context, incentives and sanctions are readily adaptable to bureaucratic planning. Bureaucratic planning embedded in such behaviorism happens even though the most modern insights of physiology, learning theory, psychology, and sociology indicate that human development, cognition, inequality, etc. are more central to understanding human behavior than behaviorism. Thus the models that one is likely to learn in a university class based on "the latest research," are different than the ones assumed by a school principal trying to maneuver a school of dozens of teachers, and hundreds (or thousands) of students through the days of the school year.

Goldstein et al (1996, 9) describe why children are different from adults in their book *The Best Interests of the Child: The Least Detrimental Alternative*:

1) Unlike adults, children change constantly, from one stage of growth to another. They change with regard to their understanding of events, their tolerance for frustration, and their needs for and demands on parents care for support, stimulation, guidance and restraint . . .

2) Unlike adults, who measure the passing of time by clock and calendar, children have their own built-in time sense, based on the urgency of their instinctual and emotional needs, and on the limits of their cognitive capacities . . .

3) Unlike adults, young children experience events as happening solely with reference to their own persons . . .

4) Unlike adults, children are governed in much of their functioning by the irrational part of their minds—their primitive wishes and impulses . . .

5) Unlike adults, children have no psychological conception of the blood-tie relationships until quite late in their development . . . What matters to them is the pattern of day-to-day interchanges with adults who take care of them . . .

There are of course interests in adapting these understandings to the administration of childhood which occurs in the schools. Here is an example of how this works for 5–8-year-olds (Table 4.1).

The point is not to question the efficacy of such a table for understanding groups or even individual children. It works as any other simplification or "ideal type" does, in the sense it is an artificial construct reflecting every individual and, as such, no single individual. Rather it is to point out that such rationalization is inherent to the operation of a bureaucratized school system. Such tables are important not because they reflect the normative child—and is the means by which administrators can abstractly "see like a state" from 30,000 feet. This normative child becomes the standard for which school curricula are designed, against which all those individual children are then measured, and for which school curricula are designed. And vice versa. Children from such a context are both unstandardized

Table 4.1 Stages of Child Development.

	Brain Physiology	Physical and Motor Development	Cognitive Development	Social and Emotional Development	Developmentally Appropriate Activities
Age 5 (Kindergarten)	Rapid myelinization; Dendritic complexity increases	Balance beam; skipping, cutting and pasting; lacing shoes; etc.	Can count and compare; think ahead; name the days of the week; recognize numerals 1 to 5; vocabulary of 2,000 or more words; puzzles of 15 or more pieces	Best friends; prefer small groups; play well without adult supervision; need consistent rules and enforcement	Read aloud chapter books; build vocabulary; discuss and draw pictures from a story; play silly simon sez
Age 6 (First Grade)	Mylenization process continues; dopamine levels are near that of most adult brains improving focus; longer-term goals possible	Skate; jump rope; skip with both feet; draw a diamond; hold writing utensil with three fingers; tie shoelaces	Ask many questions; value quantity of work rather than quality; good starters but don't always finish; solve problems; mix colors	Competitive, lack good sportsmanship; want good friends; throw tantrums; get upset when criticized	Read aloud every day; practice matching; play mystery letters, hokey pokey, and the chicken dance; jumping jacks; push-ups, duck duck goose, pick up sticks

Age (Grade)					
Age 7 (Second Grade)	Synaptic density of the frontal lobes peak; better impulse control; greater independence; myelinization in new parts of the brain; brain interconnectedness increases	Well-established hand-eye coordination; jump, leap, swim, bike, and ride scooters	Relate several ideas in their heads; understand number concepts; know daytime and nighttime; know right and left hands; can count backwards; upset if they cannot finish a task; able to tell time to the quarter hour	Cry easily; moody; one friend at a time; enjoy being alone; are affectionate; are polite and sympathetic; becoming aware of their own emotions	Read aloud; assess phonemic awareness; play "alphabet war"; create a leveled library; practice rhyming; discuss reading with expression, accuracy, and at a level rate
Age 8 (Third Grade)	White matter exceeds grey matter, accelerated growth of the prefrontal cortex, brain is 90 percent of its adult weight; glucose uptake begins to decline; organization for memory begins	Wiggle and clown around; make faces; many accidents; need 30 minutes physical activity	Want to know the reason for things; can retell a story; find math useful; see many points of view.; have well-developed time and number concepts	Articulate feelings; keep secrets; tend to dramatize; eventually obey; like instant gratification; may develop a close friend of the same sex; enjoy school; somewhat possessive of their things	Read aloud; write letters to characters in stories; write and illustrate a book; wrote journals; read stories that ask for points of view; tag and freeze tag; insist upon cooperation in sports (relay teams); jump ropes; Frisbees; balance beam

Adapted from Sprenger 2008

(i.e., not normative), or standardized (normative). Or, to put it into Durkheim's terms, they are normative or deviant. This is of course a *habitus* that children themselves become very sensitive to; among the first questions asked of each other are references to their place in the bureaucratic order, e.g., "How old are you?" and "What grade are you in?" These questions are asked so that they can place each other into the preexisting hierarchical order with all its preexisting expectations.

Such classifications/assumptions are rules that by their very nature are about conformity and compliance, they are designed to efficiently process children into becoming independent, worthwhile, and respected adults (see Goldstein et al 1996, xiii). This is what state-curriculum standards and "average yearly progress" are about. But there is a problem in a country that also values each individual child and exalts each child's sentimental worth in a manner that assumes they are literally priceless (Zelizer 1985, 23) and therefore none of the low quality blueberries can be discarded.

Unstandardized Childhood

A child starts out life as an unpredictable creature. Behavior is ruled by the emotions of the moment, whether it is joy, wonder, dreaminess, sadness, frustration, aggression, or any other range of human emotions. In the modern United States, such emotions are embedded in the normative stereotypes of a modern culture, which measures such qualities against an idealized adulthood emphasizing the opposite—i. e., control of emotion and reasoned behavior.

Against this assumed idealized adulthood, first graders are called "leaky" because they cry, sniffle, and "leak" unexpectedly. Third and fourth graders socialized to comply with the demands of the institution do not leak so much—but have yet to enter puberty—and most importantly are responsive to the demands of the adult-dominated institutions in which they find themselves. Adults in such a context find joy at both the spontaneity of "clowning around" as nine- and ten-year-olds seek to please adults. In contrast, teenagers whose physical powers are at their peak are defined relative to a more "adult" standard, as alternately exuberant, moody, defiant, and impulsive for similar behavior (see Currie 2004). Adults tend to place blame on the cerebral cortex, which his not myelinized in the same fashion as a 30-year-old adult. But the paradox remains: What a few years earlier was a source of delight in the third grader's small body becomes a social problem in the teen years.

This happens in a world where adults hold up their own assumed qualities as the normative standard and are therefore intolerant of developing children who do not comply. Indeed, they designed schools to cope with such deficiencies in children in sustained and predictable fashions.

But, there is also an inherent paradox embedded here: How is it possible to romanticize spontaneity in the context of routine bureaucratic tasks? This is indeed the challenge of the school as it slowly makes the unpredictable predictable, a task they are asked to do so with a minimum of product wastage, i. e., no defective ingredients can be taken off the assembly line, under the assumption that as the legal doctrine states, "No Child Left Behind."

The problem of course is that ultimately, romanticism aside, childhood emotions are qualities poorly suited for a bureaucratic institution. Thus, much of the hidden curriculum of any school is about creating a child—or rather an adult—who complies enthusiastically, willingly, with fervor and automaticity to the preexisting standards established by the culture. Self-discipline, which reflects positively on preexisting laws, regulations, rulebooks, curricula, and examinations, is highly valued. To make this process as efficient as possible, the mechanisms of the institution are ever-perfected, as teachers and administrators seek to control childhood.

Standardizing Childhood

The question then is how is an institution—a school—created that takes unpredictable children and creates predictable adults? Schools are granted some 1,000 hours per year for a period of 12–13 years to do this, and school administration is in large part wrestling with this problem. How do you focus the strengths of a modern bureaucracy to deal with the emotional world of the five-year-old and create an adult? To undertake this task, the field of education emerged and established standardized "Age Graded Curricula" to deal with what child psychologists insist is a developmentally changing "whole child," but parents insist is "sacred" even though by definition, no individual "whole child" sacred or otherwise fits into a preexisting bureaucratic box without removing the very edges of what makes them "whole."

Bureaucratizing a Child Who Is Sentimentally Sacred and Bureaucratically Whole

Logically can a child be both sacred and therefore unique and undertake an age-graded curriculum at the same time? Of course it is possible, at least it is by bureaucratic fiat! The sacralized child who is special, unique, treasured, and a source of wonder for its parents, is made whole by the graded system. These two concepts, rooted in the language of emotion and science, respectively, are in tension with each other, even as they persist in the American school. To provide a sense of how these bureaucratically rationalized categories are transformed into sentimental cultural categories, it is useful to show how the concepts of "stages" borrowed from science, combine with the categories of popular culture. For illustrative purposes, I will relate a few of the categories gleaned from literature and popular culture: Leaky First Graders, Cute Third Graders, Junior High School Queen Bees and Wannabees, and Defiant Teenagers on the Road to Whatever. Together these categories reflect what can be thought of as the "sacralized child." In effect, such categories are the "hidden curriculum" of how schools deal with the emotions of childhood.

Leaky First Graders

Jonathan Kozol wrote letters to a teacher, Francesca, completing her first year of teaching, and who in doing so bounced between the worlds of her six-year-old charges, the school administration, and the world of a diversity conference where she was sent by administrators intent on ensuring that a mandated diversity curriculum was taught, presumably to her first graders. Kozol (2007: 84) wrote in response to her letter:

> But I also like the fact that even in the midst of all the indignation that you voice [about the distance between the diversity conference and the classroom] you did not leave out the sweetness and the many, many hours of sheer happiness you've known this year, as well as certain of the funny details you tucked in about the real life of a teacher in the elementary grades. I tried to imagine the reaction of the audience when you said that six year-olds are "leaky little people" because of the many "accidents" they have. I wonder how many presentations made at education conferences ever mention matters quite so interesting as the great importance of the distance of the nearest bathroom from the classroom door. "First graders leak! as you explained this to me later, "either from their eyes" when they have painful quarrels with each other "or from their dribbly noses" when they're coming down with colds—or, as you put it, "from the other end more frequently."

Kozol and Francesca are of course wrestling with the ironies of unbureau-cratized children that the school system sees only through the lenses of their age (six years old), the grade (first), and what the leaders of the conference want them to know about (diversity). Francesca sits at the crossroads of these paradoxes, and at least for the time being seems to have a good sense of humor when confronted with six-year-olds who leak, have accidents, and wonder how far away the bathroom might be.

Cute Third Graders

Phillip Done (2009) is a third grade teacher who expresses his appreciation for the exuberance of his students. He writes about their enthusiasms, sociality, and eagerness to please the teacher. Third graders have social hierarchies, but they are not yet rooted in the meanness of the older children, gossip, and sexuality. And while they still might "leak" a little bit like the first graders, he can also teach them about the water cycle, gardens, and the class bunny. Done has many sentimental stories to relate about third graders to illustrate his affections for them, among which are:

> If a child cannot think of what to write, he will shake, twirl, tap, drum, and poke his pencil. The longer it takes to think of an idea, the more shaking, twirling, tapping, drumming, and poking there will be . . . Students are like dogs. They make lots of noise when their master is away, display frantic greeting behavior when he returns, and follow him around the classroom when he is back . . . (2009, 320–321)

Third graders, judging from the descriptions of people like Done, are the cute ones—grown up and not quite grown up at the same time.

Queen Bees and Wannabes: Junior High Drama

Junior high schoolers are known for being obsessed with popularity issues. Objectively, they are also every bit as "magical" as they were in the first and third grades, though the cultural stereotypes that order junior high school life may not recognize this. Certainly sixth grade teachers are likely to be less tolerant of shaking, tapping, twirling, and drumming by 12-year-olds than Philip Done was for his 9-year-old third graders. Roseann Wiseman (2002) who wrote the self-help book *Queen Bees and Wannabees* about the nature of girl cliques in the sixth to eighth grades describes what she finds when making presentations to groups of middle school girls:

> For some girls, popularity is magical. Popularity conveys an illusory sense of power. Some girls think that if they can achieve it, all their problems will disappear. Some become obsessed and measure the popularity barometer daily, then issue constant weather reports. Others dismiss it, thinking the

whole things is ridiculous. Some are angry and deny they care, although they really do. Some feel so out of it they give up.

One of the funniest things about teaching girls about cliques and popularity is their paranoia . . . if they even have a clue as to what I'm there to talk about, most are convinced they're being unfairly singled out for being particularly exclusive and mean, and that the teachers have called me in to set them straight . . .(82)

Cliques and popularity outside the standards generated by the state school board are of course a key part of the clandestine curriculum of the sixth through eighth grade, as every junior high school vice principal (and everyone else) knows. Even though it is not part of the school curriculum, the emergence of social-stratification systems in the context of a graded school system is critical for understanding broader American society as well as that of the American high school. Unlike Phillip Done's third graders, the teacher is not the center of social life; rather the peer group is the most profound and meaningful element in their social lives (Adler and Adler 2003, 253). Patricia and Peter Adler describe these groups in the following fashion:

Children from all the schools we studied describe the arrangement of members of their grade into a hierarchy based on peer status . . . For every age level, within each gender group, and in every school with a population of more than eighty students per grade, the social system was composed of four main strata: the high, wannabe, middle, and low ranks. At the high end was the popular clique, comprising the exclusive crowd. Below them were the wannabes, the group of people who hung around the popular clique hoping for inclusion. Next was the middle group, composed of smaller, independent friendship circles. At the bottom were the social isolates who found playmates only occasionally, spending most of their time by themselves (255).

The bureaucracy struggles with this implicit challenge to its authority by hiring consultants like Wiseman, but the emotions embedded in junior high–type relations are often more powerful, and indeed, become embedded in the bureaucratic structures of a graded system in which, as is described in chapter 5, children are sorted into their destinies in a class-bound order. And this order for adults, of course, reflects the same *habitus* that the Adlers observed in their "four strata."

High Schoolers: Compliant and Defiant

High schoolers, Ted Sizer (1984, 59) writes, are managed through two powerful incentives: Students (and their parents) want a high school diploma, and the students want to respect themselves and be respected. Little he writes is about being "hungry" for education or zest for learning. Rather it is out of fear of failing to graduate, becoming a stigmatized "dropout," and the potential loss of respect that makes high schools into manageable institutions. The result though, is that the student who is valued is often docile, or as Sizer (1984, 54–55) writes,

> No more important finding has emerged from the inquiries of our study than that the American high school student, as student, is all too often docile, compliant, and without initiative. Some who have initiative use it to undertake as little engagement as possible...Such students like to be entertained . . . The constructive skeptic can be unsettling to all too many teachers, who may find him cheeky and disruptive. Questing can be costly.

Writing about problem children in high schools, some of whom may be inclined to "questing" but others to being knuckleheads, Elliott Currie in *The Road to Whatever* describes how students who do not comply with the standard are pushed out by the bureaucracy, often not for academic problems, but for an unwillingness to submit docilely to the authority of the schools. Referring to a large study of behavior problems, Currie writes:

> Most studies of schools' responses to discipline problems and academic failure show that students in trouble often have a range of remediable problems that appear early in their school careers, and it suggested that schools could benefit by taking a more attentive approach to these problems and developing strategies to prevent them before students get into serious trouble . . .(2004, 198)

But such a seemingly common-sensical approach assumes that there is a working bureaucracy able to deal with the vagaries of the junior and senior high school social world, in which the outcasts are pushed to the periphery where they become the stigmatized "dropout." Currie notes that "again and again, the schools' response to such evidence of trouble vacillated between the ineffective use of suspension and expulsion" (2004, 197), or in other words, the schools sought to, just as would be expected in a bureaucracy, push the bad blueberries out. However, because it is still a school, they cannot do it explicitly or efficiently. Instead, the miscreants resort to a false consciousness of sort and blame themselves for not fitting into the preexisting *habitus* of the system, or as Currie described "Mickey," one of the children he interviewed. "Part of her understood her parents' point of view, and she often blamed herself for her failure to make 'better choices'" relative to the rules enforced by the vice principal. In other words, this student, chronically in trouble with school authorities, acknowledged the legitimacy of the high school in enforcing standards (2004, 191).

The problem is that the emotional child is pushed into the preexisting expectations of the school institution, whether it be as a leaky first grader, cliquey sixth grader, or defiant high schooler. But they always exist in the context of an ideal type, which is the "whole child" that the school attempts to create. But this whole child, invented at the turn of the twentieth century, is ultimately a creation of the bureaucratic minds of school administrators everywhere, where it is assumed there is a "whole" in each child, which balances the cognitive, physiological, and social measures of childhood, with the age-graded opportunities offered by the institution. This can perhaps be thought of as a mix of the scientific approaches emerging from the traditions of the pragmatist Dewey, Piaget's (1970) *Science of Education and the Psychology of the Child*, and Rousseau's *Emile*, which are then bureaucratized. Given such a complicated kaleidoscope, it is not surprising perhaps, that the bureaucracy, with its impulse to simplify, can never quite create the institution of its creators sacred dreams.

The Emergence of Educational Standards and Behaviorism

Emotions aside, at the heart of bureaucratic action is the idea that standard inputs will result in predictable outputs. This was at the heart of the factory models for schools promoted by G. Stanley Hall and others at the beginning of the twentieth century, as it is today. In a bureaucratic factory an efficient, predictable, and calculable manufacturing process led to the great production of wealth by capitalist enterprises. For the captains of new school systems, the productivity successes of capitalism, with the underlying logic of the competitive marketplace and free expression of choices presented a compelling logic. They believed individual action result in the efficient production of what people wanted and needed. This happened through a system of incentives and deterrents which they believed underlay modern society. This was expressed well by Stanford University's Ellwood Cubberley who in the early twentieth century wrote that:

> Our schools are, in a sense, factories in which the raw products (children) are to be shaped and fashioned into products to meet the various demands of life. The specifications for manufacturing come from the demands of twentieth-century civilization, and it is the business of the school to build its pupils according to the specifications laid down. (see Cuban 2005, 1)

Reformer Jane Addams approvingly passed along a similar message from business about what schools were to do in an 1898 address to the National Education Association:

> Teach the children to write legibly, and to figure accurately and quickly; to acquire the habits of punctuality and order; to be prompt to obey, and not question why; and you will fit them to make their way in the world as I have made mine. (Cuban 2005, 1)

President George W. Bush's Secretary of Education Rod Paige in 2003 only put it a little differently:

> Henry Ford created a world-class company, a leader in his industry. More important, Ford would not have survived the competition had it not been for an emphasis on results. We must view education the same way. Good schools do operate like a business. They care about outcomes, routinely assess quality, and measure the needs of the children they serve." (Cuban 2005, 2)

And the newest Secretary of Education for the Democratic President Obama, Arne Duncan had little to add to this idea of schooling as being an appendage of capitalist values in 2010:

> President Obama's top priority has been to turn around our economy. He knows we have to educate our way to a better economy. He understands that a country that out-educates us today will out-compete us tomorrow. http://www.chron.com/disp/story.mpl/metropolitan/7145455.html

Sociologist Donald Bills (2004, 21–26) in summarizing such views pointed out that such cultural views, while not necessarily part of the explicit curriculum, are at the heart of the American system; there is an assumed connection between education, meritocracy, and culture:

> The point is not that American culture is consistent or unambiguous (Mark Twain's devastating parodies of the Alger novels demonstrate this pretty clearly). Americans are apparently quite able to believe both the American dream of schooling as the means to advance and the evidently opposite adage that "It's not what you know, it's who you know." The point rather is that the impulse of education as a means of social mobility has always been a part of American culture, an impulse that is by all accounts increasing even since the endorsement given it by Mann, McGuffey, and Alger. (Bills 2004, 23).

In other words, an economic model focused on competition fits well with early twentieth century ideologies rooted in a social Darwinism emphasizing that the effective and good survived, while the deficient did not at whatever preconceived, age-appropriate standard there might be. From this logic, it is only a short leap to behavioristic reasoning that inducing desirable behavior in individuals is done through systems of incentives and deterrents, in which the excellent is rewarded and the undesirable discarded. Particularly in the United States where big business viewed the schools as primarily the source for one of the factors of production—skilled labor—behaviorism, with its emphasis on rewards and deterrents, is attractive. After all, school reformers reasoned, if incentives worked in capitalist labor markets, why shouldn't it work in school life?

Such behavioristic reasoning is embedded in a taken-for-granted system of bureaucratic rewards, grades, praise, and promise of ultimate reward in the form of high-status jobs. The other half of the behaviorist equation, deterrents, are also typically straightforward, bureaucratized, and start with denying recess time, corporal punishment, trips to the principal's office, "bad" grades, suspension, and expulsion all in the assumption that as "Mickey" described above, it is simply up to the student to make "better choices," and be accountable, as if teenage development is simply a question of buying a better tool for the job at Home Depot.

The language of market accountability thus often accompanies the sanctions: Common is the assertion that a miscreant "gets what they deserved," earned their grade, competed ineffectively, failed to make better choices, and so forth. Such language also fits in well with the inherently simplified manner that school bureaucracies use to think of their mission from 30,000 feet. Left out though are two major concepts that which are seemingly assumed away by thinkers like Frederick Hess, who put a behavioristic models at the very front of his argument for "mean accountability" and school reform. First concepts of *human development* are left out. Second, the definitions of the "fundamental requirements of further education, work, or good citizenship" are assumed. The developmental problem is that a leaky 6-year-old is much different than a surly 14-year-old, both as an individual and ideal type, especially when viewed from the bureaucratic heights where simplification rules. The hidden curriculum loses track of this.

From Developmentalism to Human Ecology

Developmentalists know that an approach to a six-year-old does not work the same as with a first grader and a twelfth grader; six and seventeen-year-olds do not evaluate incentives and deterrents the same way. This is why psychologists (and others) also talk about the importance of child development. Thus while children as groups are known to change in a predictable fashion as their physiological, psychological, and sociological relationships shift (see Table 4.1), children as individuals—the whole child—are different again, regardless of the uniformity of product assumed by school bureaucracies.

At its most rudimentary, such developmentalism emerged from Erik Erikson's eight stages of sociopsychological development, forms of which have been widely taught in psychology classes since the 1960s. Erikson (1950) and his successors (see e.g. Bennett et al 1999) hypothesize that humans pass through stages in which they develop an identity and personality across the life cycle (See Table 4.2). Emotions change and evolve in this context, and are elaborated upon in the type of typologies with which this chapter began. As noted, this in turn corresponds with normative physiological changes in the individual and the development of social environments, starting with the family. At the center of this are a range of developmentally specific emotions focused by many of the same institutions; thus infants, toddlers, and young children view the family differently than do adults. But the behavioristic logic occurs only in the context of a changing psychological and social context both inside and outside the individual. In essence there is, to borrow the language of Uri Bronfenbrenner (1979), an "ecology" to child development, which shapes the child socially, psychologically, physiologically, and culturally based in preexisting belief systems. In this context, ideologies, cultures, and sub-cultures explain and legitimize specific stages of life and other putatively physiological states, in the category they themselves created. Or as Bronfenbrenner writes:

> The macrosystem refers to the consistence observed within a given culture of subculture in the form and content of its constituent micro-, macro-, meso-, and exosystems, as well as any belief systems or ideology underlying such consistencies. Thus cultures and subcultures can be expected to be different from each other but *relatively homogeneous internally in the following respects: the types of setting they contain, the kinds of settings that persons enter at successive stages of their lives,* the content and organization of molar activities roles, and relations found within each type of setting, and the extent and nature of connections existing between setting entered into or affecting the life of the developing person In addition, these consistent patterns of organization and behavior *find support in the values generally held by members of the given culture or subculture.* (emphasis added, Bronfenbrenner 1979, 258)

In the modern United States, the school bureaucracy codifies the values that shape the members of the culture. Ultimately the environment that

Table 4.2 Erikson's Eight Stages of Human Development. Variations of Erikson's original typoloty of the psycho-social states have been widely developed. What they share in common is the idea that normative psychological and social development occurs in a predictable fashion during a life cycle measured by chronological age.

ERICKSON'S PSYCHOSOCIAL STAGES

Stages	Crisis	Positive Effect	Negative Effect
Childhood			
1st year of life	*Trust vs. Mistrust*	Faith in the home environment and security	Suspicion and fear of future events
2nd year	*Autonomy vs. Doubt*	Senses of self-control and adequacy	Feelings of shame and self-doubt
3rd through 5th years	*Initiative vs. Guilt*	Ability to be a "self-starter," and therefore initiate one's own activities	A sense of guilt and inadequacy to be on independent
6th year to puberty	*Industry vs. Inferiority*	Ability to learn, to understand, and organize things and events	A relative sense of inferiority at understanding and organizing
Transition years			
Adolescence	*Identity vs. Confusion*	Seeing oneself as a unique and well-integrated person	Confusion over who and what one really is, and where you belong
Adulthood			
Early adulthood	*Intimacy vs. Isolation*	Ability to make enduring commitments to others, and to love	Inability to form affectionate relationship and enduring relationships
Middle age	(*Generativity vs. Self-absorption*	Concern for the broader social world, including family and society	Selfish concerns only for self-one's own well-being and personal prosperity
Aging years	*Integrity vs. Despair*	Sense of integrity, fulfillment and a willingness to face death	Dissatisfaction with lived life, and despair about death

Adapted from Erik Erikson, *Childhood and Society* (1950, 247–274), and multiple on-line sources the school bureaucracy creates provides the ecology for social and physiological development. The problem for the school bureaucracy is that physiological, psychological, and social maturation that change in individuals make sense only in the context of a standard developed by school officials hired to "see like a state." But individuals themselves mature unpredictably, as indeed the legal doctrine embedded in "Individual Education Plan" recognizes. Likewise, family and neighborhood social relationships change with time.[1]

The problem of course is that bureaucracies like, and even demand, predictability even across generations, which means that they like things to be as they were measured and calculated in the past, whether it was for a normal growth chart at the pediatrician or a rule about gum chewing developed decades earlier. Thus there is a developmental paradox in how the schools and childhood are administered. Bureaucracies assume a predictability and constancy in human behavior because it is well suited to bureaucratic action, even if the insights of physiology, psychology, and sociology indicate that cognition, inequality, etc. have changed in the past, and will logically do so in the future.

The marks of this paradox are spread across the public schools bureaucracies of the last century, as schools struggle with the difficulty of creating systems to address needs for the bureaucratic predictability anticipated by developmental models, while existing in a world focused by changes in what it means to be a child, whole or otherwise. The bureaucratic response is, the age-graded system in which all children with a particular birthdate are isolated together in a classroom in order that "age appropriate" curriculum is efficiently and predictably applied. In the process though, a new kind of child is created as, predictability, that variation from the preexisting model is discouraged and compliance and docility in the context of that model rewarded. The child becomes predictable because the bureaucracy needs predictability to function. That the child is predictable though is still a result of the bureaucracy and its needs for simplification, and not innate to childhood, or for that matter child development.

Behaviorism may not reflect the latest in scientific reason, but it does reflect a cognitive model easily adaptable to the management of large groups of people through the use of incentives and punishment, and legitimate rules for managing large organizations. Sometimes, cultural *habitus* trumps the laboratory bench of the developmental sciences. It seems to do so in the case of beliefs about school management and its love affair with behaviorism. Thus a "self-fulfilling prophecy" emerges as the child pushes against the demands of the school bureaucracy for adequate yearly progress, school frameworks, and age appropriate behavior, all of which are rooted in the bureaucratic habits established in past decades.

Bureaucratizing the Whole Child:
Age-Graded Curricula

Developmentalism may point to complexity in how individual humans change across the life course. But bureaucracies deal poorly with such complexity; rather they seek a principle, and then embed it in a preexisting frame, which in turn creates an institutional *habitus*. Indeed, this *habitus* is taken for granted in discussions of what school accountability is all about. Frederick Hess (2006:78) provides a good example of how the efficacy of incentives and sanctions are used in schooling in his advocacy of what he calls "mean accountability," and is rooted in behaviorism:

> Mean accountability . . . uses coercive measures—incentives and sanctions—to ensure that educators teach and students master specific content. Students must demonstrate their mastery of essential knowledge and skills in the areas of math, writing, reading and perhaps core disciplines . . .
> . . . school performance no longer rests on fond wishes and good intentions. Instead, such levers as diplomas and job security are used to compel students and teachers to cooperate. Mean accountability seeks to harness the self-interest of students and educators to refocus schools and redefine the expectations of teachers and learners . . .

This is clearly the language of behaviorism that points to efficiencies relative to the overall goals established by preexisting authority. In this respect, the model is very much like an assembly line in which students and teachers are assumed to be rational actors seeking only diplomas and job security. Laws, rules, regulations, and tradition created around this assumption result in quantitative indicators, which in turn become bureaucratized understandings of child and educational development.

But what came first, the assumption about education needing a very specific 12 years or the understanding of child development? The answer is clear: The bureaucratic assumption came first, and the "sciences" of child development and education responded to that world.

Creating Age-graded Curriculum—Nineteenth Century American Pragmatism and Egalitarianism

As described in chapter 2, nineteenth-century schools included students with a range of capabilities and ages. Thus, it was not unusual to find 17-year-olds learning to read in the same classroom with nine-year-olds and being taught by a 16-year-old school marm like Laura Ingalls.

School was valued, but did not necessarily take precedence over the demands of the agricultural cycle. Schools were also small, reflecting the low-population density. Instructional years were brief, the curriculum idiosyncratically organized by McGuffey and his fans, and the cultural demands of a rural populace.

But newly bureaucratized standards emerged in the cities where there were masses of immigrant children, and a social system stratified by social class. School administrators created laws and instructional practices that reflected the understandings and beliefs about how such children learned developed from understandings of factory-based manufacturing or the experimental schools of large universities.

Mixing older and younger children in the same classroom came to be seen as disorderly, and ideologies about the importance of isolating younger from older children emerged—in large part to facilitate control by adults. Much of this was rooted in new understandings of child psychology and the common-sense observation that it was older (and larger) children who became bullies and victimized younger children.

Such assumptions were a basis for a coherent system that reflected the range of new beliefs about social, psychological, and physiological development. Birthdays were to be used to determine what repetitive tasks specific to a particular age level were most effective. This matched nicely with findings about child development, used to rationalize and bureaucratize teaching in a fashion that was efficient, calculable, and could be controlled from a central office by reducing tasks to a series of check lists. It was out of this movement that achievement standards emerged from universities, which sustained a veneer of rational science, and school board rooms, which provided political justifications.

Two examples from California are presented here, for English and math. Note that these standards share an assumption that there is a natural progression out "there" and assumes that a capable administrator delivers a program proscribed by a state board of education. Embedded in such rules are administrative checklists and benchmarks designed to facilitate administration.

California's Age Graded Curriculum, Reading, and Math

In evaluating California's curricula, note that the standards, grade levels, and "strong consensus" reflect a political wishlist as much a "scientifically" derived understanding of child development. Despite the origin of such standards in the sentiments of political meetings, all mentions of sentimental leaky first graders, or defiant teenagers are left out. Remaining only is the rational language of education science.

California English Standards, K–12

California's 1998 standards for English reflect the demands of the bureaucracy to organize and rationalize the language arts programs into an articulated system, which reflects standards specific for each grade.

It is important to think about the timeline behind the promulgation of such standards. These standards were announced in 1998 based on a law passed in 1995. Assessment was to begin in 2001 (as indicated below), and the curriculum continues to be used throughout California in 2011. The fact that this process is rooted in a law first passed in 1995 means that it is based on research conducted in the 20 years or so preceding that date, i. e., 1975–1994. Such research in turn was undertaken by educators and researchers who themselves attended elementary school between roughly 1925 and 1955. The legalese is left in the quote in order to emphasize has deeply rooted in the broader bureaucratic-legal framework, into which concepts of child development have been inserted.

> The *English-Language Arts Content Standards for California Public Schools, Kindergarten Through Grade Twelve* represents a **strong consensus** on the skills, knowledge, and abilities that all students should be able to master in language arts at **specific grade levels during 13 years** in the California public school system. **Each standard** describes the content students need to master by the end of **each grade level** (kindergarten through grade eight) or cluster of grade levels (grades nine and ten and grades eleven and twelve). In accordance with *Education Code* Section 60603, as added by Assembly Bill 265 (Chapter 975, Statutes of 1995), the Leroy Greene California Assessment of Academic Achievement Act, there will be performance standards that "define various levels of **competence at each grade level** [and] gauge the degree to which a student has met the content standards." The assessment of **student mastery of these standards is scheduled for no later than 2001.** (Emphasis added; Source: http://www.cde.ca.gov/be/st/ss/documents/elacontentstnds.pdf)

Implicit to the regulations described above are the emphases on the combination of grade level and standards, and a compulsory education law enforced beginning at age five. Embedded in this of course are assumptions about what is "age appropriate" achievement, a conclusion putatively derived from scientific studies but, in reality, necessarily derived from the strong political "consensus" promulgated by state school board and the Legislature to match bureaucratic capability. The combination of standards and grade levels creates a momentum of its own, and in the process becomes a self-fulfilling prophecy, as Campbell's Law (see chapter 8) predicts.

This self-fulfilling assertion of student mastery of English standards (scheduled no later than 2001) results in specific curricular content for each of the 13 years. The most important section is the part of the law that insists in classic bureaucratic fashion that the schools will define level of academic competence at each grade level and then determine whether each student has "mastery." Excellence in this context becomes tautologically justified and legitimated by citing the rationalized and bureaucratized legal codes in the reports that school districts make to the state. In other words, success is bureaucratically defined, rather than being a result of a "scientific" understanding of education or child development. Compliance with such standards is not an objective definition of "excellence," irrespective of what the bureaucracy may claim. Rather excellence is a construction of the political forces of previous decades, which in turn emerged out of politically derived definitions of morality, which in this case were finally codified between 1995 and 1998 for use on into the future.

Math Standards, K-12 in 2011

Numeracy standards for California are structured differently than reading standards but are still embedded in similar assumptions about the progression of a child through a 13-year curriculum. Again California state standards:

> The mathematics content standards for kindergarten through grade seven are organized by grade level and are presented in five strands: number sense; algebra and functions; measurement and geometry; statistics, data analysis and probability; and mathematical reasoning. Focus statements indicating the increasingly complex mathematical skills that will be required of students from kindergarten through grade seven are included at the beginning of each grade level; the statements indicate the ways in which the discrete skills and concepts form a cohesive whole.
>
> The standards for grades eight through twelve are organized differently from those for kindergarten through grade seven. Strands are not used for organizational purposes because the mathematics studied in grades eight through twelve falls **naturally** under the discipline headings **algebra, geometry, and so forth**. Many schools teach this material in traditional courses; others teach it in an integrated program. To allow local educational agencies and teachers flexibility, the standards for grades eight through twelve do not mandate that a particular discipline be initiated and completed in a single grade. The content of these disciplines must be covered, and students enrolled in these disciplines are expected to achieve the standards regardless of the sequence of the disciplines. (Emphasis added; Mathematics Content Standards, State of California 1997, (http://www.cde.ca.gov/be/st/ss/documents/mathstandard.pdf)

A slight difference for the math standards is for the high school levels of grades eight through twelve where it is presumed that disciplinary headings of "algebra, geometry, and so forth" will order the curriculum, rather than an age-graded curriculum. Whichever way it is framed though, missing is the concept of the unique "leaky child" or cute third grader; in its place is a simplified bureaucratic category, "the learner," placed on the assembly line of grade level, learning strands, and disciplinary headings. Flexible perhaps, but still an assembly line.

There is a rather odd assumption in the math standards this progression is "natural," although there is no mathematical principal that *naturally* assumes the order of algebra, geometry, etc. Rather there is a bureaucratic need for standardization and homogenization of the curriculum. Nevertheless, these bureaucratic necessities run counter to other cultural values, including those rooted in an appreciation for individual identity, the whole child, individual creativity, and the freedom to develop and independent course. Bureaucracy and uniformity necessarily created the need for developmentalism; the school system was not adapted to the findings of the developmentalists.

Bureaucratized Instruction to Individual Education Plans (IEPs): Bureaucracy confronts the Spoiled Blueberry Problem

Ultimately, English, mathematics, and curricula are about compliance and conformity. But disability and deviance are in conflict with this. But there is still the problem of what to do with the children who do not fit well onto the preexisting factory line but still must be served by the school bureaucracy because they cannot be discarded. Not surprising, the response is bureaucratic: More rules and programs are developed to define the rights and responsibilities of the myriad of possible exceptions to the rules.

Most explicitly this came in the Federal Americans with Disability Act, which specified that every child with a disability is entitled to an "Individual Education Plan" (IEP) that satisfies individual needs. How this is done is spelled out in excruciating detail designed to fit any imaginable contingency with a salient bureaucratic category. Thus, "Individual" is a process and no longer a reflection of what are logically speaking, infinitely variable, but a formulaic process seeking categorization. This is negates the very nature of "individual."

TITLE 34—EDUCATION
. . .
Sec. 300.320 Definition of individualized education program.
(a) General. As used in this part, the term individualized education program or IEP means a written statement for each child with a disability that is developed, reviewed, and revised in a meeting in accordance with Sec. Sec. 300.320 through 300.324, and that must

include—

    (1) A statement of the child's present levels of academic achievement and functional performance, including—

        (i) How the child's disability affects the child's involvement and progress in the general education curriculum (i. e., the same curriculum as for nondisabled children); or

        (ii) For preschool children, as appropriate, how the disability affects the child's participation in appropriate activities;

    (2) (i) A statement of **measurable annual goals**, including academic and functional goals designed to—

        (A) Meet the child's needs that result from the child's disability to enable the child to be involved in and make progress in the general education curriculum; and

        (B) Meet each of the child's other educational needs that result from the child's disability;

      (ii) For children with disabilities who take alternate **assessments** aligned to alternate achievement standards, a description of **benchmarks** or short-term objectives; (3) A description of—

        (i) How the child's progress toward meeting the annual goals described in paragraph (2) of this section will be **measured**; and

        (ii) When periodic reports on the progress the child is making Toward meeting the annual goals (such as through the use of quarterly or other periodic reports, concurrent with the issuance of report cards) will be provided.. . . (emphases added)

In essence the inherent unpredictability of childhood (e. g. leakiness) became a codified rational legal rights, specified in a fashion only a bureaucracy can recognize. Even Jamie Vollmer's "blueberry problem" is assumed to be rationalizable, as disability becomes defined relative to a legalistic norm and is conveniently shoved into a category of its own. Implicit to such regulations is the presence of "normal" children and age-appropriate activities. In other words, such standards inherently reflect moral values, despite the patina of science reflected in terms such as benchmarks, measurable annual goals, and so on.

Child and Adolescent Development: Psychological, Social, and Institutional

The Twentieth-Century Child as a Psychological Creature

School itself creates normative expectations that become rooted in every child's psyche to the extent that the first question at school becomes,

"How old are you?" And also the second question, which very likely is, "When is your birthday?" also reflects this. Age and an awareness of legitimated rights, responsibilities, and capacities associated with age are acquired even before a child arrives at the schoolhouse door because they were born between four years and nine months to five years and eight months previously. There is of course nothing sacred about such a number; still it quickly becomes the quantitative measure around which school life is organized and becomes the standard against which the child is held.

This of course is a response not to the needs of the child asking the question, but a broader need established in the nineteenth century to organize bureaucratic schools in a rational and efficient fashion. Indeed, it was out of this world that psychologists and educators began to routinize normative expectations for child development, such as those described on Table 4.1 above. A normative sequence correlated with birthdate emerged and was codified in the laws and regulations of the modern state and in the *habitus* of the population. This in turn was correlated with particular types of brain physiology, physical and motor development, cognitive development, social development and emotional development. The point is that the bureaucratic demand came first, and the "science" to implement the bureaucratic dream followed.

The Social Child

The physiological and psychological sciences lend themselves as ways to justify standards for normative behavior. These justification in turn lend themselves well to bureaucratized public school policies. Or as Goldstein et al put it:

> Their healthy development requires that they be in the direct, intimate, and continuous care of adults who are committed to nurturing and protecting them. From the relationships with their important adults, children gradually develop their own internal regulating, self-guiding, and self-approving faculties enabling them to become independent, worthwhile, and respected adults—members of family community, and society. . . .Each child develops in response to the environmental influences to which she is exposed. Her emotional, intellectual, and moral capacities unfold—not in a void, and not without conflict—within her family relationships. (1996, xiii, 8)

This indeed is why the graded system emerged as it did. Social relations focused by age were created, and recreated, in predictable ways inside and outside of schools. Such relationships begin with the primary relations within the family to peer groups, and in the teen years to an emphasis on dating and pairing off in high school. These relationships go beyond the individual and is the stuff making up social life.

The context for such relationships—defined as healthy development—is typically codified in the rules and regulations of the school. This involves everything from the definition of bullying, requirements for school spirit, norms for group work and sharing, and of course limitations in junior high schools on "public displays of affection." Much of this social world is shaped by implicit curriculum, which defines what type of relationships are permissible and impermissible on an age scale.

The Twentieth-Century Child as a Product of Schools, Nation, and Bureaucracy: A Behavioristic Project in a Developmentalist World

The problem of the school bureaucracy then is how to manage the moving developmental target created by the physiological, psychological, and social environment. Technically, this is done with the templates of the developmental stages. The underlying idea is that if an administrator can isolate enough variables and the outcome can be explained, as indeed, the template for developmentally appropriate curriculum demonstrates, the desired product is created. In essence, add the correct ingredients, mix, and you get what is desired in an 18-year-old adult, albeit with some "spoilage." This is indeed, the type of project that bureaucracies are designed to produce. So ultimately the bureaucratic model implies behaviorism, irrespective of the scientific advantages of developmentalism. The problem with developmentalism is that it is rooted not in inputs but in dialectical interactions with the previous stage, the origins of which are rooted in emotion and sentiment. And this presents a paradox for the administrators of any school bureaucracy. The bureaucracy, from its 30,000 foot elevation, recreate issues of individual, physiological, intellectual and social development as rules and regulations, not the emotion or sentiment seen up close.

The rationalized rules, which are inevitably simplifications, are then passed on to an army of hired bureaucrats—i. e., teachers and their supervisors. Most notoriously, rules about sexuality and relationships are enforced in similar fashions for seven and seventeen-year-olds with a result that a second grader is occasionally accused of "sexual harassment." But this is only a symptom of what is inevitable as a bureaucratic system seeking to guarantee equal treatment for all. The problem is that bureaucracy is at best a blunt tool for dealing with relationships having origins in the emotions of developmental change, which as a result edge their way into the "hidden curriculum" I wrote about at the beginning of the chapter. Another way of seeing this is to note that a bureaucracy by definition is not created for individuals but for impersonal groups, which require an abstraction and assumptions about how people will respond in particular situations to incentives and deterrents. In short, behaviorism.

The Docile Adult

Implicit to the school project is the creation of the docile and disciplined adult, which Goldstein et al (1996) called "independent, worthwhile, and respected adults." Such adults comply habitually and predictably with broader social expectations. One not only has the *habitus* of the curriculum but also a *habitus* that requires acquiescence to broader morality (Durkheim) and its hierarchy (Bourdieu). In the individualistic culture of the United States, this implies a *habitus* that glorifies the autonomy of the adult individual, while at the same time docilely accepting the demands of the broader society. At its most cynical, this docility creates what Max Weber (2002, 178) described as "narrow specialists without mind, pleasure seekers without heart." On a more optimistic level, this docility is the happy-go-lucky person of the sitcom world of "Happy Days" or "Cheers," who complies at the office and school, while living for a weekend when individuality can be hedonistically expressed at drive-ins, beaches, bars, and sporting events albeit in a predictable fashion.

Irony emerges because even as individual creativity is ostensibly nurtured, the modern capitalism demands a willingness to offer 40 or more hours per week at a tedious task. Underpinning this are the habits of mind and beliefs in the goodness of the system itself. This system, as with the school, is deeply embedded in behavioristic values in which the rewards are salaries, sustenance, and social status. Deterrence is withholding of salary, social sanctions, ostracism, or at an extreme, the sanction of incarceration.[2]

The Twentieth-Century Child as a Psychological Creature

Child and adolescent development has been evaluated from psychological, sociological, and economic viewpoints, among others. In an individualistic society, such as the United States, most prominent are psychologists, with self-help books advising parents how to parent for school success, how to raise high achievers, how to get a smart child to reach their full potential, and so forth. Such approaches include a range of developmental, physiological, and behavioral guidelines. Prominent are the how-to books that urge parents to fit into current society/school, in a way that anticipates the nature of a future society built on the older ways of honor, identity, and self, which will create a healthy and disciplined adult.

Shaping the child to fit society/school are summarized well in how-to books like Sylvia Rimm's *Why Bright Kids Get Poor Grades,* which starts with the assumption that life and society are competitive and that learning and honor at school are about doing well on the standards developed by the school:

> Learning to compete effectively is central to achievement in school. Underachievers have not internalized this basic competitive message. Instead, they manipulate their families and school environments in fear of failure. They learn to avoid competition . . . (1995, 9)

At the root of this categorization are questions about what a healthy and psychologically disciplined adult will be. This is of course a moving target and ultimately unknowable—the disciplined adult of 30 or 40 years hence has inherently yet to be defined. But this does not mean that adults do not look deeply into their own souls and identify what they think this will be. What is more, this look into their own souls will have an effect—an echo—on what is actually possible.

In today's world, globalized and "flat" as it may be, it is easy to forget that until the twentieth century, many people did not leave the immediate area where they were born. They lived and existed their whole life in the confines of one valley, district, or canton. Life was focused by family and clan, not a vast global society. Each clan was similar; in fact, they were once so similar that a famous writer compared the premodern peasant family of France to the bag of potatoes. Each potato was a clan, similar in its capabilities and interests, lacking in an effective division of labor, but together they are a heavy bag of potatoes. Take one out, or add one more, and the bag of potatoes was not much different—only a little heavier or lighter. This is a very different metaphor than that of modern differentiated society, in which the clock rules, and each small part helped create a whole. The irony is that this is the antithesis of an individual.

Youth Culture as a Byproduct of the Bureaucratized Curriculum: Leaky First Graders, Cute Third Graders, Defiant Teenagers, Jocks, and Nerds

The values, judgments, and stereotypes created for our school children reflect their capacity to comply with the implicit and explicit curriculum found at the school. This in turn reflects not only the behavior of the children but also the emotions, judgments, and morality we associate with children at particular ages. It seems useful at this point to return to those popular responses to the stereotypes—social constructions—that teachers and parents use to view the social world of the school. How is it that the leaky kindergartners and first graders, so adored by their teachers, become surly teenagers? Why do they go out and create cliques of people like nerds, preps, geeks, and jocks, when the factory that created them, the public school, only wanted to make was a compliant, docile adult? And how is it that indeed, so many of those surly teenagers do actually end up being docile adults at age 30? Look inside any modern adult, and the marks of a leaky first grader, cute third grader, cliquish middle schooler, and defiant hedonistic teenager remain, waiting to be passed on to the next generation.

Leaky First Graders

Compliance with school expectations is created in the context of a still-developing physiological identity in which the context of broader social relationships have yet to emerge. But first graders are, as the teacher Francesca observed, "leaky" because they cry, sneeze, and even wet their pants in unexpected times and places. Not to mention, they have a hard time sitting through the standardized test by which the school measures its own achievement. To preserve the integrity of the institution, first grade teachers accommodate the unpredictable by creating such categories (Kozol 2007, 84). Rationalizations and standardization mean that the first grader has a new goal to achieve while failure to reach that goal—by leaking unexpectedly—is a minor aberration, unworthy of sanction, as it would be for older children.

Cute Third Graders

Still not dealing with rapid physiological development of the teen years, third graders develop the social skills that please adults like third grade teacher Philipp Done. Still small in stature, they are of little threat to adults, and their miscues are thought to be cute and nonthreatening. They are also compliant and have the reputation for being "balanced" in the sense that their psychological, physiological, and social capabilities complement adult expectations for them. What this really means is that the standards for third graders match well the expectations adults have for the age group—in other words, they are compliant.

Cliquish Sixth Graders

But if first and third graders are somehow compliant and "under control" of adults, sixth graders are starting to slip the bonds. They start to create their own cliques independently, and even in defiance of that which the adults created for them. In this, their peer groups are labeled dysphemistically as cliques, and the jockeying for social position intensifies and shifts from year to year as the groups form and reform around "Queen Bees and Wannabes." Such groups are not approved of by adults, who recognize with less-than-fond memories, their own preteen anxieties.

But this interaction is still very much a *habitus* that is within the larger culture. After all, every sixth grader was once a cute third grader or, for that matter, a leaky first grader. Sixth graders create the next category, which causes the most anxiety for adults and their school system: teenagers.

Defiant Teenagers

Defiant teenagers are a product of the first six to eight years of school socialization. Isolated from the broader world in schools, the boys in particular develop physiological strength, and can present a threat to the physical and social status of adults. They are also at a stage of psychological development in which moral judgments modeled on those of adults are expected. In the case of boys, this is reflected in the high rates of punitive incarceration in the hopes that in behaviorist terms, they will "learn their lesson." Particularly in the context of high schools, where the almost-adults are segregated using the laws of *in loco parentis*, unique youth cultures emerge. These are known by various euphemistic and dysphemistic terms like cliques, gangs, and so forth.

High School Cliques

High school culture is neither inevitable or biological. Rather it is the culmination of the psychological, physiological, and social conditions created in previous years. Segregated from older age cohorts as well as teachers, youth turn to each other and create a society in opposition to adults. But in fact the cliques that emerge in American high schools reflects the values the broader culture holds dear and the manner in which these values are reproduced into the next generation.

Examples common in the late twentieth-century high school are jocks, nerds, stoners, gangsters, and preps—just a few of the subcultures that are created. Notably, they even come to define not only each other but adult culture as well.

Jocks. Groups reflecting a working-class focus on sports. Often associated with deviance and defiance. Jocks do not need to do well in school to gain status. The focus in sports is on the utility of team sports as a reflection of an assumed adult world, on the one hand, and the importance of "individual character," on the other.

Nerds. The brainy ones who are aware of the explicit rules of the high school but oddly ignorant of the hidden curriculum of social life, cheerleaders, football, and so forth, that their peers are so sensitive to.

Preps. Conformists and student government types who obey both the explicit and implicit rules and believe in the justice of the preexisting system.

Gangsters. Mainly males who associate with each other in opposition to established authority (see Klein 1995).

Stoners. The deviants who mark out the edges of what is right and wrong. In the United States, these groups are closely associated with drugs and sex, the two issues that the broader culture finds frightening (see Wooden and Blazak 2000).

Note that each social status has its roots in response to broader values about individualism, group identity, and utility. Putatively, individualistic though they may be, in fact such school groupings are still a response to the broader society and do not exist in a vacuum. Each is incubated in a public school system that is designed to accommodate all and that purports to discourage inequality. Nevertheless, nerds, jocks, preps, and stoners are all responses to the *habitus* of this broader culture.

This brings back a central point of this chapter, which is that schools have both an explicit curriculum, and a hidden one. Central to the hidden culture is the fact that as Bourdieu wrote, education is about the reproduction of preexisting power relations. This is much more than simply a survey of high school cliques, rather it is about how schools are used to sort students into the categories the preexisting elite needs.

Chapter 5

The Sorting Function of Schools: Institutionalized Privilege and Why Harvard Is a Social Problem for Both the Middle Class and Public School 65 in the Bronx

Status Privileges: Birth and Educational Achievement

Competition for status privilege in the broader society—what some call the "*latent sorting function*" of schooling, is perhaps the deepest purpose of the hidden curriculum. In the United States, this sorting system is ostensibly meritocratic and assumed to be rooted in valid and reliable measures of smartness, achievement, productivity, and other measures that resonate with the cultural *habitus*. But of course, it is also about reproducing preexisting powers relations (Bourdieu and Passeron 1977/1990) in the hidden curriculum by sorting for those who are most like themselves and best able to reproduce the status quo. Such a sorting system abhors difference and by implication change. Or as Bourdieu writes:

> The dominated perceive the dominant through the categories that the relation of domination has produced and which are thus identical to the interests of the dominant. (Bourdieu 2009, 456)

This chapter is about identifying how stratification systems work and reproduce themselves using the categories of elites to both sustain their own position, as well as to organize those lower in the social order. Notably such stratification systems go beyond simple comparisons of annual income or accumulation of wealth but are also wrapped up in issues like honor, status, and prestige; this distinction is important because schools operate in a context of abstract concepts of status hierarchy.

How Stratification Works in School Systems

The school systems play a key role in the reproduction of status hierarchy. While this function is widely acknowledged, it is still only implicit to mission statements, which assert that education is rooted in learning, care for children, visions of the future, and so forth. But teachers also assign grades and routinely decide when to promote (or demote) students. In other words, if Sally gets an A, and Mark gets a B, Sally is deemed smarter and more deserving of reward than Mark. This of course has implications for the reproduction of existing systems of economic and social inequality. This happens even though this "latent" sorting function is not explicitly part of any school's mission statements, which instead vaguely address opportunity, equality, ideas, mastering basic skills, and searching for knowledge.

Mission Statements: Elite Harvard, Middle-Class Chico, and Working-Class Butte College

Education is an inherent paradox. At its most explicit, it assumes that students are trained for a fair, meritocratic, and competitive labor market in which learning is valued without reference to who they are or their social connections. This is why fair markets are "anonymous" and do not recognize who adds value. But schools do not operate in anonymous markets. Schools emphasizing the visible honors of academic achievement and, teacher-student relationships are often the opposite. The tensions between the utility of skills in an anonymous labor market while monopolizing the distribution of visible status honors in the broader community is at the heart of the educational enterprise (see Weber 1920/2010).

As anyone who has ever perused *US News and World Reports* college rankings issue knows, raw anonymous human capital is not the only thing peddled at elite colleges—so are "connections," status, and *habitus* of elites. Ross Douthat, in fact addressed this tension—that between visible honors and the anonymous labor market in which productivity is the measure—at Harvard

University. He concluded that any success he would have in the future was related to connections as much as anything else:

> I understood the secret of Harvard's success—which is that it doesn't end with college, that it still exists out in the wider world, and that all of my adult life, all the people I would know, the jobs I might have, and the worlds I would conquer, would be nothing more than an extension of my four years in Cambridge . . . Harvard had made me to be elite and connected, and successful, to be inside, you might say . . .(Douthat 2005, 250).

In other words, education at Harvard is not simply about the creation of skills, brain power, and wisdom as sorted out in an anonymous meritocracy; it is, as Bourdieu wrote, also about the dominant preserving the dominant. Elites depend on institutions like Harvard to create the habits and symbols with which they can recognize each other. These symbols determine which worlds can be conquered. The Harvard pin is ultimately about inclusion for insiders who share and recognize a style of life, and exclude the rest of us.

And such habits echo downward in the stratification system. Just like the Harvard pin, the symbols, habits, and styles of life of working and middle class lives described in Annette Lareau's book *Unequal Childhoods: Class, Race, and Social Life* reproduce social class among middle- and working-class children in Pennsylvania. The difference is that the elite set the standards that reflect the overall shape of the status pyramid. Harvard sets the tone for the game; what is valued at the top reflects downward, shaping the *habitus* of those lower down and what they think, say, and do.

Mission Statements: Elite, Middle Class, and Working Class

Despite Ross Douthat's bluntness about understanding "the secret of success" being rooted in Harvard's role in sorting people, there is nothing about elite exclusivity in the mission statement of Harvard College. Instead qualities like productive cooperation, full participation, and even the liberation of students (or at least Harvard's students) is emphasized, even as they try to sneak in a statement about "self-reliance." In fact the entire subject of elites is missing, buried in abstract statements about the centrality of advancement, encouragement, and rejoicing about responsibility:

The Mission of Harvard College
Harvard College adheres to the purposes for which the Charter of 1650 was granted: "The advancement of all good literature, arts, and sciences; the advancement and education of youth in all manner of good literature, arts,

and sciences; and all other necessary provisions that may conduce to the education of the . . . youth of this country. . . ." In brief: Harvard strives to create knowledge, to open the minds of students to that knowledge, and to enable students to take best advantage of their educational opportunities.

To these ends, the College encourages students to respect ideas and their free expression, and to rejoice in discovery and in critical thought; to pursue excellence in a spirit of productive cooperation; and to assume responsibility for the consequences of personal actions. Harvard seeks to identify and to remove restraints on students' full participation, so that individuals may explore their capabilities and interests and may develop their full intellectual and human potential. Education at Harvard should liberate students to explore, to create, to challenge, and to lead. The support the College provides to students is a foundation upon which self-reliance and habits of lifelong learning are built: Harvard expects that the scholarship and collegiality it fosters in its students will lead them in their later lives to advance knowledge, to promote understanding, and to serve society. (http://www. harvard.edu/siteguide/faqs/faq110.php)

Harvard's latent mission is very clearly an elite one, untethered to the pragmatic utilitarian goals of a more anonymous marketplace as, say, the community college system, where the message is about "skills," and not "responsibility."

Butte College provides quality education, services, and workforce training to students who aspire to become productive members of a diverse, sustainable, and global society. We prepare our students for life-long learning through the mastery of basic skills, the achievement of degrees and certifications, and the pursuit of career and transfer pathways.

Or at the middle class Chico State where I teach, just down the road from working class Butte College, a middle ground is sought in which graduates will both assume responsibility and also be "useful":

California State University, Chico is a comprehensive university principally serving Northern California, our state and nation through excellence in instruction, research, creative activity, and public service.

The University is committed to assist students in their search for knowledge and understanding and to prepare them with the attitudes, skills, and habits of lifelong learning in order to *assume responsibility* in a democratic community and to be *useful members* of a global society. (emphasis added)

Robert Frank and the Consequences of Relative Inequality

The missions of Butte College and Chico State do not exist in a vacuum, because middle-class values are profoundly influenced by the actions, wants, and needs of those above them and even those at socially distant Harvard. Robert Frank's book *Falling Behind* (2007) is among the most articulate in describing the very nature of economic inequality and the ideological interrelationships that develop in a fashion that, in Bourdieu's words, "are identical to the interests of the dominant." In other words the values of Chico State satisfy the needs of Harvard for midlevel managers who will be "useful members of a global society." And finally down to the graduates of Butte College who can do the tasks that require "mastery of basic skills" and are needed by those above them in the system of hierarchical dominance.

Frank points out that the greatest amount of status envy is found between adjacent status groups, not between extremes. This envy is about both the cost of items, and the meanings attached to particular scarce items. Thus middle-class people desire the status markers of the upper-middle class, the upper-middle class of the lower-upper class, and so forth, all the way up to the super wealthy. As Frank writes, this means that what Bill Gates buys matters since the next poorer billionaire competes with Bill; the multimillionaire compares themselves with the billionaires, the mere millionaire with the multi-millionaire, all the way down to what the Marx called the *lumpenproletariat*, who envy those just above them, while using the same categories that the distant dominant Bill Gates and those just below him set in motion. In schools, things like SAT scores, math and science classes, grades, AP classes, classical music lessons, athleticism, clothing, and the other markers, which America's upper class value and use to evaluate themselves and others, are passed downwards.

Perhaps the best way to think about how this works with the education system is to look at Robert Frank's description of how consumption and status envy heighten inequality with reference to consumer goods. Frank writes particularly about societies in which there is a steep slope between different levels of the "pyramid." As an economist, Frank focused on money and consumption. But I think that his principle can be used to evaluate the educated-status pyramid, which has at its top Harvard University, too. Thus where Frank wrote about how increasing house sizes (among other indicators) for the very wealthy distorts housing markets for the middle class, he might as well have been writing about the outsize effects that Harvard's admissions office plays in sorting out who gets admitted to the club at Cambridge structure the curriculum in a place as socially remote from Harvard as "Public School Number 65" (P. S. 65) in the segregated Bronx. Harvard effects P. S. 65 because the categories of the dominant and successful, which in the case of Harvard means that SAT scores measuring their verbal reasoning and mathematical skills, structure not just who gets into Harvard but curriculum below. These goals for verbal reasoning and math skills in turn are presented even at P. S. 65 as the lode star of an anonymous meritocratic system. But of course it is not anonymous; rather it reflects what the Harvard students value from their own social worlds.

The residue of Harvard's predispositions and *habitus* filters down from Harvard to P. S. 65, where students are convinced of the meritocratic system where the rules set by others are fair.[1] The problem of course is that ultimately such a status system is a row of dominoes, with each domino desiring to be as big as the next one in the row. Thus, the ultimate standard (Bill Gates) is the most important, even though few middle-class people desire to have a house like Gates does. The problem is that they *do* want a house as big as the boss, who in turn wants a house as big as his or her boss. In this way, the super wealthy set the steepness of the pyramid of wants; and the further that the apex is from the base of the pyramid, the more risky the leaps to the next level. Frank in particular writes about how Victoria's Secret markets fancy bras in a fashion that takes advantage of this principle. By setting the standard high each year with one bejeweled piece of underwear priced at several million dollars, they create more demand for the $150 bra by those would have spent only $80 in the past. Harvard does this too for higher education by keeping the admission standards for its entering class high, elusive, and distant. The community college at Butte copies Chico, and the faculty at Chico seek out "comparable to envy, which is the lower tier of doctoral schools. In turn these lower-level schools ape Berkeley, which in turn is envious of Stanford, and Stanford finally looks up to Harvard. And as a result, just as Bill Gates sets the rules of competition for wealth in motion by his rules, so does Harvard set in motion the goals of schools all the way down to Public School 65 in the Bronx.

This is really easy to see in the case of legal education, which has one of the most transparent ranking systems, rooted in the numbers generated by undergraduate grades and LSAT scores and its close correspondence with those considered for Supreme Court appointments. The pinnacle is set by Harvard and Yale University law schools, which, truth be told, train people for the same anonymous pass/fail bar exams and licensing regime as every small unaccredited law school in the country. In other words, on its meritocratic surface, the law school attended is not important in becoming a lawyer; all that is really important is that you pass the bar exam. But the legal profession is not anonymous the XXXX. Nevertheless, because of the accumulated prestige, Harvard and Yale law schools play the most important role in determining where every law school in the country is in the meritocracy is focused upon. In unusually blunt terms, Supreme Court Justice Antonin Scalia acknowledged that when he said at a speech in 2010 at the Washington College of Law regarding the hiring of Supreme Court law clerks:

> "By and large," he said, "I'm going to be picking from the law schools that basically are the hardest to get into. They admit the best and the brightest, and they may not teach very well, but you can't make a sow's ear out of a silk purse. If they come in the best and the brightest, they're probably going to leave the best and the brightest, O.K.?"

The data bear out the hard truth that Justice Scalia described, as he followed his own tautological reasoning to its logical conclusion:

> Over the last six years, the justices have hired about 220 law clerks. Almost half went to Harvard or Yale. Chicago, Stanford, Virginia and Columbia collectively accounted for 50 others. No one from Washington College of Law made the cut. (http://www.nytimes.com/2010/09/07/us/politics/07clerkside.html)

But examine closely the broader implications of what Scalia is saying about the nature of status and schooling in the selection of the United States legal profession and its elite. In effect, he is saying that the pool from which Supreme Court Clerks (and Justices[2]) are selected is defined by undergraduate grades and LSAT scores accumulated by the age 22 or 23. Scalia's assumption is that these two measures are valid and reliable measures of the "best and brightest," as he said. This, Scalia implicitly asserts, is the critical factor determining how a lawyer will be evaluated for the rest of their career, not the quality of legal teaching, scholarship, judging, or whatever else a lawyer may do in the 40 or 50 years after graduation. This is what Bourdieu (and Durkheim) are writing about when they point out that education systems are about the perpetuation of a preexisting status quo before other factors. "The dominated" do indeed come to ape the ideology that reflects the interests of the dominant.

Thus, even though neither Harvard nor Yale Law School have as part of their mission statement "our goal is to create a pool of legal talent that will staff the United States Supreme Court," both do this, and the 198+ other law schools in the United States do not. Nor, for that matter do rural high schools have as their explicit goal creation of a pool of young people who will enlist in the US military at graduation, but 44 percent of the US military is made up of recruits from rural areas (Washington Post, Nov. 4, 2005). In short, educational institutions matter for the structuring of opportunities. America does this by letting some schools preselect those destined to rule from the Supreme Court, and others preselect those that go into the military. Schools play the critical role in establishing which place in the social hierarchy a student will exist.

From this perspective, it is not so surprising that those with the advantages of birth and youthful association strive to preserve the advantages their parents provide via birth and the educational system. Indeed, it was at its heart the reason why the Civil Rights movement of the twentieth century focused so persistently on issues of access to education and the role in preselecting the young for specific future?. The categories of the dominant are established, bureaucratized, and reinforced through the hierarchy of the educational system.

Seeking Honor Through Education: The Steepening Pyramid

Status and money are interrelated in large part because the cultural habits that bring high status are a consequence of conditioning and styles of life beginning in childhood (see Weber 1920/2010). Where and to whom a child is born matter a great deal in the development of educational opportunities, cultural capital, and position in society. Thus, the highborn can be poorly educated, and the lowborn can become highly educated. But, by and large, the two are interrelated; as it is well known, the highborn are more likely to achieve educationally, while the lowborn are not (see Bourdieu and Passeron 1977/1990; Collins 1971). What is more, the very nature of inequality means that there is inevitably an "arms race" across time, as educational achievement with its emphasis on exclusivity narrows and raises the definition of excellence.

The educational arms race in American schooling has clearly shifted the nature of the status pyramid during the nineteenth and twentieth century. This is evident particularly in the case of high school diplomas, which at the beginning of the twentieth century were a high-status achievement and a ticket to upper-middle-class status. But by the end of the century it was associated with working class. The same happened with the Bachelor's degree, as my students are Chico State are well aware. A Bachelor's degree was a ticket to the managerial upper-middle class in the mid-century, but useful for only the next level down by the beginning of the twenty-first century when one-third of American adults had one.

But of course, the educational stratification system is much more than a straight-forward meritocratic collection of degrees (see Figure 5.1). It is about the hidden curriculum, the system that separates those who are self-defined using their own categories as "the best and smartest," as Justice

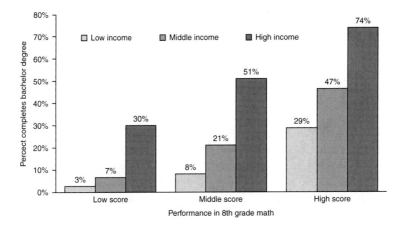

Figure 5.1   Educational Outcomes and Socioeconomic Status http://www.epi.
org/economic_snapshots/entry/webfeatures_snapshots_20051012/
Source: Fox, Connolly, and Snyder 2005

Scalia said, from the rest of us. It is also about preserving systems of domi-
nation. In the case of American legal talent, and probably other fields, this
results in a steepening slope similar to what Robert Frank described for the
class system.

Self-Defining Prophecy: Elite Achievement as Meritocracy

But how is the ideal that acquired meritocratic achievement as measured by
things like SAT tests and grade point averages is sustained, while also preserving the privileges of the wellborn? The answer is that merit is defined
by success on exams emphasizing the English verbal and mathematical
skills, which also happen to be the skills cultivated by upper-class families
and prep schools. But the selection of such skills is not natural and does
not occur in a vacuum, as Bourdieu noted. Effectively deemphasized are
skills likely to be associated with the children of anyone who is not advantaged. A bright and talented person who speaks another language, farms,
fixes automobiles, plays an obscure musical instrument, studies a type of
mathematics not found in the US curriculum, or even studies sociology is
unlikely to be rewarded in such a system. Indeed, Daniel Golden (2006),
Nicholas Lemann (2000), Jerome Karabel (2005, and Ross Douthat (2005)
all wrote entire books demonstrating how seemingly objective measures
of merit used in college admissions, are routinely corrupted in ways that
ensure that the wealthy continue to dominate education systems, while

admitting only those from the middle and lower classes who are most likely to accept the legitimacy of the selection process itself. The problem is that as Bourdieu points out impishly with the recursive syntax quoted on p. 119, definitions of "merit" are tautologically self-defining prophecies. While blind markets may indeed be used to do the sorting, the fact of the matter is that the markets themselves are simply expressions of values, and not the values themselves. Fashion provides an excellent example of this. Markets bid up the value of items deemed "fashionable;" the monetary value reflects values of consumers, not the relative utility of a particular style of dress. The fact that verbal and math skills are on the SAT test (and not say art skills, Spanish, or astronomy) reflects the value of verbal and math skills to elites and is not intrinsic to the nature of the skills measured.

So where do the values tested for come from? Bourdieu's answer of course is that they come from the powerful who created the past, who define categories of excellence, and who dominate their world through the categories they themselves create. In other words, the merit of the past defines the desired future. People who themselves do well in this system (like Justice Scalia), evaluate themselves and their progeny and conclude inevitably that what has worked for them, *ipso facto,* is meritorious and design a system that bureaucratically seeks out similar people. Thus people who did well on the LSAT, had high grade-point averages, and attended Harvard and Yale, seek out other people who have a similar background when hiring Supreme Court clerkships.[3]

The only irony in all this is that work and long hours at school or office have come to play such an important role in how the elite perceive themselves, as well as others. Indeed, in the past it was leisure and lack of economic activity that defined the wealthy; but in the post–World War II United States, this resulted in a rather odd phenomenon described by David Brooks in his book *Bobos in Paradise* and his newspaper columns: The first hard-working upper class focused on the responsibilities of maintaining the status quo.

> The information age elite exercises artful dominion of the means of production, the education system. The median family income of a Harvard student is $150,000. According to the Educational Testing Service, only 3 percent of freshmen at the top 146 colleges come from the poorest quarter of the population. The educated class ostentatiously offers financial aid to poor students who attend these colleges and then rigs the admission criteria to ensure that only a small, co-optable portion of them can get in . . . .
>
> The educated elites are the first elites in all of history to work longer hours per year than the exploited masses, so voracious is their greed for second homes. They congregate in exclusive communities walled in by the

invisible fence of real estate prices, then congratulate themselves for sending their children to public schools. They parade their enlightened racial
attitudes by supporting immigration policies that guarantee inexpensive
lawn care. They send their children off to Penn, Wisconsin and Berkeley,
bastions of privilege for the children of the professional class, where they
are given the social and other skills to extend class hegemony. (http://www.
nytimes.com/2005/05/29/opinion/29brooks.html)

The class system today teaches the wellborn to work long hours, use large
vocabularies, and believe that the root of their success, and that of their
own children, is in their capacity to succeed on standardized tests. How
did the ideology of the meritocracy come to displace older beliefs about the
rights of inheritance via birth?

Meritocracy Displaces Birth, but Birth Trumps Meritocracy

Nicholas Lemann[4] wrote about the history of the SAT exam and college
admissions in *The Big Test: The Secret History of the American Meritocracy*:

> The people at the top of a society almost always believe themselves to be
> genuinely superior to the rest, not just luckily born, and to have earned their
> place. Societies that we now think of as having been obviously more aristo-
> cratic than meritocratic—such as the United States between the world wars,
> or Victorian England—were run by people who thought that they deserved to
> be in charge. How could prosperous people in the past possibly have believed
> this about themselves? Usually they had participated in a limited-context
> meritocracy. . . . members of a small, restricted group compete all out for the
> best prizes, the winners justifiable entitled to them, and the great mass who
> could never enter the contest are off somewhere far away, invisible.
>   Today's upper-middle-class American Mandarins have taken in this set
> of attitudes. The notion that they are participating (and succeeding) in a
> great broad, fair, open national competition is at the heart of their idea of
> themselves, and indeed you do have to be very able and intelligent to get the
> most prestigious of the billets distributed by the meritocratic machinery. . . . .
> It is perilous, though, to assume that every corner of this vast society . . .
> People who have done well in the system too often declare victory for a few
> thousand people a year. The truth is that the Mandarin class is by now so
> well established that the range of possible outcomes for those born into it
> is quite narrow and so is the size of the opening to people who are not born
> into it. (Lemann 1999, 342–343)

Ideology extends beyond the small restricted group at the top, and as a
result, what Harvard thinks is important matters for the Bronx, but
not vice versa. Jonathan Kozol describes how as a result in the world of

P. S. 65 you get poor children in a segregated school chanting meritocratic liturgies of "If it is to be, it is up to me," and "Yes I can, I know I can" as a testament to a system that they believe seeks out the best and the hardest working and the brightest based on a test of will. Meanwhile, those across town, who indeed will make the decisions of the future, are ensconced in the "Baby Ivies" of the upper class, where instead of a liturgy praising the meritocracy, there are small classes, music lessons, and sports instruction for first and second graders.

Thus the American school system rewards privilege on the basis of birth, even though to do so violates deeply held beliefs about equality of opportunity and the meritocracy at the heart of American *habitus* and culture. Birth and inheritance do matter for who goes to P. S. 65, and who thus goes to Harvard; education becomes "human capital," which is directly translated into value for employer and employee alike by the marketplace.[5] The edifice of the meritocracy, the SATs, rationalization of test scores, and so forth, are the temple to the idea that "intelligence plus effort" results in a worker who is valuable to employers in the free (but fair) market. Poor boys made good are rewarded by such a system; it is meritocratically reasoned.

Michael Young, who coined the term "meritocracy" in his 1958 novel *The Rise of the Meritocracy* actually viewed the meritocrats with disdain. His book satirized how he thought the late twentieth-century upper classes would game the meritocratic education system they created for themselves in a fashion that preserved their own advantages by easing their young into the "less exacting professions," like stock brokering and law:

> Upper class parents with dull children did everything possible to hide their handicap. They usually made up by their own frantic determination for any lack of will on the part of their children. For instance, they bought places at private schools which would never have been awarded on merit. They spent, for the sake of stimulus, even more on books and travel than other rich people. And when the combined pressure of home and school had produced, as it often did, a person superficially not too dull, the parents eased the loved one into a cosy corner of one of the less exacting professions, such as law or stockbroking. These anti-social parents were able to keep a hold on the old professions and also on family firms which for one reason or another enjoyed some small buy effective monopoly. The old upper class found jobs for nearly all its children, while most of the additional jobs in the new professions, especially in science and technology, went to cadets drawn from the lower classes . . .(Young 1958, 98)

The connection between educational outcomes, particularly at the college level, and income is so well known as to be almost trite. But its triteness belies its origins in the attitudes, *habitus*, and assumptions, not of policy, but of the broader culture.

Buried in such tales are the home experiences described in Annette Lareau's book *Unequal Childhoods,* which is about the nature of social class and class inequality in Pennsylvania. She writes about the manipulations of meritocratic systems by the social class that created measures of meritocratic achievement in the first place—the upper classes.

Meritocracy as Dystopia

One of the biggest ironies of the modern meritocracy is that its discoverer (or inventor), Michael Young, viewed it with dread. In *The Rise of the Meritocracy (1870–2030),* he described the emergence of a passionless exam system, which rewarded intelligence and merit without respect to parental status. Ironically, in the system he imagined, Young describes the abstract faith that the system would, like Scalia said, identify mechanistically the best and the brightest. The problem is that, in the process of creating a ruling class that did well, a new caste system, in which status is monopolized and the masses excluded, is created as the competition is effectively limited to a preselected caste. The punch line of the book is that this system is ultimately unsustainable. In Young's novel, the meritocratic elite excludes the working class so viciously, that in the end it is challenged by the masses, who, in the year 2030 revolt and destroy the infrastructure that the meritocracy itself created to isolate and protect itself.

The meritocratic ruling class of Mandarins that Young forecast is not that different from the "Bourgeois Bohemians" that David Brooks (2001) satirically called the "SAT gods;" students whose training at private schools is directed at creating the strongest college application possible. Ross Douthat (2005, 279) described his fellow undergraduates at Harvard as such:

> Throughout our youth, we had been encouraged to look out for ourselves, to compete ferociously for the prizes and honors and scores that marked success in the meritocratic world. We had been bred into a striving selfishness, and after such an education, I wonder if even a presidential call to arms would have convinced us to subordinate our own ends to those of the nation, to lose our egos and our resumes in the anonymity of the platoon or the embassy?[6]

Or as Young (1958, 127) himself generalized about the dominance of the newly meritocratic upper class:

> Before modern society could reach maturity, ambition had to be forced ever upwards, and the ideology of the people brought into conformity to the needs of the new scientific age. In effecting this vital psychological

change—making discipline voluntary by putting a goad inside the mind—In the beginning there was Protestantism . . . the function of Protestantism [as described by Weber] was to fire the acquisitive urge.

Ever upwards of course leads to a steeper pyramid in which the gulf between rich and poor, and educated and uneducated, gets ever wider, stretching the commonalities that should hold the *Gemeinschaft* community together.

Cultivated Children, Natural-Growth Children, Segregated Children, and the Children of Hogwarts

If Michael Young describes the origins of meritocratic metric well, sociologist Annette Lareau describes the mechanism for how and why the working classes are not only excluded but come to accept this exclusion as normal and natural. Lareau compared the interactions between middle class families and their children and the working class and their children. In doing so, she focused on the habits that different styles of parenting develop.

Drawing on Bourdieu's approach, Lareau documented how different habits of childrearing are closely associated with class in the United States. Thus just as Douthat and Young wrote that the upper class comes to believe their own success is the result of self-evident merit, the working class comes to explain why children do not earn such success and accept explanations for why their children do not succeed in the context of "the system." She does this by developing a gardening metaphor that contrasts the "concerted cultivation" style of childraising by middle-class parents and their children, and the "natural growth" parenting style of the working classes. Concerted cultivation involves structured activity for children and results in adults ready to assume managerial roles, while the more free-range natural-growth parenting style encourages children to interact with their peers, sports, and television on their own, programming children for the working class.

Cultivating Little Adults vs. Childhood for Its Own Sake

These differences, Lareau writes, are rooted in behaviors and relationships that begin early in life. In *Unequal Childhoods: Class, Race, and Family Life,* she writes that the "cultivated" children of the middle class do well in a structured world because they are socialized to adult norms, even as toddlers. Middle-class parents encourage conversation on adult topics, and the children negotiate with adults and social institutions. Often this happens in the context of organized sports activities, music lessons, parent-teacher conferences, and so forth, all of which mimic the habits of the middle class and the wealthy. The point is that their relationships to the dominant social institutions are fundamentally different than those of the working-class children described below; middle-class children learn that there is a give and take between powerful institutions that can be appealed to through mastery of bureaucratic reasoning. These things are taken for granted by the time they get to high school. School by such families is seen as another bureaucracy to be negotiated. As such school becomes a place to train for mastery in the adult world (Lareau 2003, 239).

This is in contrast to what Lareau describes as the more free range "Natural Growth Children" of the working class who are raised without the plethora of *organized* sports activities, cultural activities, and so forth. Most importantly, as Lareau writes, they have different relationships to adults and the dominant institutions than the cultivated middle class. Parents organize their children's lives so that they spend time around home, and in informal play. They have more opportunities for child-centered play than the cultivated children, but they also tend to view adults as a source of unquestionable authority and not open to reasoned negotiation (Lareau 2003, 238). For the working class parent/student, as Lareau describes, the teacher becomes another often arbitrary authority who cannot be questioned or negotiated with, and is to be sullenly resisted when appropriate. This *habitus* of schooling reflects what happens at home.

But, Lareau writes, working-class families raised in such a context, do indeed have values and orientations—which are admirable—but unlikely to be rewarded with a high SAT scores, GPA, or even a high school diploma. In such families, there is a strong emphasis on kin. Sports and other activities are less likely to be cultivated for skill and college applications. Sports are considered to be activities for children for their own sake, without any purposive goal.

When challenged by untenable situations, natural-growth children are urged to either withdraw or, in an extreme, to defy authority. Negotiation is avoided. Lareau's best example of this are the lessons working-class children are offered to "hit back" when confronted by a bully, rather than to enlist authority. As Lareau writes, interaction between such working-class, natural-growth children and adults, is focused on words of affection, commands to do particular tasks, or behave in a particular way. Reasoning and negotiation are not seen as tactical responses. Television socializes such children, and preferred programming often reflects the role of chance (e.g. game and reality shows) and sullen compliance in the face of school power (*The Simpsons*). Upper-class adults who bully opposition into submission, (e. g., Donald Trump and Jerry Springer) are admired. Social scientists who focus on language acquisition note that such children have smaller vocabularies than "cultivated" children beginning at about age two to three (Lareau, 2003, 129–132).

The point that Bourdieu, and implicitly Lareau, make is that such children develop a different *habitus* than the "cultivated" children of the middle class, whose activities are focused on the nature of success borrowed from the adult world. They dream of achieving the goals of high SAT scores and grades. The irony is that working-class kids, in acquiescing implicitly, acknowledge the legitimacy of the existing status system. Thus, while natural growth childhood is warm, pleasant, and family oriented, the consequences are not rewarded on exams emphasizing vocabulary and reasoning, the exact skills cultivated in the harried household of the upper-middle-class child, and especially the private schools the elite enter as toddlers. So in the end, the children of the working class are meritocratically pushed back into the working class.

Notably, despite the obvious nature of such tracks, in the egalitarian world of the United States all three sets of children are still encouraged to "go to college," i. e., the category at which the elite excel. Thus when working-class children raised in "natural growth" habits are in high school, they still express expectations for college attendance, regardless of the fact that the high school culture is focused on the *habitus* of the here and now, whether it be sports, work, care of younger siblings, or family events. These are all significant activities reflecting the world of the working-class, natural-growth child. But they are cultivated at the expense of math skills, vocabulary skills, and other habits, which lead to success in college, or in the academic realms of high school. In this context, the oppositional culture of "passive aggressiveness" is sharpened.

But particularly for the working class, this appearance of docility often translates into pranks, drug abuse, and juvenile delinquence, which are both a resistance and acquiescence to a dominant culture. This opposition is perhaps why working class and poor children are present in drug-rehab programs, have children at earlier ages, and go to prison at higher rates than the nerds and geeks who are the products of the upper-middle-class concerted cultivation. Nevertheless, because the number of children with such a natural-growth *habitus* numerically dominate many high schools, the cultivation of academic achievement is often stigmatized, at least for a time. Ultimately, the temporary dominance of the natural-growth child established in the social world of the comprehensive high school disappears, as what Mary Wollstonecraft called in 1792 a "false refinement," reasserts itself.

Thus in the school world, a *habitus* emerges from the shared experiences of the four-year bachelor's degree—which inherently teachers have, but 60–70 percent of parents do not. In such a context, the Bachelor's degree becomes a critical status marker. To the working-class parent, the degree is a source of legitimated authority and an accomplishment separating the teacher from the majority of their students and their parents. The different *habitus* are accorded different values by significant social institutions, particularly the schools, which exist at the intersection of child-rearing habits.

Teachers of course straddle this divide. They themselves are the product of universities, deferred gratification, and typically cultivate their own children intensively. But they also are typically in a high school world dominated by a majority raised in the world of what Lareau calls the working class.

From P. S. 65 to the Baby Ivies in York City

But the place where birth really usurps meritocracy is in the segregated reaches of the inner cities and rural areas where, beginning at birth, children are excluded from the cultural activities, personal interactions, and accumulation of social and cultural capital, i. e., the type of behavior rewarded in school and on standardized tests designed with success at Harvard in mind. This is perhaps where the sorting function of schools is most visible. Orfield and Lee (2004) are among those pointing to segregation of students by race and economic group in American schools. Indeed, segregation has intensified since the 1980s; as schools became more racially segregated, it was less likely that an African American student would attend a majority white school in the 2000s than in the 1980s; even in some inner-city schools in places like Los Angeles, New York, and the US South, it was even unlikely that they would attend schools with any significant number of white students. Indeed in 2001–2002, the average black student attended a school that was 53 percent black and 30 percent white, at a time when the national population was 12 percent black. The average white student meanwhile attended a school which was 79 percent white and 9 percent black (Orfield and Lee 2004,17; Kozol 2007).

Jonathan Kozol in particular has written about the consequences of African American children attending segregated schools in the twenty-first century. For example, he described "Pineapple," a student from P. S. 65 in the South Bronx who he kept in contact with for several years. The level of repair on the school plant was often decrepit in the segregated New York City schools that Kozol wrote about, with inadequate seats in the classrooms and classes conducted in condemned buildings. A pastor of a local church pointed out that the children of P. S. 65 lived in a world of their own. When they went shopping in nearby Manhattan, they might find themselves surrounded by white children, and also "very scared" (Kozol 2007, 16).[7] This contrast is starkest perhaps in a large city like New York, which also has a large elite that has spawned the "Baby Ivies"—kindergartens for well-heeled parents intent on preparing their five-year-olds for an Ivy League college 13 years hence. But nevertheless, Pineapple is still part of the *habitus* of college attendance, and he and his classmates still see school and themselves in the context of college attendance, and other categories created for them. Pineapple believes he should be able to go to college, but Kozol's description makes it obvious that this is unlikely given the segregated nature of his school.

Nevertheless, the mantra of attending college, Kozol wrote, was drilled into the children at P. S. 65 even though they were personally aware of only the community colleges at the very lowest rung in *U.S. News and World Report*'s ranking system, and were completely unaware of the high-status universities like New York University and Columbia University, just a few miles away in Manhattan.[8] More irony is seen in the self-exhortation sessions in which children at inner-city schools chant rhythmically things like "If it is to be, it is up to me," or "Yes I can, I know I can!" in a world assumed to be ordered by a blind meritocracy. Such chanting, Kozol writes, is justified in the pseudo-psychological assumption that the individual's "will to fail" (or succeed) explains low achievement, and not the advantages of tutoring programs, organized sports, helicopter parents, and the other crutches of the "cultivated child" of upper-middle and especially upper classes. In such a context, poor children are conditioned to believe that they earned their fate.

This belief reflects Durkheim's inherently conservative definition of education itself, i. e., that schooling is about preserving and passing on the older legitimated values, customs, morality, and hierarchical systems, no matter how aggressively people like Paolo Freire (*Pedagogy of the Oppressed*) and Ivan Illich (*Deschooling Society*) may dream of empowering the poor via schools.

Hypercultivated Children of the Upper Class: The Misery of Hogwarts

Far above even the level of the harried cultivated child of the middle class are those who will rule the companies of the future. They have what might be called the *habitus* of the Bohemian Grove, Davos World Economic Forum, or the Renaissance Weekend. Such habits are acquired in a limited number of preparatory high schools and elite universities. Annette Lareau has not written a comparable ethnographic study of children with upper-class fathers who attended Bohemian Grove functions. But, G. William Domhoff has written about these schools in his *Who Rules America?* books and emphasized that it is in such places the assumptions about life in the upper class are developed. Such attitudes in particular focus on the legitimacy of upper class ways of doing things. In particular, as he writes, it is in elite schools, and at a young age that the upper class becomes "cohesive" and comes to think alike about issues that both preserve and justify their own privileges:

> From infancy through young adulthood, members of the upper class receive a distinctive education . . . Schooling . . . during the elementary years at a local private school called a day school. During the adolescent years the student may remain at day school, but there is a strong chance that at least one or two years will be spent away from home at a boarding school in a quiet rural setting. Higher education will take place at one of a small number of heavily endowed private colleges and universities. Large and well-known Ivy League schools in the East and Stanford in the West head the list, followed by smaller Ivy League schools in the East and a handful of other small private schools in other parts of the country . . . the system of formal schooling is so insulated that many upper-class students never see the inside of a public school in all their years of education . . . This separate educational system is important evidence for the distinctiveness of the mentality and life-style that exists within the upper-class because schools play a large role in transmitting the class structure. . . .

Quoting Randall Collins, Domhoff continues:

> Schools primarily teach vocabulary and inflection, styles of dress, aesthetic tastes, values, and manners . . . only 1 percent of American teenagers attend independent private high schools of an upper class nature. (Domhoff 1998, 80–81)

Such upper-class institutions are what sociologist Erving Goffman called "total institutions" that isolate their members from the outside world and establish a set of routines, traditions, and automatisms that increase the levels of cohesiveness among people raised in this fashion. Ultimately, Domoff writes, such separateness results in feelings of superiority and exclusivity for having somehow survived the rigors of an expensive and rigorous education (see Domhoff 1998, 82), *a la* Harry Potter's fictional school at Hogwarts.

Less fictional is the elite private school I once visited, Rosenberg Academy in Switzerland, where my daughter was scheduled to take an SAT exam on a Saturday morning in November 2007. I read on the

Internet that the recommended budget for a student attending there was $50,000–60,000 per student per year, including pocket money of $10,000–15,000.

We arrived early, and were asked to wait in a room outside the dining commons. As we sat there, the boys aged perhaps 12–16, but dressed in suit and tie, and the girls, in conservative pantsuits, arrived for the 7:30 a. m. meal. Despite the suits, the boys were squirrelly, just like other teenagers. Except . . . Before the meal started, they lined up behind their chair. They sat down when a hand-bell rang, and the younger students ate feverishly until the bell was rung again, and they were dismissed at 7:45. Only the older students were allowed to remain for a more leisurely Saturday morning breakfast. My wife and I sat in the anteroom watching this for the hours my daughter was taking the exam. We listened to uniformed teenagers chatting in four or five languages (French, Italian, English, German, and maybe Russian) as they passed through, ignoring our presence. I remember spending some time gazing at the school's trophy cabinet, which had the standard trophies for tennis, golf, and so forth. But also one for the school's race car team, even though under Switzerland's laws, students the under 18 were too young to qualify for a driver's license.

My daughter claimed that Rosenberg reminded her of Hogwarts School of the Harry Potter series and took particular amusement at the young man who asked if he could loosen his tie while taking the SAT. Hogwarts is particularly relevant, I think, as a literary metaphor for the isolated upper class. J. K. Rowling's use of Hogwarts as a literary device, is an acknowledgment that the upper class think and act differently than we ordinary mortals do, even if their kids chafe at the discipline. But the point of such private schools is to create a *habitus* of privilege. Boys growing up in such a place feel uncomfortable without a suit and tie, even at Saturday breakfast, and will intuitively seek out others with similar feelings.

Such markers of caste are perhaps most obvious in a place like Rosenberg. But they are also found in culture created in American schools where bureaucratic "measurable standards" and culture are established to separate and track the natural-growth children of concerted cultivation, segregated inner-city children, and Hogwarts-bound children into their meritocratically correct slots.

Hogwarts' Triumph: Harvard's Hard-Working Rich Meritocrats

Ironically, the center-right *New York Times'* Ross Douthat is among the most articulate in expressing how cultural differences lead to the systematic exclusion of most of us from the upper reaches of the American class system.[9] Douthat (2010) writes:

> But cultural biases seem to be at work as well . . . while most extracurricular activities increase your odds of admission to an elite school, holding a leadership role or winning awards in organizations like high school ROTC, 4-H clubs and Future Farmers of America actually works against your chances . . . This provides statistical confirmation for what alumni of highly selective universities already know. The most underrepresented groups on elite campuses often aren't racial minorities; they're working class whites (and white Christians in particular) from conservative states and regions. Inevitably, the same under-representation persists in the elite professional ranks these campuses feed into: in law and philanthropy, finance and academia, the media and arts. p. A21.

There is of course nothing particularly wrong with rewarding the skills and habits that worked for the United States in the past. After all, the skills valued today are in many ways both more refined and bureaucratized than those valued in the past. The privileges of the pre–World War II era is gone; simply being born wealthy is no longer a straight forward shortcut to power and prestige; instead we at least *believe* that the meritocracy is triumphant. But still there is a de facto demand for there to be special treatment for the special 10 percent, while the rest of us are left behind. The imprimatur extended by higher education is also at some level necessary. But it is also the basis for the new systems of this Mandarinate, the type satirized by Michael Young, i. e., elite meritocrats isolated from the broader culture, even as they sustain the legitimacy of their superior position, which is embedded in morality: "Castes or classes are universal, and the measure of harmony that prevails within a society is everywhere dependent upon the degree to which stratification is sanctioned by its code of morality" (Young 1958, 152).

In describing this caste, Young's character asserts how and why the winners in the meritocratic game deserve the conveniences and financial successes in much the same way that a Wall Street banker of the early 2000s might have thought about their own privilege:

> We are thinkers . . . We are paid to think. Well, what do we need to do our work well? We need quiet—no man who is disturbed by noise can devote himself to single-minded concentration. We need comfort—no man who is forced to consider little physical irritations can scale the heights of achievement. . . ." (Young 1958, 157)

But oddly enough, the elite universities founded by the soft sons of the past elite are at the forefront of this shift, as the new meritocrats become what David Brooks calls with some irony, the first hard-working upper class ever.

Harvard, the American Hogwarts, has for the time being positioned itself at the pinnacle of the American meritocracy where it produces Mandarins steeped in a Protestant Work Ethic. Nevertheless, such position is still relative, and there is in effect a positional arms race as the curriculum they announce continues to have a disproportionate effect on the education system through the phenomena described by Annette Lareau and Robert Frank. This is the world where the children of P. S. 65 in Brooklyn mindlessly chant slogans about attending college, but where children are more likely to spend time at the local jail than a four-year college sometime in the next ten years.

Chapter 6

Teachers, Parents, and the Teaching Profession: The Miracle of Bureaucratized Love

Searching for the Next Jaime Escalante: Miracle Teachers, Parents, Children and the Bureaucratization of Love

There are three million teachers in the United States, 70–100 million parents, and more are grandparents, all interested in children in different ways. To begin with, each of the parents focuses their hopes and dreams on one or two, but not many more, of the 50 million children attending the K–12 schools. Each one of the teachers are focused on 20, 30, or in the case of high school students, groups of 150–160 students. Parents also have the advantage of getting to keep their own child for a number of years, whereas the focus shifts every year as teachers are asked to cope with a new group of children.

Nevertheless, the teacher becomes a pseudo-parent both legally and emotionally, particularly in the case of the lower grades. Indeed, there is even a bureaucratic legal doctrine reinforcing this concept. The school is presumed by the law to act in the place of the parent, *in loco parentis*. This bureaucratic legal simplification, while convenient for the administration of schools, obscures a major disconnect between the dreams of parents and the capacities of teachers since, after all, a teacher is not a parent. Perhaps as a result, the miracle teacher, capable of transforming the strengths and weaknesses of America's children into perfect scores on the AP Calculus test, is a staple of American popular culture stepping in where parents, culture, and society fail. The belief is that somehow, the energy, wisdom, and love of a teacher can make up for the deficiencies of the broader culture through a mix of charm, wit, and hard work, even though such a conclusion defies reason.

Teaching is a highly skilled profession, in which both academic knowledge and practice improve quality. Teachers specialize in order to do this, by withdrawing from other possible careers and committing themselves to teaching. As a career, they are then isolated in a classroom year after year with other peoples' children, where they are evaluated both by bureaucratized metrics like test scores of their employers, and perhaps more importantly, with the words and emotions of the children they share the classroom with. In exchange for this, they receive the salary, which is their, livelihood, as well as the prestige that accompanies a middle-class status, and a level of education that is above that which most other students will ever achieve, or for that matter what the students' parents achieved. In this context, teachers respond as do other coping professions. Traditionally, this means that they seek establishment of a monopoly on the right to teach via credentialing requirements, protection from political interference through seniority protections, and during the last 30–40 years, via unionization. As with other coping professions, social activity is often with those who share their profession, and schedule, i.e., other teachers.

The fact that teachers are indeed a profession, and teachers have the same financial interests as other professionals, still does not belie the fact that teaching is an emotional task that involves separating a child from their parents. An important consequence is that the teacher as charismatic miracle worker becomes the ideal, even in a context where there are industrial-style labor relations.

Dominance of Charismatic Outliers

Thanks to Hollywood portrayals, and even a few real-life examples, the hero-teacher is able to slay the bureaucracy is a staple of popular culture. The idealized teacher-heroes resist bureaucracy, which is bad. This leads in turn to the idea that, as in the name of a popular documentary movie from 2010, the schools are simply "Waiting for Superman," that is the teacher (or administrator) who will come along and miraculously rescue the children from the incompetence of the mediocre teachers and bureaucrats.

Thus, in the movies, TV, and even sometimes even in real life, the miracle teacher is assigned to the most difficult kids on campus, whether in high school (television's 1970 sitcom *Welcome Back Kotter* and the 1988 movie *Stand and Deliver*), in an impoverished kindergarten or preschool where no child speaks English and all are neglected (Francesca of Kozol's *Letters to a Teacher*, and the popular program "Teach for America)," or maybe in a middle school where children have fallen behind (Knowledge is Power Program/KIPP). The new teacher, program, or even an administrator, like former Washington DC Superintendent Michelle Rhee, salvages what was neglected in the past, i. e., presumably the capacity to care, and pushes aside the seemingly arbitrary impediments created by "the bureaucracy." Caring teacher is good, and bureaucracy is evil; only the new teacher-hero leaves no child behind. Not even Vinny (John Travolta) on the 1970s sitcom *Welcome Back Kotter* or the Fonz (Henry Winkler) on *Happy Days* are left behind by these teacher-hero. Indeed, final redemption for the the Fonz comes after he not only finally gets his high school diploma but ends up himself becoming a teacher.

The most recent manifestation of this "Waiting for Superman" syndrome, in which school reforming administrators and business entrepreneurs are brought in to tame the bureaucracy, fire the incompetents, and promote the hard working. The mantra is "no excuses" and that poverty and disadvantage does not matter, just like one of the stars of the film *Waiting for Superman*, philanthropist Bill Gates, presumably did with Microsoft. Highlighted are the few teaching stars who have produced high test scores.

The emotional formula in all such accounts is similar, if teacher X can do it, why can't teacher Y? The real-life lives of super-teachers like Jaime Escalante, who had students from inner-city L. A. city schools are highlighted and pointed to as exemplary. The new teacher faced with the buzz saw of "business as usual," the story line claims, confronts a system that guarantees student failure on whatever is the metric of the day, whether it be test scores, unsafe halls, juvenile arrests, teen pregnancies, scores on AP exams, etc. The point is that with a combination of hard work, long hours, parental engagement, and empathy with students, the teacher turns around the class (or school), the bureaucracy is again proven inadequate, but nevertheless in the end applauds the reform and educates happily ever after.

The problem is that the basis for the miracle teacher is in fact—a miracle. The storyline seems to point out that because of enthusiasm, hard work, long hours, and the miracle-worker, the structure of the industrial workplace created by their employers is transcended. But think about what successfully defying such a bureaucratic apparatus implies. After all, those 15,000 school district human resources offices are supervised by something like 75,000 school board members, lay people who believe that through force of their own personality and political wisdom can create a better school for *their* children. Overlapping this governance is 3,140 counties with variable powers and interests in school systems, and a multitude of city-level governments. In such a context, it is not surprising that the young miracle teachers break the rules. What competent person wouldn't? But, the miracle teacher is not the bureaucratic rule-keeper churned out by education schools; rather the miracle teacher is by definition the exception to that bureaucratic rule. What is miraculous is that not all of them are fired for breaking the rules, and therefore can last long enough to perform their miracles!

Jaime Escalante as Teacher-Hero

Journalist Jay Mathews did much to call attention to what a talented teacher can do. In the 1980s, Mathews followed math teacher Jaime Escalante around Garfield High School in Los Angeles and watched him transform children growing up in impoverished neighborhoods into calculus scholars who could master the AP testing regime. Famously, the bureaucratic examiners at AP headquarters in far-away Princeton, New Jersey accused his students of cheating and forced them to retake the test, a challenge at which they were successful, and which of course made for great cinematic drama.

Escalante did this through force of personality, and many, many long hours going well beyond the terms of his employment contract. He followed his students to their homes and conducted many hours of after-school classes. He interrupted administrators and colleagues who would not privilege his calculus program. And of course he got results! The best-known result was a book by Mathews modestly titled *The Best Teacher in America*, a paean to a charismatic personality, technical savvy, frequent bullying, and the extraordinary amount of time Escalante brought to his job as a high school math teacher. The problem of course is not so much the title itself—Escalante may well indeed have been one of America's greatest teachers—but that every single one of these parents want "the best teacher in America" for their child, but only 150 or so can have the single "best" teacher.

In playing to the dreams of American parents, Robert Bennett, President Reagan's Secretary of Education, wrote the following about Escalante: He is one of "America's true heroes. His extraordinary achievement at Garfield High offers a hundred bold lessons and one shining example for American education." Not to mention a great story for film adaptation. The problem of course is that such extraordinary individuals, by definition, are exceptions to the rule, and large bureaucratic institutions deal very poorly with exceptions. Bureaucracies prefer, again by definition, the predictable, efficient, calculable, and controllable over the "Extraordinary Hero" like Escalante. In fact, the initiatives of millions of potential extraordinary heroes are routinely and necessarily squashed.

But this theme has still been taken up by education reformers who point out that the teacher in the classroom is the most important variable for raising test scores, regardless of the fact that a teacher is actually asked to do much more. Or as Hanuschek et al (2005) put it when evaluating test scores from Texas:

> . . . results confirm that good teachers increase student achievement. The average student who has a teacher at the 85th quality percentile can expect annual achievement gains that are 0.22 standard deviations greater than the average student with a median teacher.

After all, schools cannot control for poverty, residential segregation, child neglect, so they assume them to be constants, because they are not the product of education policies. The problem is that in the world of the reformers, only the teachers are a variable raising (or lowering) test scores, and principals, using the metric of tests, can identify who to hire and fire. This is despite the fact that to have a teacher at the "85th quality percentile" there must necessarily be 84 percent who are not at that level. Or in other words, for Jaime Escalante to be the "best teacher in America," there must be 2,999,999 who are not. Simply put, for a Jaime Escalante to be a "best" teacher, the rest must be not-so-great. This though has not stopped reformers from trying to bottle and sell the charisma of an Escalante to tens of millions of parents convinced that their child too deserves the best, and that if their child does not get it, the public system has failed them.

Teach for America, KIPP, and Other Attempts to Bureaucratize Charisma

The Teach for America program was established in 1989 with the belief that great teachers make great schools. Consistent with Justice Scalia's assumption about the capacity of schools to identify the "best and brightest," Teach for America asserted that the graduates of America's best private universities (i. e., those graduates who had the highest SAT scores out of high school) would spend two or three years teaching in schools that served the poor. They would bring their eagerness, pedigree, and energy—something veteran teachers obviously lacked—to these schools for a limited period, and some proportion might enter the teaching profession, while the rest would resume their predestined job trajectory at elite law and business schools. This program in turn gave birth to further programs dedicated to the pedigree-as-excellence assumption.

The "Knowledge is Power Program" was founded in 1995 in Houston, Texas. Two teachers, recent grads of the Ivy League and Teach for America, Mike Feinberg (U. of Penn) and David Levin (Yale), created a program for schools on steroids, which used all the energy of youthful teachers, breaking down what they viewed as the limits of school hours and teacher engagement with students outside school. They insisted on Saturday schools, longer school days, parental involvement, homework, and made home visits. They also fundraised to supplement what tax dollars do not provide and worked incredibly long hours. Journalist Jay Mathews (2009) also traced the careers of Feinberg and Levin as they established schools in poor neighborhoods of first Houston, and then other cities, using the energy and talents of recent college graduates from elite colleges.

Consistent with the emphasis on charisma, Feinberg and Levin credited much of their success to one teacher, Mrs. Harriett Ball, who they found in Houston. Mrs. Ball insisted on high standards for her students and long hours for herself. Feinberg and Levin copied her "technique," which in effect was charisma plus unpaid overtime. Such successful experiments described by Mathews and others were used by school critics to frame "magic bullet" arguments. Meaning that they asserted that if only the techniques of such teachers "scaled up" and were used throughout the system, test scores would rise.

Emotionally engaged teachers like Escalante, Feinberg, Levin, or Ball are effective because they appeal to a pragmatic *habitus* inherited from nineteenth-century American classrooms. To understand how this happened, it is necessary to return to the roots of the American education system, which, despite romanticized pop culture to the contrary, is still saddled with a *habitus* of the rural school marms and hard-headed businessmen of the nineteenth century.

Upper-Class Masters, Loving School Marms, and Hard-headed Businessmen

As described in chapter 2, it was these three contexts—aristocratic privilege, rural populism, and urban utilitarianism that combined to create demand for a particular type of teacher at the nineteenth century. As Diane Ravitch wrote, such schools may seek to create a sense of loyalty to the American sociopolitical order and the habits of patriotism, punctuality, and obedience. However, the next question was: what kind of teacher would staff these new schools?

As described in chapter 2, the model for today's teaching profession was not in rural farms where the profession developed earliest but in the factories of the industrialists who funded the urban schools. There, manufacturers instilled with how the new science of management processed raw materials and made a predictable desired product. Urban schools were seen the same way. With the help of social workers, legal doctrines emerged to justify intrusion into family life and asserted that the state should act *in loco parentis* in order to protect the best interests of the child. But how to do this? Was it to be through learning, creating order, or both? As James Q. Wilson writes, how the task is framed varies, particularly between socioeconomic areas. Wilson writes:

> As Willard Waller pointed out over half a century ago [in the 1930s], the teacher faces two tasks: focus student energies to produce learning and control student energies to maintain order. In principle, the two tasks are complementary: For learning to occur, order must exist. But in practice the two tasks can diverge sharply. In some circumstances, the preoccupation with order dominates the concern for learning. There is some evidence, for example, that schools in lower-status communities display a greater concern for order than do those in upper-status ones. That relationship might exist because either community expectations or pupil behavior (or both) shape the way teachers define their jobs. (Wilson 1991 40)

Teaching as a Technical Science: Creating a Profession

By the end of the nineteenth century, business believed that teaching was a profession similar to that they were familiar with on the assembly line. Children in this context were looked on explicitly as objects to be shaped and formed, in a process like any other in the industrial world.

David Snedden, a professor at Columbia Teacher's College in New York, asserted in a fashion that would be echoed by the more philosophic Durkheim who emphasized that teachers were there to pass on the morality of the previous generation. Snedden the pragmatist in 1913 wrote, "the primary aim of education was to adjust individuals or groups to carry out their social roles (see Ravitch 2000, 81)." Thus, the needs of society determined what options were available, and it was the duty of the "educational sociologist" to train for specific social roles. Four general principles under-lay this, according to Snedden and his allies:

1) Groups, as defined by their occupational interest, required different types of education.
2) Most students by the age of 12, and certainly by 14, should be in vocational programs, since this is what society required in the long run.
3) Traditional academic programs had little utilitarian value for society, or such children, and need not be taught to the vast majority of children.
4) The first three assumptions reflect the most modern understand-ings of science, and anyone who disagreed was "wrapped up in the cocoons of blind faiths, untested beliefs, hardened customs." (see Ravitch 2000, 82)

Then as today, teachers were seen as the technicians on an assembly line designed by educational scientists to produce the learning that they identified was needed for the economic future. Given the demand to create a new school system, they began to ask of the teaching corps what indus-trialists were asking of their assembly line workers, i. e. how to efficiently get the most production out of the least inputs? Having identified the stop-watch and other tools of assembly line efficiency, they turned to school management. Given that the goals of the schools was to serve the needs of the business for literate/numerate workers and to guarantee peace in the streets, what was the most efficient way to go about doing this? Thus, the answer as Linda Darling-Hammond (2010, 237) describes the long–term effects of this on today's schools:

> Most of today's schools were designed not when the goal of education was to educate all students well, but to batch process a great many efficiently, selecting and supporting only a few for "thinking work." Strategies for sort-ing and tracking students were developed to ration the scarce resources of expert teachers and rich curriculum, and to justify the standardization of teaching tasks and procedures.

Anyone who challenges such a faith in the business principles for manag-ing teachers is tarred with the broad brush of the faithful, who change heresy, as Ravitch, others who have questioned the status quo have expe-rienced. When they questioned the management assumptions behind No Child Left Behind, the response is to excoriate them in the court of public opinion.[1]

Teachers and the Science of Caring

The irony raised in the case of Jaime Escalante is that he was hardly a bureaucrat like the fans of No Child Left Behind—in fact he was an impulsive *anti*bureaucrat, as his emotional attachment to his work and students demonstrated. What he was really good at was caring emotionally for his students. Otherwise he routinely flouted the rules, berated his supervisors and colleagues, when they encouraged his students to do anything besides calculus, and complained to the press. Educational advocacy is also rooted in emotions, feeling, rather than a science. We still pretend that there is such a thing as "education science," and expect teachers to be really good at it. Education science is of course an oxymoron—but nevertheless it is the one that is at the heart of the tension found in schools. Thus teachers must be responsive to the interests of emotionless bureaucracies focused on the impersonal discipline of testing, personnel management, and rulebooks while making an emotional connection with their students and their parents.

Teacher Sonia Nieto (2003, 48–49) recounts the story of one teacher who began interviewing personally students who were failing about their academic and home lives, and in the process became a confidante of the students. They began calling her at home, and keeping journals to please her.

> Nobody was more surprised than [the teacher] Claudia at what happened next. In the process of interviewing them, speaking to them when they called her at home, and reading the journals they shared with her, she noticed that within weeks her students were doing their homework much more consistently, and their schoolwork in general had improved. Claudia didn't see this as a miracle cure for low achievement. In fact, it initially bothered her that they were probably doing these things mostly to please her, rather than for themselves. (49)

Like Jaime Escalante, Claudia goes beyond the rationalized conditions of her bureaucratic teacher contract and "cares" as Nieto's book puts it. Caring of course is not the behavioristic give-and-take of incentives and sanctions, carrots and sticks, but an irrational emotion. Or as Nieto wrote, "Teachers in particular have an obligation to work to sustain hope and to resist giving up on young people" (see Nieto 2003, 49 quoting Herb Kohl). But of course "hope," like "caring," is an emotion, not an independent variable in the regression equation that demonstrates that "the best" teachers raise test scores, while under-performing teachers do not.

The problem is that "hope" is not something that the state or school can see or assess. So it is not there in the assessment of the teacher or the child. No testing instrument purports to measure such an emotion—if it could.

The Teacher as a Well-Qualified Businessperson Who Leaves No Child Behind

The logical conclusion to the business model for schools is the United States' "No Child Left Behind Act" (NCLB) of 2002, which is as much a business plan as it is an education plan. Because a child is inevitably left behind (i. e., blueberry discarded), the business plan kicks in with its incentives and sanctions for the teachers.

Sanctions and incentives are levied in a context where teachers are assumed to be "well-qualified in an academic field." But having a teaching credential, Bachelor's degree, Master's degree, or especially a PhD has very little correlation with the "hope" or "caring" that teachers described above instill. But the bureaucratic imagination pushes ahead anyway, emphasizing only the qualities it "sees" from 30,000 feet. As an illustration, the NCLB Act itself answers a rhetorical question about why the teachers' knowledge and its role in the assembly line are what counts, not hoping or caring:

> . . . parents and educators intuitively believe that a teacher's knowledge of subject matter is critical if students are going to achieve to high standards. As Sandra Feldman, president of the American Federation of Teachers, says, "You can't teach what you don't know well." In addition, research shows that teachers who know the subject matter that they teach are more effective in the classroom. Having teachers who know well the content they are teaching is good practice because it leads to improved student learning. (emphasis added, http://www2.ed.gov/teachers/nclbguide/nclb-teachers-toolkit.pdf page 8)

More intuition is implied in the basic symbols representing a well-qualified teacher:

> In general, under *No Child Left Behind* a highly qualified teacher must have: A bachelor's degree. Full state certification, as defined by the state. Demonstrated competency, as defined by the state, in each core academic subject he or she teaches. . . .

The chain of logic in the above list starts from the intuitive feelings and ending with teacher certification is a long and ultimately specious one. Note that in between these two variables listed above are research, knowledge, good classroom practice, high qualifications, and a bachelor's degree. The advantage of assuming such connections relevant to "student learning" is important for the bureaucracy, because it provides a convenient checklist for the administration of NCLB, as seen from 30,000 feet, to see dispassionately its work from the distance that only the state does.

This conclusion, as well as grounding the research in intuition, makes sense in a business model where variables are easily controlled and workers readily hired and fired. But it makes little sense to teacher Claudia who found that hope, generated by teachers working outside the established structure, was the key. Or for that matter, to the third grade teacher Philip Done, who wrote:

> On the first day of school, kids usually fall in love with their new teacher by first recess. But for me, it takes about a week until they are mine. I always miss the old ones. I look at row two, second seat from the end, and I still see Jesse from last year leaning back on his chair. I look at row one, right on the aisle, and I still see Alexandra with her hair in her mouth. I look at row three, middle seat, and I still see Mark surrounded by pencil sharpener shavings. But Mark is sharpening his pencils, Alexandra is eating her hair, and Jesse is falling over in another classroom this year. They all have their new favorite teachers now. (Done 2005, 13).

Philip Done's is not the language of a businessman or worker in the labor market, school administrator, nor for that matter is it that of a parent. It is honestly and straightforwardly intuitive, and the language is that of a teacher, who by omitting the words of market efficiency is rebelling against the business model that assumes that the product has no emotional pull to the teacher that produced them.

Sorting, Rationing, and Tracking Function

The problem is that the bureaucratic school of today was not designed with the development of "individual responsiveness" as Linda Darling-Hammond (2010, 237) points out and NCLB assumes. Rather it was designed at the turn of the twentieth century for sorting and selecting students into different tracks at an early age, with one narrow track for "thinking work," and the other broader track for everyone else. This was done with the assumption that there is a need to ration the limited resources, which are skilled teachers and a rich curriculum. This in turn justifies the "standardization of teaching tasks and procedures." In the United States, of course, this quickly means that allocation of scarce resources is stratified by ability to pay, as is any other scarce resource. This results in stratification by race and class as is the case with other scarce resources in the United States.

But in the context of the school, the question arises: Who controls the scarce resource, which is the "expert teacher and rich curriculum," and who wants it? The partial answer of course is that the school administration, which funds classes and curriculum, does so in the context of their school-level bureaucrat, the principal, while it is typically the student (and parent) who seeks access to this resource. But this also relates back to chapter 5 in which scarcity and stratification is focused on. For in schooling, inequality is also reflected in the competition for the status markers.

In such a competitive context it is perhaps not surprising that those who master the middle-class ethos of the college-educated teacher, or what Lareau called "concerted cultivation," are best able to seek advantage, or as Darling-Hammond (2010, 51) writes, there emerges:

> Unequal access to knowledge . . . structured in a variety of subtle and not-so-subtle ways. In U.S. schools, far more than those in high-achieving nations around the world, this occurs through the allocation of different programmatic and course-taking opportunities . . . Sorting and tracking often begin as early as kindergarten or 1st grade, with decisions about which students will be placed in remedial or "gifted" programs . . .

Dispassionately sorting and tracking are ultimately what teachers do, or even primarily do. This creates an inherent conundrum for anyone hired in a labor market to teach the children of others. In the privacy of the classroom, they must emotionally bond with the children. But in the public arena they are dispassionate sorters and recalcitrant employees.

Protecting the Teacher and Establishing the Profession

The compromises made in the creation of the teaching profession are a near-impossible job description for the teacher. They include caring parent, rational scientist, pedagogue, practical politician, and manufacturer. And they *care*. To ensure these mixed messages are delivered effectively, if not efficiently, there were bosses at the education schools, the district office, the state, PTA, local school board, and the local school administration.

The incapacity to reconcile all competing interests make teachers vulnerable to parents, school boards, and the business community, as each competes to influence classroom content. Such vulnerability is inconsistent with the dignity of a profession for which scientific training and education is required.

> Teachers resent being treated like children, and they become incensed at the lack of respect they are shown by administrators. The reluctance of

administrators to involve teachers more substantively in school reform efforts is certainly not a new problem. . . . [what is more] [t]he general public's disregard for the professional and intellectual abilities of teachers is another sore point. There is widespread belief, for example, that teacher education students, and teachers in general are simply not as smart as other professionals. . . .Related to this, the idea that teaching takes skill and intelligence is not broadly shared. Let me first start off by saying that I enjoy teaching and I believe it is my calling. I also love my students. But the system does not provide with the support of the opportunity to grow . . . Reading this chapter, you might think that being a caring competent teacher means you need to be perpetually angry . . . (Nieto 2003, 71, 73)

This conflict is anticipated in Wilson's (1991, 169–170) description of such "coping professions and their supervisors. He writes about the frustration inherent to the jobs of the school principal, and police lieutenant, who occupy similar supervisory positions in "coping organizations," like the police and schools:

Some agencies can observe neither the outputs nor the outcomes of their key operators. A school administrator cannot watch teachers teach (except through classroom visits that momentarily may change the teacher's behavior) and cannot tell how much students have learned (except by standardized tests that do not clearly differentiate between what the teacher has imported and what the student has acquired otherwise). Police officers cannot be watched by their lieutenants, and the level of order the officers maintain on their beat cannot readily be readily observed, or . . . attributed to the officers' efforts. . . .

How do you improve your educational product when you can neither describe the product nor explain how it is produced? . . .

Where both outputs and outcomes are unobservable there is likely to be a high degree of conflict between managers and operators in public agencies, especially those that must cope with a clientele not of their own choosing. . . .

Thus, the frustrations of teachers are reciprocated by administrators who have little practical control over what "their" classrooms "produce." Still administrators are held accountable for such production. The result is an uneasy truce in which principals are asked to "get the back" of teachers, in exchange for bureaucratic indicators of progress, which only teachers and their students can produce in a closed classroom.

Indeed, the fact that such conflict is embedded in the nature of the job means that unionization and confrontation in the political sphere is likely. This at times leads administrators to hubris in stating their own capacity to shape large institutions and the relative effect of "teacher quality" on classroom performance. Writing in 2010 after an election-year setback when DC Mayor Adrian Fenty was defeated after aggressively promoting school reform, 16 major school superintendents published the following manifesto asserting the importance of the statistical view of learning and the classroom. They saw it through the simplified lens of their human resources offices:

> So, where do we start? With the basics. As President Obama has empha-
> sized, the single most important factor determining whether students suc-
> ceed in school is not the color of their skin or their ZIP code or even their
> parents' income—it is the quality of their teacher.
>
> Yet, for too long, we have let teacher hiring and retention be determined
> by archaic rules involving seniority and academic credentials. The wide-
> spread policy of "last in, first out" (the teacher with the least seniority is
> the first to go when cuts have to be made) makes it harder to hold on to
> new, enthusiastic educators and ignores the one thing that should matter
> most: performance. (http://www.washingtonpost.com/wp-dyn/content/
> story/2010/10/08/ST2010100802672.html?sid=ST2010100802672)

The first problem of course is that the above statement is not true. Whatever it is that President Obama and 16 superintendents may assert, a student's zip code does matter a great deal in which school they will attend, the teacher hired, and the curricular offerings. The problem is that as with other "coping professions," teachers respond to such manifestos by erecting barriers between themselves and those who they fear will attack them, be it administrators, parents, or students. Refuge is sought by turning inside and presenting a united front; and this has consequences for the *habitus* of teaching as a profession, school administration, and the structure of schooling. It becomes a *habitus* of confrontation.

The Dignity of Tenure, Job Protection, and Unionization

Employment guarantees emerged for teachers in the context of the emotional pulls as they "cope" with parents and the public, as it did for the growing civil service in the 1970s. But unlike the federal or state civil service, the "boss" was not a vast federal or state government with a centralized civil service office, but thousands of school boards, many rooted in local interests.

Protecting Teachers from Politics by Practicing Politics

Teachers quickly found in the 1970s and 1980s that as a unionized workforce, their activities could spread far beyond collective bargaining and into the state houses. They did this through the use of campaign contributions primarily to the Democratic Party, and teachers became a key element of the Democratic Party's coalition in the 1970s and after. As such, they became a player in issues that went beyond traditional labor negotiations, seeking to influence issues like tax policy and general education policy, both issues of intense concern to the business interests, which began to coalesce under the Republican banner. To further ingratiate themselves with the Democratic Party coalition, teacher unions also lined up behind other areas of traditional Democratic interest that had little to do with education, such as environmental issues, civil rights, welfare policy, and occasionally even foreign policy. By becoming partisan, teachers offered themselves up as a political punching bag to be critiqued by Republicans. Thus, the irony of the situation is that in the process of protecting teachers from competing political pressures, teachers sought power themselves. In this role they set the political agenda not only for negotiating working conditions but also education policy.

Teacher's associations and unions turned the status of teachers as professionals trained and experienced in the subject of "education" to their advantage, when it came to curriculum choices, and testing regimes. This was resisted by a public and corporate culture, which instead blamed the most visible adults on the playground, as being at fault for what they believed were the dismal condition of the schools. Partisan politics resulted in a tug between teacher advocates claiming a professional monopoly, and business interests concerned with whether the workers produced suited the pragmatic utilitarian needs of the broader economy. In such a context, the California Teacher's Association editorialized:

> So why is it that teachers are being bashed on the one hand and seen as rescuers on the other? The trend of teacher bashing also seems to coincide with teachers being viewed as "superheroes" that can raise student achievement in a single bound. Never mind the fact that teachers are mere mortals. As superheroes they should be able to singlehandedly close the achievement gap . . . If students succeed, it is the teacher who did it. If students get low scores, it is the teacher's fault. If teachers are both the cause of low performance and the cure for low performance, nobody has to focus on poverty, housing, unemployment, health care, immigration or other societal issues. Then again, it's easier to play the blame game than to have a real discussion about the complex issues facing today's students. (Posnick-Goodwin 2010)

At the same time, equally partisan critics asserted that business principles were more suitable for school administration and advocated the use of management models and technology in a fashion that will serve needs for the "productivity" of schools, which is assumed to be only rising test scores. Powerful patrons emerged in the form of successful businessmen who control large philanthropies like the Gates and Annenberg Foundations. Frederick Hess describes the demands for business-like accountability well:

> The nation continues blithely to operate schools in a fashion that was dated in the 1970s and that today would be deemed irresponsible in a toothpaste factory . . . we pour money into technology with little thought to how these tools might be used most sensibly . . . The technology that makes the easy sharing of information possible is the engine that makes tough-minded accountability, school choice, and visionary leadership a possibility . . . Using new technological tools to relieve educators of routine functions will help them focus on those roles that add substantial value—enhancing their contribution, making the organization more productive, and thereby increasing both the benefit to the customer and the resources available to reward employees. (Hess 2006, 219–220)

Ultimately such conflicting views are not inherent to teachers per se, but is a product of what James Q. Wilson described as being a "coping profession," which reflects the fact that teachers, and administrators, are in fact "coping" with the culture and do not by themselves turn the raw product, which is children, into a product that is predictable, much less theirs alone.

Protecting Teachers from Parents

There is a natural tension also between parents who are interested in what happens to their one child, and teachers who are concerned with the destiny of that same child, only insofar as it effects their professional ability to guide an entire class. In addition, the teacher has power, because they are the gatekeepers for status markers—grades and promotion—that parent and student desire.

Besides the tension over grades, for most parents there is also a status differential between them and the teacher. Teachers with BA degrees are typically better educated and have a higher status than the parents. As described in chapter 5, this status difference gives middle-class children an advantage in dealing with schools that working-class children do not have. Annette Lareau (2003, 248–249) described this tension well:

> Differences in educational resources are important as well. Middle-class parents' superior levels of education gave them large vocabularies and more knowledge. More education facilitated concerted cultivation, particularly with respect to interventions to institutions outside the home. As I have shown, poor and working-class parents had difficulty understanding key

terms bantered about by professionals . . . Middle class parents' educational backgrounds also gave them the confidence to criticize educational professionals and intervene in school matters. For working-class and poor parents, educators were social superiors. For middle-class parents, they were equals or subordinates. In addition, research indicates that middle class parents tend to be more sensitive to shifts in child-rearing standards . . .

The nature of confidential student records of course reinforces the inequality. Teachers control not only the release of grades and other status markers, but use the language of the profession to obscure the underlying logic of a system in which they are privileged relative to students and parents. Again, this is something that wealthier, rather than poorer, students are likely to be attuned to.

Principals Protect Teachers

As J. Q. Wilson has written, teaching is a profession that demands independent process from the operators, and this is inherently difficult to supervise. In this relationship, principals and teachers inevitably have a strange relationship. Principals are rewarded for "leading" skilled teaching, but do not do teach themselves. They have little control over what actually happens once the classroom door is closed.

> The operators will be driven by the situational imperatives they face—the teachers' need to keep order in the classroom or the [police] officers' desire to create order on the street or restore order in the quarreling family. The managers will be driven by the constraints they face, especially the need to cope with complaints from politically influential constituencies. (Wilson 1991 169)

This creates unusual power relationship between the teacher and principal, which are oppositional, and to the outside seem focused by the fact that the principal is expected to "have the back" of their teachers. The success of the principal is dependent on the performance of the teacher and students in a classroom that the principal cannot control. Indeed a leading textbook *The Principalship* (Sergiovanni 2006) does not even have a section on classroom dynamics, presumably because, as every study has shown, what happens on an hour-to-hour basis in the classroom is not under the purview of the principal, even as laws are created that assert that there is. Thus, students have little formal recourse when challenging teachers and principals acting *in loco parentis*. Solidarity of the teacher corps created through an oppositional system, absolute power in assigning grades, and the need of principals to "have the back" of the teacher, means that school yard discipline is, from the student's perspective, arbitrary. This happens in millions of circumstances as the rights of the teachers and principals to exercise authority *in loco parentis* and conduct discipline is rarely questioned.

A byproduct of such arbitrary authority is the nihilistic subculture of youthful defiance, which includes the "Road to Whatever" described by Elliott Currie, or perhaps more elegantly in defiant songs like Pink Floyd's "Just Another Brick in the Wall" about the monotony of school life for young people, or the defiance expressed in nihilistic band Motley Krue's 1985 hit "Smokin' in the Boys Room." Each of these expressions of youthful angst create a "teacher figure" who is an arbitrary all-powerful authority to be evaded often with the help of drugs and only in an extreme defiantly confronted.

But if defiance is a byproduct of the conformist subculture of *in loco parentis*, more common is the docility of the high schools described in chapters 2 and 4. Teacher authority may be absolute, but it is widely accepted in the American high school, with its pleasure-focused youthful subculture of sports, dances, and youthful sexuality in which the teacher, the devious figure who Pink Floyd sang about, is really a benevolent figure, and even at times a pseudo-parent, seeking to peacefully, creatively, and conservatively recreate the existing social order.

The Limits of Teachers *In Loco Parentis*

The ultimate problem is that three million teachers hired as well-educated specialists to process 50 million students cannot care as much as 70–100 million parents. In the process, "caring" is replaced with regulations and rulebooks derived from the organization of a blueberry factory, in which students, teachers, and parents are assumed to respond to a the mix of incentives and sanctions in the same fashion that factory workers do. Again the faith is that somehow, the energy, wisdom, and love of a teacher can make up for the deficiencies of the broader culture through a mix of charm, wit, and hard work, even though such a conclusion defies reason

Darling-Hammond and Berry (1988, 5) provided a tongue-in-cheek description of the nature of the behavioristic reforms emerging out of the bureaucracies of the 1980s. They wrote that school reforms *du jour* focused on raising teachers salaries in exchange for more centralized control over curriculum, but it could have been written about any of the reforms of the last 150 years: "The second wave reformers [of the 1980s] suggest greater regulation of teachers . . . in exchange for the deregulation of teaching."

Whether we are on the second, or third, or fourth wave of school reform, the paradox is still the same: There are limits to what teachers can do *in loco parentis*, no matter how much legal doctrine may wish otherwise. The charismatic teacher Jaime Escalante, with his rebellious commitment to hard work and emotional engagement with his students is certainly a very positive example of what can be done. But in the larger context of a nation's school system, he is an outlier. The problem is that Escalante is the teacher that every parent believes their child deserves.

And inevitably in such a context Hollywood responds by creating yet another film focused on a miracle teacher like Jaime Escalante, with a nemesis as either a time-keeping villain counting the days until retirement or a rule-keeping administrator. The point being that for the national discourse to continue, there must be what educator Deborah Meier recently wrote about on her "Building Bridges" blog regarding a film made about a music teacher she knew well:

> They needed a "knight on a white horse" to make the story a popular hit. "Music of the Heart" (with Meryl Streep) was merely following the long-before, laid-out script about public schools and teachers and the organizations they fight to create.
>
> There's a long line of such films that highlight the lonely life of the great teacher. In fact, if they are indeed sometimes lonely, it's because they are breaking the rules— (http://blogs.edweek.org/edweek/Bridging-Differences/2010/09/blog_-_thursday_sept_23.html)

For the individual in this broader system, be they the parent, teacher, administrator, or child there will always be a frustration with the unachievable goal, because that is what you get when rationality of the broader bureaucratic system, is mixed with the need to love and care for a child. Assertions to the contrary by the bureaucratic enterprise, caring indeed works in education. But this caring is not best provided by a teacher, but by a parent. Sure, at times a charismatic outlier, like Jaime Escalante, will emerge to slay the dragons, and ironically, become the hero of the bureaucracy that seeks to replicate the unreplicable.

But the vision that somehow, the energy, wisdom, and love of a miracle-creating teacher can make up for the deficiencies of the broader culture through a mix of charm, wit, and hard work, defies reason. This defiance of reason is what is at the heart of the tension at which teachers are at the center.

Chapter 7

The Child Savers

Introduction: Natural Experiments and Social Science

In conventional science, a theory is proposed, and a prediction made. If the experiment is successful, the previously irresolvable resolves itself, as it moves toward the predicted equilibrium. This is the basis for controlled experiments in a laboratory or other environment controlled by the scientist. Meaning that, based on particular observations a theory is created, a prediction made using theory, and then the theory is tested to observe whether the predictions are realized.

Social sciences, except in rare circumstances, do not have the luxury of such controlled-lab experiments. But they do sometimes use "natural experiments" in order to evaluate a larger system. They do this by searching for trends, outcomes, and then assessing why or why not the trend did not reach a "natural" conclusion. In testing a policy, social scientists compare a population that has adopted a policy as a "treatment" in one place or time, and compare and evaluate the results using logical comparisons. In the process of doing this, you begin to understand the principles underlying a particular phenomenon, including logical trends, and make a good prediction about how the situation resolves itself. In the case of this book, the phenomenon being studied is the relationship between a *habitus* of school bureaucracy, modern childhood, and the interaction between the two. Behind this is an implicit question: What happens when children are raised by only the parents, or alternatively, only by the bureaucracy? This chapter is about evaluating what a modern school independent of the bureaucracy looks like, and alternatively, what happens when the bureaucracy tries to raise children without parents.

Or more to the point, what happens when parents fire the bureaucracy and homeschool? Or what happens when the state fires the parents and takes over parenting using a bureaucratic institution, such as foster care or juvenile courts? Evaluating these—which are in effect natural experiments—helps identify why the odd combination of parents and bureaucracy, suspicious of each other though they may be, are nevertheless persistent and even elemental to modern society.

Experiments in Saving Children

Homeschooling is where parents fire the bureaucracy and take on personal responsibility for educating their children. By the same token the bureaucracies sometimes take over parenting duties too, and parent via institutions staffed by employees hired in the labor market. These include fostering institutions, orphanages, and juvenile halls. By looking at these "natural experiments," the logic and *habitus* underlying the overall system can be understood better. What this natural experiment tells us about the persistence of bureaucratic schooling is the subject of this chapter.

The homeschooling movement grew rapidly in the United States after the 1980s, as some parents grew increasingly disillusioned with the public school systems,which had emerged in the early twentieth century, and particularly in the generation after World War II when the goal of universal high school education was realized. Focused on by the critical parents was the regimentation of the bureaucratic school. As a result a few parents refuse the efficiencies implied by bureaucratic activity and take on the duties of the school themselves, often by investing a great deal of time from the mother. A similar argument can be made about the nature of charter schools, in which parents fire the bureaucracy, and set up schools in order to escape at least some of "the bureaucracy," while still using public funds.

But we can take this thought experiment the opposite direction too. For not only do parents fire the bureaucracy, but the bureaucracy also can fire the parents. This happens in foster care and the juvenile justice system routinely. The state asserts its interest in protecting "the best interests of the child," typically from child abuse, child neglect, abandonment, or delinquency. In such circumstances the state assumes responsibility for raising the child not only via the public school system but also outside the school system. The parents effectively are fired by the state from participating in the raising of their child, and indeed, the state assumes financial responsibility.

But then why aren't the parents or bureaucracy fired more frequently if the situation is so bad? If indeed there are such advantages to either firing the bureaucracy or parents, why hasn't this happened more universally? Why have not more parents "fired the bureaucracy" by homeschooling their children, or at least starting their own charter schools, or as many do, place them into private schools where they can take control from the state? Why do only 1–2 percent of parents decide to homeschool, and only about 2–3 percent use charter schools despite extensive campaigning to "break the monopoly" of the public school system? Another 10 percent or so have consistently used private schools, many of which have a religious affiliation with Catholic or Evangelical churches (See Table 7.1).[1] But in fact 85 percent of parents continue to send their children to public schools, even as they lament the conditions there (see Table 7.2). This proportion has not changed notably since 1970, which was when compulsory education for high schoolers laws were finally enforced, even in the remotest areas of the segregated South.

In other words, despite the rationalized scientific control over childrearing implied by the institutionalized rearing of children, why has this proven effective for only a very small proportion of children, and indeed, catastrophic for a large number?

Table 7.1   The Growth of Private Schools in the United States, 1989–2010.

Private School Statistics at a Glance

PK–12 Enrollment (2009–10)	5,488,000
	(10% of all US students)
Total number of Schools (2009–10)	33,366
	(25% of all US schools)

Where do private school students go to school?

	89–90	09–10
Catholic	54.5%	42.8%
Nonsectarian	13.2%	13.6%
Conservative Christian	10.9%	15.2%
Baptist	5.8%	5.0%
Lutheran	4.4%	3.7%
Jewish	3.2%	4.8%
Episcopal	1.7%	2.0%
Seventh-day Adventist	1.6%	1.1%
Calvinist	0.9%	0.6%
Friends	0.3%	0.4%

Source: National Center for Education Statistics, Council for American Private Education. www.capenet.org/facts.html

Table 7.2   Nontraditional Public Schooling in the United States, 2010.

	(2010 Total Students)	2010 (%)
Homeschool	1–2 million	2%
Private Schools	5–6 million	12–15%
Charter Schools	3–4 million	3–5%
Foster Care	400,000–500,000	.08%
Juvenile Halls	100,000	.02%
Public Schools	About 50,000,000	85%
Total	About 60,000,000	

Source: http://www.census.gov/compendia/statab/cats/education.html

Homeschools, Charter Schools, Foster Care, and Juvenile Courts

Having said that much, I would like to point out that by examining the logic and consequences of such natural experiments, we learn something about the *habitus* of public schools today. Very different institutions like homeschools, charter schools, foster care, juvenile courts, and so forth do indeed share an important thing in common: All are in fact a reaction to the elephant in the room, which is the persistent and unloved public school system. All involve someone announcing that the public school system is inadequate whether due to the child, parents, or the institution, and investing in an expensive substitute. Oddly enough, this means that by looking at how such institutions critique the public schools, the limitations and strengths of not only homeschools, charter schools, foster care, and juvenile courts are understood, so are the actual advantages of the public school system of which they are so critical. In essence, why is the school system so persistent, while also being unloved?

Thus, this chapter is about what happens when the tension between bureaucratic action and the emotions of parents boil over and confront each other, with the result one party walks away from the other in the name of saving the children.

Saving the Children by Firing the Bureaucracy/Firing the Parents

Thus at extremes, two things happen. In a burst of individualism, parents fire the schools and assume responsibility for educating their children in the ways of the broader social world. This happens particularly in the United States, where parents educate 1–2 million children at home, while only loosely acknowledging the role or rights of the state in childrearing. In homeschools, parents refuse taxpayer subsidies of the public schools and the efficiencies of the school bureaucracy, while claiming to create a superior school. Substituted are the efforts of a parent, typically a mother, who organizes a curriculum that is nominally in tune with state requirements.

Firing the School Bureaucrats

Since the extension of mass public education after World War II to the high school level, two major challenges to the "public school monopoly" emerged. Most radical is the homeschool movement, but also significant is the charter school movement. Homeschooling emerged out of the 1960s countercultural and conservative Christian circles, while charter schools are typically a less radical middle-class effort to use public funds to create schools outside the public school system, in exchange for some supervision from the state. The two approaches are at different points in the "fire the public school" continuum.

Firing the School Bureaucrats I: Love and Homeschools

Homeschooling in the United States was discouraged by a range of laws and policies as recently as 1983 (Gaither 2008, 175–200). This changed quickly, and by 1993, homeschools were legal in all 50 states in response to a well-organized "homeschool movement," much of it organized by churches who believed that Christian education should be central to school curriculum. By 2004, over one million students were being homeschooled at any one time (Mathews 2009). Still this was only a little over 2 percent of the total. But the fact that many more children were at one time homeschooled, or partially homeschooled by parents, reflected what many more parents thought of themselves and their children's schooling. Much of this was focused by a nostalgia for a time when it was assumed that all education was done at home.

Homeschools had their roots in an odd alliance between the 1960s counter culture, and the objections of the conservative Protestant churches to what they viewed as a godless secular curriculum in the public schools. The reasons cited by parents for homeschooling are well described by Gaither (2008). Most persistent were concerns among conservative Protestant Christians about what the corrupting influence of public schools on religion and home life. By the 1980s Protestant Christians, many associated with Calvinistic groups organized by Rush Roshdoony and Focus on the Family's James Dobson, churned out materials adapted to home use and their conservative Protestant viewpoint. Intense publishing and marketing led to their dominance of what became a homeschooling social movement. The movement was made possible in particular because, as Gaither writes, the context of changing conditions in house size, women's goals, and the Protestant religious revival of the late twentieth century. In this context, a room in the house often became a formal "school room." Stay-at-home mothers, many of whom were well-educated, sought a larger role in the lives of their children as a way to protect them from corruption by the larger culture.

The homeschool movement organized by Dobson, Rushdoony, and their followers, became a social movement, with magazines, advocacy groups, and others seeking to develop community. By the 1980s and 1990s, homeschoolers allied themselves with the Republican Party coalition, and dominated the development of homeschool curricula. This alliance became tighter as school boards and superintendents sought to slow the legislative success of the homeschool movement by using the courts to compel school attendance, particularly in the early 1980s. A wave of social activism leading to the explicit recognition of a parental right to homeschool in all 50 states was tied not only to the small homeschool community, but more importantly to the growing power of the evangelical churches within the Republican Party.

Homeschool advocates dominated the collection of data about homeschooling, at least until recently (for recent exceptions, see Gaither 2008; Kunzman 2009). Focus was on the successes that homeschool parents had, even though they rarely calculated the costs associated with the practice, particularly those associated with "opportunity costs," i. e., the fact that homeschool mothers were focused on homeschooling rather on more lucrative economic activities in the labor market. What advocates cited were successes on standardized test scores and success at college of homeschool children. Advocates pointed out that colleges regularly target homeschoolers, on the assumption that "home schoolers were self-motivated . . . and high academic achievers." (HSLDA 2010), which indeed is often true. This has led HSLDA to trumpet the following results on the Iowa Test of Basic Skills on their website in 2010, citing an article by Lawrence Rudner (1999):

> On average, home school students in grades 1–4 perform one grade level higher than their public and private school counterparts.
> See http://www.youcanhome school.org/starthere/default.asp?bhcp=1, accessed October 30, 2010.

Rudner himself though is more circumspect in explaining his findings than are the advocates at HSLDA:

> Major findings include: the achievement test scores of this group of home school students are exceptionally high—the median scores were typically in the 70th to 80th percentile; 25% of home school students are enrolled in one or more grades above their age-level public and private school peers; this group of home school parents has more formal education than parents in the general population; the median income for home school families is significantly higher than that of all families with children in the United States; and almost all home school students are in married couple families. Because this was not a controlled experiment, the study does not demonstrate that home schooling is superior to public or private schools and the results must be interpreted with caution. The report clearly suggests, however, that home school students do quite well in that educational environment.
>
> (Rudner 1999)

But as recent academic studies have shown, on average homeschools probably do not do much better than traditional schools on achievement tests, and to a certain extent, it is like comparing apples and oranges. Homeschools are hyper-small, with teachers of various abilities and skills who do the activity as a part of parental commitment, not as a job sought in the labor market. They are focused on a small number of children to which there is an intense preexisting personal bond. And of course the achievements of those specific children, not a group, is the goal of the "school." In contrast, the bureaucratized public school hires teachers in the labor market who have specialized training, and do not necessarily have a preexisting connection to any particular child in a class.

Having said that, if a statistical comparison is insisted upon (which both homeschool advocates and academics have undertaken), the real difference is probably in terms of variation around similar means. There is more variation within the homeschool community than in the public schools, meaning that there are more homeschoolers who do fantastically by conventional measures, but also large numbers who do poorly relative to public schools.

But all this is really besides the point in arguing whether homeschool can be adapted for mass modern education, and here the evidence is incontrovertible. By its very nature, homeschool is not appropriate for a modern society in which the division of labor (see description of Adam Smith's pin factory in chapter 2) underpins production—there are too few parents in a modern society willing or able to make the investment in time or home space to be intimately involved in their child's education. Homeschooling also does not confront the "blueberry problem," which the public schools must. This does not of course mean that anecdotal comparisons will not continue to be made—they will be; and anecdote being what it is, such argumentation will always involve making a comparison between the little David, which is the homeschool movement, against the awkward Goliath, which is the public school system. And while the Davids may win the argument, they still do not challenge the efficiencies and utility of the public school bureaucracy in educating 85 percent of all children rather than 2 percent or so who are homeschoolers. In the end, Goliath dominates.

Firing the Bureaucracy II: Charter Schools

If homeschooling is a complete rejection of the bureaucracy, charter schools are a partial repudiation; unlike homeschools they are an attempt to generate local solutions to what are believed to be local problems. But the system of charter schools, is a national system underpinned by a national *habitus*, which must respect state mandates about the separation between church and state and racial and socioeconomic equality. As with homeschools, valid comparisons between charter and public schools are difficult in large part because they have fundamentally different ways of dealing with the "blueberry problem." Meaning that charter schools self-select students; even if there is a lottery involved, only applicants who believe in the particular mission of the charter apply in the first place. This selects for motivated students with engaged parents, and against children whose parents are not engaged with the system, and by default follow the path of least resistance, which is inevitably the local public school. This latter path of course 85 percent of American children set off on each year regardless of opportunities or the presence of other charter schools.

The general idea of charter schools is that public funds are utilized for new programs, with the approval of an elected school board, but without the bureaucratic controls and accountability to all of the requirements of state law. In many cases, this means that the charter schools are an end-run around the teacher contracts, which administrators claim hamper efforts at reform. And indeed, charter schools with their emphasis on experimentation have often prove more successful in terms of testing results than similarly situated traditional schools. Such results are quickly pointed to by politicians and others interested in school reform. This has been especially the case since 1988 when the first "modern" experimental charter school was established in New York City with the support of American Federation of Teacher's union leader Albert Shanker.

But despite the excitement and controversy surrounding the charter school movement in the early 2000s generated by both the Republican

George W. Bush administration, and the Democratic Obama administration, the charter school movement is not particularly new; indeed, the charter school movement in fact has a long pedigree, going back to at least John Dewey's demonstration schools at the University of Chicago in the early 1900s. Charter schools use public money but are "chartered" at the request of parents and teachers seeking an innovative curriculum for a specified type of child or curriculum. In this sense, like the demonstration schools of the past, they are typically "boutique" schools, specializing in one particular approach to education rather than mass instruction. Likewise, by definition they are an outlier—the exception to the rule. As with homeschools, the ideas developed through charter schools can be creative and influential. But often they are reliant on a charismatic figure like the KIPP schools were on their founders rather than the routines of mass bureaucracy. The reliance on charisma means that the reform is always perceived as "new" despite the old traditions that such experimental schools have in American education.

As a result, despite heavy promotion, charter schools even after 20+ years, do not exceed more than 3 percent of the school-age population, despite widespread promotion by presidents, governors, mayors, and superintendents. More importantly charter schools do not necessarily confront the "blueberry problem" found in mass public education in which "no child can be left behind," or at least cannot be easily discarded. Unlike charter schools, the public school is the only institution that cannot avoid taking children who do not have familial support or the special needs that make up the population of "bad blueberries."

Nevertheless there are of course powerful proponents of charter schools. The proponents of charter schools like President Barack Obama and his Secretary of Education Arne Duncan believe that the charter schools demonstrate ways to improve learning and made the approval of charter schools a key qualifying factor for federal funding by the states. Often this is done with reference to the presumed efficiencies of market-based models. Using the hyperbole of the advocate, Duncan said in 2010:

> The charter movement is absolutely one of the most profound changes in American education, bringing new options to underserved communities and introducing competition and innovation into the education system.

Key to the proposals of Obama and Duncan were competition in the awarding of federal contracts to the most deserving and/or compliant. In this respect, the focus is squarely in the tradition of the American cultural emphasis on markets and behaviorism—there is an assumption that, in the marketplace of ideas the best and most resilient emerge. Thus, using the bully pulpit of the White House, Obama created in 2009–2010 a "Race to the Top" competition for federal education funds in which states changed laws and administrative policies, particularly with respect to teacher rewards for performance (as measured by student improvement on test scores), and the elimination of laws restricting the expansion of charter schools.

On the other hand, Diane Ravitch, who was previously a proponent of charter schools, by 2009 had become a critic, highlighting the fact that there was no one single thing such as a "charter school" that could be compared to public schools:

> Have charter schools lived up to the promises of their promoters? Given the wide diversity of charter schools, it's hard to reach a singular judgment about them. In terms of quality, charter schools run the gamut. Some are excellent, some are dreadful, and most are somewhere in between. It is in the nature of markets that some succeed, some are middling, and other fail (Ravitch 2010, 138).

In effect, Ravitch is pointing out that the "on the one hand and on the other hand" nature of charter school research is too easily dismissed in the hurly-burly of partisan politics. As Ravitch wrote, it is in the nature of competitive markets that some will succeed, and some will fail, as she wrote above. The problem is that the real failures (and successes) are apparent only after the 13 years a child is in school or, to stretch this point to its logical extreme, life cycle of a child, which lasts 60–80 years after they matriculate in kindergarten. Regardless, it is not the two-year political cycle. In large part, this lack of consensus is to be expected given the mismatch between short political cycles, the capacity to promote reform in large bureaucracies, and the life cycle of an individual student, which is 13 years. This creates a real conundrum for schools that serve all children, not only those with active parents.

So ultimately the problem with charter schools, in particular, and education, in general, is that political promises are made and evaluated in two-to four-year-election cycles. But evaluation of a new type of school takes a generation or two. In this environment, charter school proponents are even at a bit of an advantage—they are comparing the new programs that are in a start-up phase to the older public school system, which has the accretion of decades of bureaucratic critique. Such "competition" is of course particularly difficult for an institutions like the public school, whose goals are a moving target highly dependent on political winds and whether success is measured by quickly generated test scores, diversity scores, employment statistics, graduates' postgraduation salaries, delinquency rates, or so forth.

Many of these are only imprecisely measurable, and all may or may not be shaping children for a future, which has yet to arrive.

Under such pressure, it is not surprising that charter schools routinely meet the expectations identified by advocates as measures of success, which is indeed a criteria for future funding. Campbell's Law (see chapter 8), Weber's Iron Law of Bureaucratic Persistence, and Orwell's *Animal Farm* mean that charter schools will always generate the data to persist, even though in the process the same ossification will inevitably occur. Such pressures are analogous to the grade inflation that is seen in schools or, more familiar to most readers, employee evaluations done by human resource departments. They are tools used for supervision, and not abstract, replicable, and objective measures of quality.

The problem of course is that charter school efforts are inherently rooted in "exceptions" or outliers to the rule, rather than the rule itself, and often rely on anecdote as evidence. This is indeed why author Jay Mathews can publish a book called *Work Hard. Be Nice. How Two Inspired Teachers Created the Most Promising Schools in America*, in 2009 about the KIPP charter schools founded in the 1990s, i. e., before the schools were able to measure "results" in terms of the outcomes they promise, which indeed take 20–30 years to become apparent (or not). Charisma does indeed work well with education. But charisma is also a quality that by its very nature is not replicable on a mass scale. Firing the school and establishing your own small school with public money may indeed be possible, but it does not mean that in the long run the charter school has any more control than the bureaucracy it replaced. But it is not possible to do this without replicating the bureaucracy as well. And in this fashion, the charter school movement bumps up against the same limitations that the homeschool movement does.

Firing the Parents I: Foster Care as a Bureaucracy and Parent

But homeschool parents, and the charter school movement are not the only place where society's child savers are found. An older tradition, rooted in American beliefs in equality of opportunity asserts that society as a whole has a responsibility to ensure that parents do not abuse or neglect their children. That if parents do not provide a nurturing environment that includes a right to an education, control of destructive behavior, adequate housing, food, etc., the state has an obligation to step in and provide. A wealth of laws and governmental institutions emerged to assert state rights over childrearing and were given the power to "fire the parents" and take over parenting duties. The institutions established to deal with this include the juvenile courts, child protective services, and foster care programs, which care for 400,000+ children at any one time, along with another 100,000 youth housed in juvenile detention facilities.

But firing the parent is costly for the state and society. There are two ways of looking at how this cost increases: Either the state is losing the *de facto* subsidy that parents invest in their own child—parents are far more financially efficient than the government at delivering "parenting services," particularly when it comes to coping with the emotions of childhood in the context of neglect and abuse.

Also foster care, juvenile detention, and other consequences of firing parents are inherently expensive even when it involves taking "normal" children and providing them with full-time care. Of course, most children who enter foster care, juvenile detention, and so forth do so because of an accumulation of neglect and abuse, which requires the hiring of expensive professionals to deal with specialized positions. This is why in 2008, the California Youth Authority was spending on average $252,000 per year, per ward to incarcerate California's most incorrigible youth. Foster care, while often cheaper, in large part due to the subsidy of poorly paid foster parents, is nevertheless expensive. Federal subsidies in 2003 for Title IV-E children was about $18,000 per child. But then again, the need for such institutional care is hardly new.

Almshouses of the 1700s, orphan trains, and the Children's Aid society of the 1800s, are all predecessor's of today's child-welfare system. For that matter, the schools established by New York City's businessmen for the immigrant poor and former slaves in the early nineteenth century are the predecessor not only of public schools but also foster care systems. The earliest of these programs were under the command of judges who housed children in the same institutions as the poor, elderly, mentally ill, and others who had come to the state as the placement of last resort. All shared a common interest in recreating a nurturing family atmosphere for children who met criteria for abuse, neglect, or abandonment (See Jones-Gore 2009:1). In short, government institutions have long been available to fire the parents, and in the process assert society's broader interest in protecting infants, children, and adolescents.

Firing the parent is undertaken typically via law enforcement agencies, who report abuse and neglect of children to an agency such as Child Protective Services. In doing so, the government assumes the duties of the parent, *in loco parentis*. This legal doctrine, rooted in English Common Law, asserts that the state has a responsibility not only to families but specifically children. What this means in practical terms is that courts look at the need for "the child's need for continuity of relationships," privileging this need over blood/genetic relationships (see Goldstein et al 1996, 19). The modern legal doctrine underpinning the body of law involving child placement is called "the best interest of the child" and was a departure from previous doctrine focused on reinforcing parental rights. The question for the judge and legal system is thus, what is in the best interest of the child, which intrudes not only into the family but also schooling. Indeed, as described briefly in the discussion of homeschooling, the question is what ultimately is the role of the government in the raising of the child? Foster care occurs when the state assumes responsibility for abandoned, neglected, and abused children. Recent figures indicate that about 500,000 children are in foster care situations in the United States at any one time, a number large enough that every state has a bureaucracy to deal with the placement of such children, as well as make payments to foster parents.[2] This is just under 1 percent of all school aged children. As with teachers, foster parents operating *in loco parentis* are hired in the labor market and take on the role of parents; as with teachers, they are asked to care and love, even as their services are evaluated in the cash-based labor market.

But what is also clear, is that in assuming such responsibilities, the state takes on a process that is financially very expensive. A child is taken out of a situation where a parent pays for raising the child with love, attention, and relatively little cash, and is placed into a system in which the state purchases all three in the labor market. As mentioned above, this costs just the federal government at least $18,000 per child per year from Title IV, with state and local municipalities paying additional costs. What is more, the children accepted into such programs are rarely "cheap" in the sense that inherently they are likely to suffer from the consequences of emotional, psychological, and physical abuse/neglect. In other words, firing the parents is indeed expensive for the state, at least in a utlitarian cost-benefit calculation. This happens even in a context where foster parents assume some of the costs associated with care as a matter of sentimental attachment.

What is more, there is widespread agreement among child psychologists that there are long-term emotional consequences for children in foster care, particularly when older children and multiple placements are involved. Whether this is caused by the deficiencies of parents or state is immaterial to the broader question asked here: What happens when the state assumes responsibilities for child care beyond the demands of the K–12 school system? The answer is that state-funded parenting is inherently an expensive substitute in terms of competency, cost effectiveness, and long-term social development. Examining these circumstances reveals that at least in a broad sense, foster care systems, or their equivalent, are not a substitute for effective parents.

Firing the Parents II: Juvenile Detention Facilities and Foster Care

Foster care results from the civil courts firing the parents. But criminal courts do this as well, in response to the delinquent activity of minors.

When this happens the juvenile court system, with its own bureaucracy, assumes the legal role of the parent; but as a bureaucracy, there is an expectation that the new "parents" will be paid. In other words tasks undertaken outside the marketplace by parents must be paid and accounted for in the labor market. In the case of juvenile lockups, this implies both facilities to school the child—after all, this is the purpose of the juvenile court system—and the capacity to restrict children in a juvenile jail. This in turn implies guards and counselors who are present 24 hours per day, 7 days per week, as indeed there are in juvenile facilities. And that care is paid for in the labor market. What is more, it assumes the state pays the costs associated with medical care—which can be substantial, particularly in the case of the psychologically damaged cases the juvenile courts often assume responsibility for. Given this need to maintain health facilities, school facilities, and escape-proof living facilities, it is not surprising that costs per year range from about $40,000 for the simplest cases, to over $200,000 per year for the most complex.

In short, no governmental institution efficiently replaces a well-functioning household in the raising of children, even if that household is, by a bureaucratic standard, inefficient in its utilization of resources. And when government does this, it tends to be very expensive, while damaging the sense of security that a family creates in order to nurture the child.

Necessity and School Bureaucracy, Necessity and Parents

This chapter was a thought experiment in comparative sociology—it asks first what happens when parents "fire the school bureaucracy" and assume responsibility for education themselves, and second, what happens when the state "fires the parents," and the state becomes responsible for raising children. The comparisons, for different reasons, point to the fact that effective childrearing on a mass scale is most effective, at least in the context of mass modern society, when it is done by parents, with public schools.

From a purely financial standpoint, both firing the school or the parent is ultimately very expensive—the results are "boutique" solutions that discard the efficiency of bureaucratic action. In the case of homeschools, and even charter schools, the costs are borne by parents who pay in terms of "opportunity costs" for the labor-intensive schooling that replaces what the school does in classrooms of 20, 25, 30, or more. Evidence indicates that the wherewithal to do this does not stretch far beyond 2–3 percent of the parents; many, if not most of whom, do so only out of a special religious calling, which effectively isolates them from mainstream education circles and the reproduction of society, which indeed Durkheim called the core function of schooling. This level of commitment is not widespread, and there is little indication that it will become so despite 30 years of experimentation.

In the case of public charter schools, the costs are also high, even though they are often hidden in terms of parental involvement, wealthy philanthropic donors, effective exclusion of "expensive" children whose parents are uninvolved in schools, and the *de facto* admissions tests rooted in application procedures. In other words, such schools are not mass, but "boutique." Charter schools are more complex than homeschools and involve public money, but still they are nevertheless boutique and do not have the economies of scale necessary for mass education and the reproduction of all of society, including its inequalities and preexisting power structures. Indeed, in spite of these effective subsidies as Diane Ravitch wrote, there is little evidence that charter schools do that much better than public schools as a group when measured in terms of achievement scores. And when evaluated in terms of capacity to educate masses, they of course fail relative to bureaucratically organized public schools—despite decades of experimentation and promotion, charter schools still only educate only 2–4 percent of the American school children. The antibureaucracy that is the charter school movement is logically unable to take on the huge bureaucratic task of education in excess of 50 million children per year. And even if by some stretch of the imagination it did, it is likely to itself become what it abhors: a massive bureaucracy for the simple reason that this is still the only way to organize such a task.

However, while it is true that boutique methods of schooling are unlikely to supplant school bureaucracies, neither are the bureaucracies able to supplant parents. What the example of bureaucracies supplanting parents indicate is that parents, despite 150 years of expanding public school bureaucracies, are as key to raising children for mass society as they were in the past. Ultimately, this is because children are not simply widgets in the factory, as is assumed to the modern-school bureaucracy, but are also small human beings, emotional creatures who still form special bonds to parents and teachers, and are not reducible by the simplifications of the state whether it be as a "learner," Full-Time-Equivalent-Student (FTES), or other bureaucratic category. Were they, the dollars spent on foster care and juvenile halls would be much more effective than they are, and the "product" much more likely to fit the goals of the system designers. Instead all they see is the collection of misfits, jailbirds, and drug dealers, which dominate the statistics generated for advocacy purposes.

Not even bureaucratic childrearing, even with the commitment of loving foster parents, is a replacement for the love and commitment of a stable home. Were foster care more appropriate for the reproduction of the preexisting society, far more parents would be contracting out childcare in the open marketplace, as the state indeed does, whether it is via foster parents or juvenile hall staff hired in the labor market.

So again, there is a conundrum. In this case the conundrum is that parents and the bureaucratic schools *need* each other, despite the fact that the tension between parent and school is irresolvable. This is because children are both creatures of the market and society at the same time, just as their parents were. Children and society are as inseparable as Durkheim's definition of education implies. And ultimately at the root of this paradox is the old American conundrums between individualism, egalitarianism, and utility.

This is indeed is why such issues will continue to be in the political realm now and into the future. The *habitus* of bureaucratic pragmatism inevitably intrudes into individual parental choices about childrearing. In the process, the *habitus* of emotional parenting pushes into roles as not only parents, but as citizens who are active in the political sphere as well. The questions that emerge are old ones: at what point do the rights of the parents begin and end? At what point do the rights of the state for guaranteeing the safety of future citizens begin and end? And more importantly for this book, what does this tell us about the *habitus* of thought that results when state and individual interact?

But, this does not mean that parents are unneeded. Far from it. If anything, the examples of institutionalized parenting found in orphanages, foster care, and juvenile detention centers indicate that it is far too expensive in terms of money and emotional commitment to replace what effective parents offer their children. Just as homeschooling and charter schools are unlikely to replace the education bureaucracies anytime soon, the bureaucracies are unlikely to replace parents anytime soon.

Rather school bureaucracies and parents are tied together in a continuing but uneasy dance, utterly dependent on each other, and mixing only imperfectly. Each in their own way, seeks to save *their* children. But the irony is that, despite legal doctrine to the contrary, they are not anyone's children; rather they are a future that will create their own world.

Chapter 8

Seeing Like a State: Efficiency, Calculability, Predictivity, Control, Testing Regimes, and School Administration

Our statistics reflect . . . the values that we assign things . . . Treating these as objective data, as if they are external to us, beyond question or dispute, is undoubtedly reassuring, but it's dangerous because we get to the point where we stop asking ourselves about the purpose of what we are dong, what we are actually measuring, and what lessons we need to draw. . . . We begin to march ahead blindly while convinced that we know where we're going (Sarkozy in Stiglitz et al 2010, viii)

Introduction: Seeing Like a State

"Seeing Like a State" is a concept that was developed by James Scott who pointed out that

> . . . state simplifications, the basic givens of modern statecraft, were, I began to realize, rather like abridged maps. They did not successfully represent the actual activity of the society they depicted, nor were they intended to; they represented only that slice of it that interested the official observer . . . they were maps that, when allied with state power, would enable much of the reality they depicted to be remade (Scott 1999, 3).

Or put into the language of schools, it means that the simplifications, especially the standard tests bureaucrats use, represent only that slice of schooling, which is important to people sitting in the state capital or Washington DC, and not necessarily what happens on the ground. As Scott goes on to note though,

> The lack of context and particularity is not an oversight; it is the necessary first premise of any large-scale planning exercise. To the degree that the subjects can be treated as standardized units, the power of resolution in the planning exercise is enhanced. Questions posed within these strict confines can have definitive, qualitative answers [needed by planners].

And indeed they do, in the case of the schools, have quantitative answers that turn around and define the choices that the bureaucrats have. In bureaucratic reasoning, if there is no "metric" the phenomenon is not measurable, and therefore literally not part of the equation. As a result it cannot be questioned or analyzed.

In such contexts, the state develops fads in how it "sees"—but these fads occur in a predictable fashion, which demands a certain type of efficiency, calculability, predictivity, and control. States primarily see their schools using the glasses of such calculability, even if six-year-old children and their teachers do not. Notably, they do not want to see like either a parent, child, or even a teacher; they see only the spreadsheets through which mass institutions can be understood. What might be thought of as the "street level bureaucrat," the teacher, is in turn caught in between. Thus at one time, they are quoting the statistics of their education professor, while at the same time expressing their belief that, like teacher Philip Done (chapter 4), they can fall in love, on command, with 30 new children each September.

Statistics and Seeing Like a State

"Seeing like a state," requires the level of abstraction best created with numbers. Policy for any major bureaucracy is made by people who see the results of their decisions only from afar. Their "seeing" is necessarily through the prism of reports, laws, numbers, rules, budgets, human relations offices, and test scores, not abstract classroom engagement. The only way for a politician or administrator to "see" an entire school system is through such prisms; it is also why Diane Ravitch emphasized that working at the Department of Education in Washington DC is like viewing the nation's school system from 30,000 feet. From this elevation, the most complex of units, the individual child, become viewed as interchangeable units.

This is necessary because as de Tocqueville (1836/1990, 13) humorously wrote in the 1830s, only the Deity has the power to see into the individual minds of teachers and hearts of students; sadly school administrators do not have this supernatural ability:

> The deity does not regard the human race collectively [as we mortals do]. He surveys at one glance and severally all the beings of whom mankind is composed; and he discerns in each man the resemblances that assimilate him to all his fellows, and the differences that distinguish him from them. God, therefore, stands in no need of general ideas; that is to say, he never feels the necessity of collecting a considerable number of analogous objects under the same form for greater convenience in thinking.
>
> Such, however, is not the case with man [i. e., administrators]. If the human mind were to attempt to examine and pass a judgment on all the individual cases before it, the immensity of detail would soon lead it astray and it would no longer see anything. In this strait, man has recourse to an imperfect but necessary expedient, which at the same time assists and demonstrates his weakness.
>
> Having superficially considered a certain number of objects and noticed their resemblance, he assigns to them a common name, sets them apart, and proceeds onwards [to ennumerate them].
>
> [But such] general ideas are no proof of the strength, but rather of the insufficiency of the human intellect; for there are in nature no beings exactly alike, no things precisely identical, no rules indiscriminately and alike applicable to several objects at once. The chief merit of general ideas is that they enable the [bureaucratic] human mind to pass a rapid judgment on a great many objects at once; but, on the other hand, the notions they convey are never other than incomplete, and they always cause the mind to lose as much in accuracy as it gains in comprehensiveness.

But this creates a problem for the schools, which, unlike God, indeed routinely reduce individuals to a "common name" and then proceeds to count every single one in a manner that reflects a general idea like "learner," "student," or "child" efficiently. In the process they become devoid of what the school system wants to reproduce in the first place: the morals and values that Durkheim wrote about.

Seeing Like a Bureaucrat

This though involves an often unacknowledged sleight of hand. Seeing like a state gives those necessarily watching from afar the impression that they can look into a classroom, the mind of teachers, and the heart of students and exercise control. Diane Ravitch, the leading historian of American schooling, began her most recent book with a lament about her own involvement with the accountability and standards movements of the 1990s and early 2000s. At that time she became deeply involved in a reform movement (2010, 1–14) which assumed that bureaucracy was a problem that could be solved by applying the principles of the free market and its "total quality management" (2010, 8–9).

As a policymaker with both the George H. W. Bush and Clinton administrations, Ravitch came to share the beliefs of Republicans and Democrats that business principles, accountability, and efficiency standards could be applied to schools in the same fashion that they were to business. This happened, she writes, despite the fact that she had spent the previous 20–25 years studying the history of education reform. She wrote that given the "potion of power," she too had drunk deeply, and bought into the fads of her time, convinced that one more reform might be the silver bullet to give us the schools of our dreams (Ravitch 2010, 14).

In her *mea culpa*, Ravitch (2010, 15) wrote about "How the Standards Movements Turned into the Testing Movement," as distant administrators reduced children and teachers to test scores. What she says she forgot was that this was not the first educational reform, and likely not the last. Indeed, she goes on to write that it is the responsibility of a sound educational system to resist the fads of educational administration, and focus not on management and accountability, but on the definition of curriculum and the teaching of children.

To a large extent, I agree with Ravitch. Everything I have read and seen in a lifetime engaged in public education tells me that the fads are not the solution to school problems and that they are only the fleeting products of the powers-of-the-day. But at this point, I part somewhat with Ravitch. For while I agree that the fads are not the solution to the problems of public schooling, I do think such fads are also a byproduct of the necessary bureaucratic and political structures that hires teachers and develops curriculum. This is because schools are about the persistent hopes and dreams that Americans have for their own future, and that of their children. School fads are normal because they reflect dreams of today's society for a future, and are not something to be eliminated. Or as the politician, the French President Sarkozy quoted on p. 169 explained:

> Our statistics and accounts reflect our aspirations, the values that we assign things. They are inseparable from our vision of the world and the economy, of society, and our conception of human beings and our inter-relations. Treating these as objective data, as if they are external to us, beyond questions or dispute, is undoubtedly reassuring and comfortable, but it's dangerous. It is dangerous because we get to the point where we stop asking ourselves about the purpose of what we are doing, what we are actually measuring, and what lessons we need to draw. (Nicolas Sarkozy in Stiglitz et al 2010, viii)

Or to take one current administrative fad into account that emphasizes the use of "evidence" in decision making. The problem is that what is defined as "evidence" or a "culture of evidence" tells us much about what the culture thinks is important in their social world than it does about what will be effective in the future. But it does not tell us more about whether our children will be O.K., which is what we really care about. In *becoming* the story do the measures come to reflect values, or do the values reflect the measures? That is the chicken-or-egg question embedded in "seeing like a state" when it comes to children and schools.

Seeing Like a Parent

But if teachers, principals, and particularly policymakers must at some level "see like a state," parents never should, can, or will, at least when it comes to their own child. The relationship between parent and child is the opposite of that between a state and its citizens or a teacher and their students. Each child has typically one or two parents, who are not interchangeable standardized units—meaning one son or daughter is not exchangeable with another. The parenting literature emphasizes the role of specific bonds and commitments between a specific child and *their* parent; parent-child relationships are enduring despite what happens in the labor market. Security is important in the child-parent relationship meaning it is nonnegotiable and rooted in *emotional* attachments. Parents are special to the particular child and provide security specific to that child. The common-sensical wisdom of this, in theory, goes back in social science at least to Freud, and the others who asserted that the good child is a securely attached child (something that every grandmother is purported to know). Oddly such knowledge is expressed in the jargon of as bureaucratic state in ways unlikely to be understood by many grandmother:

> Over time, a securely attached child has learned that he can rely on special adults to be there for him. He knows that, if he ever needs something, someone will be there to help. A child who believes this can then learn other things. He will use special adults as a secure base. He will smile at the adult and come to her to get a hug. Then he will move out and explore his world. (http://www.extension.purdue.edu/providerparent/Family-Child%20 Relationships/DifferentTypesP-C.htm)

In other words, the relationship between child and parent is not negotiated via the bureaucratically administered labor market, credentialing institutions, or human resources office like that between a pupil and teacher. Most immediately it arrives via the messy improbabilities created activities like dating, courtship, alcohol, marriage, and the exigencies of duty that are the consequences of the sex act. And of course it develops from an emotional, not rational, fashion. It is rooted in emotions and sentimentality between individuals, not an individual and an institution. From this perspective, it is hardly surprising that parents see their children very differently than schools do their students.

Seeing Like a Child

The child of course is caught in the middle, as they navigate psychological and social perils created by their dependencies on emotional parents and rational bureaucratic school. The rules of developmental psychology tell us that the child will view their first grade teacher as more of a surrogate parent and fall in love with their third grade teacher as Philip Done described. By high school, their teacher is meticulously examined for their fidelity to the bureaucratic rules that moved to the center of the 16-year-old's school life where they are habitually measured in terms of test scores, fitness tests, and that all-purpose bureaucratic measure of social worth, the grade point average.

But the child of course is living in a developmentally induced delusion; their first grade teacher is in fact embedded in the same bureaucratic system as their twelfth-grade government teacher. And despite fantasies to the contrary, their first grade teacher is not a surrogate parent and is held to the same system of bureaucratic accountability as the twelfth grade teacher, and the clerk in that most bureaucratic of school-based institutions, the attendance office. This is because the school is not run as the first grader would imagine it, i. e., as an extended family; rather it is a bureaucracy.

Efficiency, Calculability, Predictivity, and Control and the No Child Left Behind Act

Much ink has been spilled in this book, and many others, about the centrality of testing to the modern-school endeavor. Or in particular, the use of *standardized* tests. It should be apparent from the above paragraphs that the use of such testing is necessary and inevitable to any modern bureaucratic endeavor which necessarily sees—and simplifies—like a state.

Schools are run as bureaucracies because as Weber wrote long ago, it is the only plausible way to undertake complex organizational tasks. And few tasks are more complex than the sustained rearing of children across a period of 12–13 years to become the adults their modern societies (including their parents) want. Only a limited number of parents do so by themselves, whether it is through homeschooling or hiring a personal nanny. So mass education is ultimately a bureaucratic task—and one that must simplify the immensity of detail, because the human mind otherwise cannot make the necessary judgments to undertake the task.

Thus, modern standardized testing emerged in a world in which bureaucrats needed numbers to say whether the qualities they were teaching children were effectively installed in the minds of millions of interchangeable units as their business plans promised. But government, even when teaching something as unquantifiable as morality, is still about planning, or as James Scott (1999, 3) wrote,

> . . . state simplifications, the basic givens of modern statecraft . . . did not successfully represent the actual activity of the society they depicted . . . they represented only that slice of it that interested the official observer.

And in the case of the school, the official observer is in the district headquarters, statehouse, or Washington where the taxes to pay the teachers are collected. And that slice they desired to see was reflected in their mission statements (see chapter 3) and not the dreams of the parents. The bureaucrats want to see that the schools produced workers, citizens, appreciation of diversity, and so forth. They do not produce love.

The Weaknesses of Bureaucratic Schools: Why We Test

But even if there are inherent strengths to the bureaucratic system, this does not mean it is perfect. Rather, it is as intensely flawed as any institution—if not more so. The reasons why are apparent when it is recognized that schools are a rational bureaucratic institution trying to do a irrational emotional task, which is ultimately as Bourdieu wrote, the reproduction of society, with all its odd taken-for-granteds. The problem is that modern society cannot divorce itself from its own systems of mass public education, no matter how contradictory this may be.

This indeed is ultimately why rationalized test measures are ultimately—irrational. To borrow a term used in chapter 3, there is irrationality in the rationality of testing. Stephen Jay Gould wrote an entire book about this contradiction, *The Mismeasure of Man*. In the book Gould demonstrates how in the United States, testing is consistently used to favor preexisting assumptions about achievement and social hierarchy. As Gould (1996, 59) points out, this means that achievement tests are consistently written in a fashion that presupposes existing values rooted in the nature of business, capitalism, and race relations, which in turn are reified as intelligence, and "the mystique of science proclaims that numbers are the ultimate test of objectivity . . . " In turn they are legitimated with the language of science because "quantitative data are as subject to cultural constraint as any other aspect of science . . . [and] they have no special claim upon final truth."

So what emerges from testing regimes are attempts to preserve preexisting cultures using measuring sticks that confirm the preexisting social order. Subjectively created measuring sticks become an objective source of wisdom for framing the problems of the masses (see Bourdieu and Passeron 1977/1990). But this results in the contradiction pointed to by Joseph Stiglitz et al (2010, vii):

> Treating these as objective data, as if they are external to us, beyond question or dispute, is undoubtedly reassuring, but it's dangerous because we get to the point where we stop asking ourselves about the purpose of what we are dong, what we are actually measuring, and what lessons we need to draw. (Cited in http://blogs.edweek.org/edweek/Bridging-Differences/2010/07/)

The point is that ultimately, all such data is not "objective," no matter how "evidence based" the quantitative indicators are. What is more, they are self-referential, so what emerges often results in a policy of nostalgia as individuals reflect back upon their own lives seeking that circle of life from *The Lion King*. But it is not a circle but the result of a *habitus* that emerges out of the contradictions in a particular society, and dialectically change emerges as tensions are resolved.

Campbell's Law and The Inevitable Persistence of Testing

Self-reflexivity is a reference to "Campbell's Law," which describes how measuring something and giving the measurement consequences effect the measure itself. Donald Campbell was a psychologist and methodologist deeply involved in the use of social data as a way to assist policymakers in making political decisions. He came to notice that the sustained use of any particular measure to evaluate success (or failure) meant that bureaucracies begin to alter behavior in a way to meet the expectations of the measure. These pressures are "corruption pressures." In the former Soviet Union, the use of such measures to command particular productivity targets resulted in shoddy work, and falsified data to meet the numerical expectations. More familiar social indicators are also susceptible, which is why independent auditors are important for checking the books. In large part, the mortgage crisis of 2007–2008 was created because mortgage lenders had corruption pressures to inflate home values, and homebuyers had corruption pressures to inflate incomes. This is Campbell's Law writ very large, which he summarizes as:

> The more any quantitative social indicator is used for social decision-making, the more subject it will be to corruption pressures and the more apt it will be to distort and corrupt the social processes it is intended to monitor. (Campbell 1976 http://www.eric.ed.gov/PDFS/ED303512.pdf)

Or, to put it into the modern jargon of the schools, Campbell's Law indicates that an evidence-based system will corrupt itself in a way that creates the desired evidence, which in the case of schools are rising test scores. Thus, in the process of becoming the point of education, the data/evidence loses its utility as a way to measure what is desired, i. e., education in the first place. For example, the SAT test is no longer a general test measuring, in a broad fashion, math skills, but the capacity of a student to exhibit the type of math skills tested for. This happens because the SAT is the gate-keeper for the social decision making, i. e., the allocation of social status via college admissions, jobs, and so forth.

But Campbell's most remarkable example is the body counts in the Vietnam War. During the Vietnam War, units of the United States army were tasked with "killing the enemy." Units that killed many enemies were rewarded, and those that failed to kill enemies were not. This created incentives for the US units to have high body counts for "enemy" dead. There were though a number of ways to do this, some of which reflected military success, and some of which did not.

The "corrupting pressures" in Vietnam emerged at each level of the chain of command. Thus at the field level, any dead Vietnamese—soldier or not—was likely to be defined as "enemy." At the next level up, there was a hesitation to investigate complaints about the illegitimate use of force in a unit that reported high rates of enemy death, because such reports indicated success and were rewarded. And at headquarters level, corruption meant that liberal standards were adopted to encourage the use of lethal force, at the expense of other policies that were more likely to contribute to the success of the American "hearts and minds" mission, but did not have an easily measurable metric like "enemy dead." In other words, the unspoken *habitus* of the army was pushed toward a goal relentlessly by the need to satisfy the assumptions behind the number.

Educational testing, whether of the recent NCLB variety, or the earlier IQ testing described by Gould, creates corruption pressures as well. Testing typically has a general goal: "evaluate learning" in a particular subject which has been identified as having special value. Thus, at the time of World War I, I. Q. testing was created in order to assist the US army with identifying the type of soldier that the army believed would make a good officer. Much of this testing focused on basic vocabulary, writing skills, and computation skills, i. e., the basic concerns of a military bureaucracy bent on shaping poorly educated and poorly nourished urban and rural masses into an army. Given especially the emphasis on English vocabulary, the officer corps came to be made up of the well-schooled, most of whom had access to the better schooling, and effectively excluded the children of the urban immigrant masses, African Americans, and rural whites. These were the tests sorting of the academically inclined, and everyone else in the 1920s.

Not surprisingly, the new exams were soon corrupted by those who understood the *habitus* underlying the new measuring stick. As in the case of kills in Vietnam, this happened throughout the system as tests designed to assess conventional upper-middle-class vocabulary skills emerged and the school bureaucracy made the mistake that Sarkozy, Stiglitz, Campbell, and others critique. They treated the test results as objective data and tried to pretend that the numbers were external to the system being measured— and in the process stopped asking what was actually being measured. Thus, a screening test first designed to create an instant officer corps in World War I became the measuring stick that shaped the futures of millions of students and their teachers. Gould pointed out that this simplification meant that the abstraction of "intelligence" became something new as a result:

> the abstraction of intelligence as a single entity, its location within the brain, its quantification as one number for each individual, and the use of these numbers to rank people in a single series of worthiness, invariably [found] that oppressed and disadvantaged groups—races, classes, or sexes—are inherently inferior and deserve their status. (Gould 1994, 56).

In other words what Gould is saying is that the abstraction of intelligence as it becomes simplified, is used to re-create the preexisting social order. I doubt that Emile Durkheim, Pierre Bourdieu, Randall Collins, or Donald Campbell would be much surprised.

The effects of "Campbell's Law" can actually be followed whenever a new testing instrument is introduced. In the years following the introduction of a new standardized tests, scores inevitably fall because teachers and students are unfamiliar with the exam and the "universe" it is meant to measure. Over a period of three to five years, the curriculum begins to align with the new exam, in a fashion that means that scores rise (see e. g. Texas as described by Ravitch 2010, 96). What is happening, is that the exam begins to drive what is taught; and as a result, what is measured is no longer "English" or "Math" but facility with the preexisting Texas Standards Exam. Or SAT exam. Or any other exam used across several years.

Such principles of testing corruption are long known. Professors of educational testing and social science methods readily point to the limited utility of their tools, and administrators believe them. But in fact there is a persistent cognitive dissonance between the scientists who design the exams and the administrators who administer them and then use results to drive decision making. This cognitive dissonance is persistent because the capacity of the testing regimes to reproduce the *habitus* of preexisting society, including the capacity to identify persistent values of the elite. Pointing out that the emperor has no clothes (as many have done for the last one hundred years) threatens the very being of that school bureaucracy. This is because the goal of any school bureaucracy is first to protect and nurture itself and the state that created it. In short, the testing regimes are the mechanism through which the school bureaucracies necessarily "see like a state," and not incidentally seek to preserve the existing state itself.

Efficiency, Calculability, Predictivity, and Control and the No Child Left Behind Act

As bureaucratic institutions, schools are embedded in the vast institutions of the modern state. As with any bureaucracy, public or private, goals are sought in an efficient, calculable, and predictable fashion (see Weber 1947; Ritzer 2008; and Waters 2001). As this happens, the bureaucracy seeks to control via nonhuman means, which in the case of schooling are the rule books, laws, and an insistence on accountability, which provide the appearance of coherence, particularly for the administrators who see children as numbers on spreadsheets rather than the child of particular parents. But the coherence of course can never be there in the same fashion that is found in a factory. As a case study of how this works, I will focus on the United States' No Child Left Behind Act, passed into law in January 2002.

The United States' No Child Left Behind Act is a classic example of how the central government responds to a problem in school administration by first setting up a measuring stick so they can "see" whether desired progress is taking place in a vast school system. The Act did this by first insisting that every child should be tested every year between the third and eighth grades, second, by insisting that decisions that are used to reform schools be made by the states and not Washington, third, that "low-performing" schools would be identified using the test scores generated, and fourth, that there would be punitive sanctions for "failing schools," which would permit students to transfer out (See Ravitch 2010, 94).

This absence of any single goal for NCLB is of course characteristic of both normal political processes, which involve coalition building, compromise, and the fact that a goal like "education" is inherently ambiguous (see e. g., Olson 1982). Nevertheless the nature of the rational bureaucracy assumes otherwise; the following paragraphs and pages use the No Child Left Behind Act as an example of how such programs are bureaucratized. In developing such an example though, I do not mean to critique only the NCLB in particular, rather the principles apply to the bureaucratization of schools generally.[1]

NCLB Efficiency. Under NCLB, school efficiency is measured in terms of students processed and test scores achieved. To be efficient, they must be measurable with a measuring stick, which is in the case of school accountability means tests scores, and graduation rates, however defined. Notably this is a shift from previous decades when the schools were seen as focused on creating a more racially just society, crime prevention, etc. Success was measured in terms of integration, measures of social justice, and so forth. Success in the business-focused 2000s, used a new measuring rod, that of the NCLB-sanctioned test score. Efficiency becomes the test score.

But a problem of efficiency with respect to schools remains the classic blueberry problem. Efficiency requires that the bureaucracy discard raw materials that do not meet the standards of the measuring stick. This routinely happens when students who test poorly are exempted from testing or moved to alternative schools, or in other words, tracked and sorted in a fashion that means scores will rise and the schools perceived as more efficient.

NCLB Calculability. Calculability is at the heart of NCLB—in no large part because that is the only way Washington, or any other central location, can see the schools. Calculability vis à vis the measuring rod is equated with the reading, numeracy, and other qualities schools are required to develop.

The only problem of course is that the corruption pressures of Campbell's Law inevitably emerge, particularly in the emotional world of the school. Or as Campbell himself wrote about an earlier generation of quantified tests used for accountability purposes:

> achievement tests may well be valuable indicators of general school achievement under conditions of normal teaching aimed at general competence.

But when test scores become the goal of the teaching process, they both lose their value as indicators of educational status and distort the educational process in undesirable ways. (Similar biases of course surround the use of objective tests in courses or as entrance examinations.) (See Campbell 1976)

In such a context, accountability becomes the point of, not the evaluation of, "normal" teaching or general competence. When this happens test-prep becomes the new normal, and the new definition of competence.

NCLB Predictivity. Bureaucracies do not like surprises. Unfortunately, children, with all their individual leaky idiosyncracy, are by definition full of surprises, the most unsurprising one being that they are creatures of hopes and dreams rather than the predictable results of the factory. Indeed, much of schooling is focused on taking the unformed and unpredictable material that is children and transforming them into predictable adults. This takes at least 13 years, and perhaps never ends.

Predictivity also implies the absence of emotions, including hope, love, and fears. NCLB and other similar programs are generated on a factory model, which seeks a predictable outcome. But children, like society itself, is not always predictable—rooted in irrational emotions of fear and hope.

NCLB Control. Schools are ultimately coping bureaucracies, not the production bureaucracies assumed by NCLB accountability models. They want to produce a predictable product (i. e. annual test score) using the financial and human resources they are supplied even though this is not possible. But instead, they seek to control as a coping bureaucracy in a state would: through a focus on enforcement of rules and procedures. The rules and procedures are the behavioristic rewards and sanctions for teachers, schools, and students.[2]

When I began this book, I was inevitably asked about testing. Was I going to show once and for all that test-driven administration of schools is an inherently flawed enterprise? The answer of course is yes; testing is indeed an inherently flawed enterprise. Test-driven administration is bound to disappoint students, publics, and administrators alike. Only people really good at tests are promoted and become the elite of the future, as Michael Young predicted in 1958 in his book *The Rise of the Meritocracy.*

Is this good for society? I guess my response is that it depends on who you ask. Those who become the conservative self-fulfilling prophecy rewarded by the standardized tests will approve because they end up validated, as they become the self-defined elite of the future. Ask Justice Scalia on the US Supreme Court, or for that matter any of the 49 US Senators who are Harvard or Yale graduates. They like the current system, because it rewards people like them; i. e., it conservatively re-creates the status quo.

This is not all that different than older status systems, which were also conservative and defined being "just like us" as being rooted in birth, race, tribal identity, or guild. Social hierarchy being what it is, the rest of us will uncomfortably probably go along with it.

The Continuing Effort to Mismeasure Man

Stephen Jay Gould in his book *The Mismeasure of Man* wrote perhaps the most prescient (and blistering) critique of how statistical measures are consistently used to perpetuate the status quo. He clearly showed that the use of psychometric tests like the SAT were consistently justified stereotypes rooted in race, class, and social status, which relegated the disadvantaged to the poorest facilities, most crowded schools, and most neglected neighborhoods. The tests he described were designed to consistently ferret out relative poverty in ways that few sociologists could do as efficiently. If you want to know where poverty is, follow the low test scores.

Gould's grasp of the history of testing shows that the "reification of intelligence" via the simplifications of the bureaucrats' standardized test is a fool's errand. Generation after generation has regretted the inevitable corruption of the meritocratic ideal as existing power imperfectly re-create itself in its own image. But still they use the tests because they can administer large programs in no other way; preexisting status arrangements, whether they are rooted in race, immigration status, physiognomy, head bumps, genetics, or any other archaic characteristics and assumed to reflect an innate intelligence.

So what are really interesting is not that the tests are consistently wrong but that they continue to be used. The problem, of course, is that the desire to "mismeasure man" is embedded in the *habitus* of our modern society. Thus, while agreeing with Gould's analysis of how such differences are misused, it is also necessary to acknowledge that they will be reproduced again in different forms as mass modern society deals with the very basic functional need to reproduce itself by transmitting the received values and morals of the past into the future. And in a grand feat of cognitive dissonance, books like *The Mismeasure of Man* are assiduously never cited in the reports, books, and studies of the many reports evaluating a massive testing program like No Child Left Behind.[3]

Thus the meritocracy gives the illusion of objectivity—which is of course why good meritocrats like Justice Scalia use test scores when selecting the "best and the brightest" to work for him. Yet, any exam is designed to reward some skills, and not others. And exams at schools are designed to reward the skills of the status quo—where else could the exams come from except the past? And the status quo, seeks to pass its privileges to its offspring, just as the aristocratic elite of medieval Europe did. Except the mechanism is not moderated by birth, but by the exams and schools. But indeed, this is a fallacious undertaking. Human capability comes in many shapes and sizes but is always dependent on social context, including that related to power and inequality. It is always fallacious to reduce human beings to simple unilinear ranking systems as schools implicitly do when administering standardized tests and assigning the quantifiable grade-point scores. But as de Tocqueville noted it is the only technique available for managing a large group of people, for those of us who are not Deity, a group which I assume includes all of the employees of the US education bureaucracies. It also has the advantage of providing a bureaucratic rationalization for justifying elite privileges as "natural"[4] and perpetuating the status quo. In the end, birth indeed often does usurp the meritocracy. In other words, you could select based on address and parental income and get a class equally well prepared to reproduce the preexisting system.

Campbell's Law Revisited

The problem of course is that in a bureaucratized school system (or any type of system), the system itself tautologically measure itself.[5] As a reminder, this is roughly what Campbell's Law predicted as described in the twisted syntax:

> The more any quantitative social indicator is used for social decision-making, the more subject it will be to corruption pressures and the more apt it will be to distort and corrupt the social processes it is intended to monitor.

This is done to, as Durkheim wrote, re-create a future that reflects past experience, including (as Bourdieu added), the need to reproduce the inherited systems of social stratification and dominance. As we saw with the Mandarins from Harvard in chapters 5, the distortions are always toward justifying the status quo in order to promote a future that preserves existing power arrangements. In this world, quality and merit become defined as what the existing upper class does best, whether it is producing SAT scores, LSAT scores, or any other measure of excellence that ultimately sits on an arbitrary and socially constructed foundation of sand.

But All *Habitus* Is Ultimately Relative

At its heart, the culture of a society is in its accumulated and shared ways of looking at its values and culture—or what Bourdieu called *habitus*. Such *habitus* is ultimately relative, too. But of course this is never as stable as the elders may wish. Thus, there is typically a nostalgia for an earlier time or enthusiasm for an exotic idea—both can be sources of the next fad, and in the process albeit slowly, the beginning of a new *habitus*.

But the problem with *habitus* is that it is always ultimately relative, and also changes with time, and across space. We have already seen how the testing movement arranges and rearranges itself in the United States often in a odd (and often simultaneous) combination of horror with past abuse and a desire to get back to the past. Or, there comes an assumption that a foreign system that generates the desired measure, or test scores will be better, if the system is adopted. It always seems like another place, be it Korea, Singapore, or Finland, perhaps has the magic key. Why can't we just borrow it? But such assumptions, assume that the *habitus* of the age, which admittedly comes from the past, can be reproduced. But can it?

Chapter 9

The Limits of the Modern American School: Rock, Paper, Scissors (Equality, Individualism, Utilitarianism)

The Limits of the Modern American School

Bureaucracies, while well suited to deal with matters of the rational mind that pragmatic American *habitus* celebrates, are in fact ill-suited for matters of the heart. Thus, bureaucracies created to undertake the tasks bump up against the three values identified long ago by de Tocqueville and that are at the heart of many continuing American dilemmas. These include first the dialectical tensions over equality, individual rights, and utilitarianism. They are the rock, paper, scissors of the American educational system. This chapter is about how this game of *rochambo* is played out in recent decades. In describing the swings, I will move between demands to eliminate the inequalities of race and poverty, protection of individual rights, and most recently, the appeal to business ethics in the administration of education programs. Three examples will illustrate the dissonance between these three values: The persistence of inequality, the persistence of radical individualism, and the persistent connection between education and business practice.

Paradoxes, conundrums, and dilemmas underlie the cultural *habitus* of the American school that drives the dreams of parents, teachers, administrators, and ultimately children. But the experimentation that began in the nineteenth century and was designed to lead to an ever more perfect school system, ultimately has practical limits rooted in the nature of its intertwined *habitus*. And this is where limits to how egalitarian, how individualistic, and how efficiently schools can be managed. Because schools ultimately seek to provide equality in a society that is not equal, individuality in an environment that is group focused, and efficiency in an institution in which inputs are not controlled, the product defined, nor flawed goods discarded.

In the case of the American school, the limits are most identifiable when institutions bump up against the underpinnings that form the *habitus* of thought and deed of both individual and the society they create. In the United States, these limits are found particularly in how schools continue to wrestle with the most salient features of American society and how it views its children. Prominent is the persistence of inequality rooted in both socioeconomics and race and the preservation these contradictions in the context of American-style business models; oddly enough, this happens in the context of an insistence on the uniqueness and rights of every individual child to seek their own potential. And so like a *rochambo* game of rock, paper, scissors, one wins and one loses, but the game never really stops. Egalitarianism, individualism, and utilitarianism echo through the schools, pushing each other aside, but only temporarily. Thus when a school becomes more egalitarian, it loses its capacity to recognize individual differences, as indeed happened in the 1980s. When it focuses on pragmatic service to the business community it tends toward inequality, which is what happened as millions of immigrants, African Americans, and others were sorted and tracked into vocational tracks during the twentieth century. And when a school begins to respond to individual needs, it becomes less efficient, and given the inequality in the American social system, it advantages the rich. In other words, over the decades, the American school system has played a game of *rochambo* as the tensions between the *habitus* of egalitarianism, utility, and individualism play themselves out.

Ultimately, though, the bigger story is not that these issues always reemerge, but that the body politic, including thoughtful historians like Diane Ravitch, are always surprised when it does. Such things are not "cyclical," as pop sociology might assume. Rather they are the result of a tension between different ideological trends embedded so deeply in American society that Alexis de Tocqueville could identify them in the 1830s. These trends result in harsh evaluations of the American school system, whether it is the observation of persistent racial and socioeconomic inequalities or the abuse of the individual rights of children or frustration with the graduating 18-year-olds. This is the result of how the broader society wrestles with the dissonance of holding incompatible ideas. Such cognitive dissonance is of course an uncomfortable feeling; it is not surprising then that society deals with this discomfort by adjusting the programs and policies that are the lode star(s) for educational policy. But lost in the political process is the distinction between what Durkheim called pedagogy and the underlying metaphysical roots of "education" in shared morality. This distinction is lost in an American system that celebrates the pragmatism of pedagogy and disdains the impractical nature of educational philosophy.

The Persistence of Savage Inequalities

At the heart of the American paradox is a toleration of inequality not seen in other rich modern societies. Regardless of the strong ideological commitment to equality before the law, competing demands of individualism and utilitarianism at times trump it. As described above, there was indeed a period following *Brown v. Board of Education* in 1954 when the society favored equality, even over the many considerations of individualism and business-like utilitarianism. Indeed, for a brief period between about 1970 and 1990, programs to ensure equal opportunity like bussing, affirmative action, and open-enrollment policies trumped the demands for individual choice in schools and cost-efficiency relative to the labor market. The result was indeed integrated classrooms brought about most importantly through policies guaranteeing a right to attend school even for the most socially stigmatized. At the forefront were policies that established schools even in the remotest and poorest areas of the large urban areas, rural Indian Reservations, and the South, often without respect for economies of scale.

But while bureaucratic goals for integration were met, they came at the expense of lowered standards for academic excellence and reduced school choice, particularly for white middle-class youth, who, in the past, were segregated from the problems associated with poverty. In an attempt to paper over these faults, schools particularly in the 1970s "dumbed-down" the curriculum by permitting an increasing number of nonacademic electives, many of which Diane Ravitch (2000, 406) believed focused on "narcissistic themes" of self-improvement catering to adolescent whims. She was particularly critical because the dilution of discipline led to a loss in the achievement levels of poor and disadvantaged students, in general, and African American students from the poorest areas, in particular. She went on to point out that:

> the dilution of academic and behavioral standards involved not just test scores, but character issues . . . [and that] The reduction in homework not only shortened the amount of time that students spent reading, writing, and practicing their schoolwork but reduced the level of self-discipline that was expected of them. Such changes, while affecting all students,

were especially pernicious for African-American students, who did not get the rigorous high-quality education that . . . advocates such as W. E. B. DuBois, William C. Bagley, Isaac Kandel, and Kenneth Clark had called for (2000, 406).

Test scores backed up her argument of declines in the 1970s. A study of high school graduates by the US Department of Education compared the classes of 1972 and 1980 and showed that test scores had fallen, and that the percentages of graduates taking an academic curriculum had declined from 46 percent to 38 percent during the period.

Ravitch's analysis was typical of that coming out of the utilitarian-business community in the late 1980s and 1990s. As described in chapter 8, Ravitch herself admits this backlash occurred, as business leaders sought control over the schools on the grounds that they no longer produced a good product, i.e., a worker that was useful to business. But in the process, the new goal of equality lost out, and as Jonathan Kozol (2007) has described, the post–*Brown v. Board of Education* goals of integration were actually reversed, and with little fanfare, schools again segregated their student bodies by race, as the values of individual choice, and utilitarianism once again trumped the *habitus* of equal opportunity (see e. g., Waters 2007, 91–94). A new synthesis emerged in which the individual choices charter schools were celebrated, and education was focused on career preparation, future salaries, and the needs of the business community. The gains of *Brown v. Board of Education* receded into the background.

Sarcastically Kozol (2007, 109) critiques the utilitarian ethos underlying this ethic in the following way:

> If the education of some children, but not others, is to be regarded henceforth as primarily a matter of commercial training or industrial production and the products of this process are children with the value that is added to them by the skills that they acquire every year in a public school, then product-testing of these juvenile commodities appears to have a simple and unquestioned logic . . .

Dollars and cents can be seen in how education is offered for some children, and not others. Thus, in Chicago, where both Secretary of Education Duncan and President Obama lived before moving to Washington DC in 2009, the Chicago School District (85 percent black and Hispanic and 85 percent low income), had less than half of the state's per pupil spending then did the wealthy Highland Park and Deerfield schools, which are 90 percent "white and others." The pattern is found throughout the country, where greater and greater inequality has become tolerated, even as claims are asserted that schooling is about a meritocracy.

Such inequality does not of course start with the schools. Rather it starts in the continuing isolation of African America– and immigrant households in urban ghettoes, where children are likely to be exposed to drug use, are heavily policed, and have high rates of single parenthood. Under the logic of *in loco parentis*, such neighborhoods, of course, should have higher funding for their schools, in order to replace what parents have not provided.

The irony is that in the context of much information about the consequences of poverty, the United States *habitus* still sees itself at the center of the ongoing individualistic "Horatio Alger"' 'nineteenth-century morality tales of poor boys made good through grit and honest hard work. Thus, the logic insists that if given the same opportunity in terms of quality of schools, school funding, etc., a poor child should do as well as a rich child—or it's their own fault. Even as funding formulae inevitably discriminate against the poor, the veneer of curricula that assumes every child can achieve and gain access to the precincts of the power elite in Harvard Yard, Wall Street, and Washington is sustained. Thus in spite of the strong assertion that equality of opportunity is elemental to the American ethos, inequality continues to be an important feature in how students are promoted. As Jonathan Kozol is fond of writing, the schools of the early 2000s are as segregated as those of the 1960s; in fact, they are more segregated than those of the 1970s and 1980s.

Radical Individualism

But for individualism, the stuff of the romantic "poor boy makes good" "Horatio Alger" novels, is still part of the American *habitus*; in this version, inequality and disadvantage are to be overcome with individual grit, not a releveling of the field by government action. The assumption is that the marketplace rewards the meritorious and is regarded as a strength of the individual and the United States itself.

This belief in individualism is the source of much of the backlash against affirmative action and other programs, which sought to guarantee equal opportunity on the basis of race. The problem was that in seeking to prevent racial discrimination, affirmative-action programs bumped up against an equally strong faith in the importance of reward for equal achievement. By the 1990s, these concerns trumped older concerns about the consequences of racial discrimination, and the American voter began to ban the use of affirmative action in hiring and university admission decisions via legal mechanisms such as California's Proposition 209, passed in 1996.

The faith in individualism is embedded in the *habitus* of the American school system. The value of the meritocracy itself, flawed though it may be, is assumed to provide individuals with the freedom to pursue dreams in ways that countries embedded in monopolies, feudal inheritance, guilds, and other structures that restrict individual initiative do not.

For example, parental rights are often placed at the heart of the American *habitus* of individuality by advocates, and have been pushed into the public school system. Indeed they are embedded in the doctrine of *in loco parentis,* which assumes that every child has a parent to protect and guide them. Complementing this are the legal promises to parents that they can intervene individually in the education of their children. The extremes are the easiest place to see the logic of such rights, and in the United States this is found with respect to doctrines focused on the parent's right to homeschool and the protection of access to education for the disabled.

Thus at one extreme is the individualism embedded in the Americans with Disabilities Act and the Rehabilitation Act of 1973, which in part requires that every child has a right to a "Free Appropriate Education" on the same terms as a child who is not disabled. These legal doctrines permit parents to demand an Individualized Education Plan for children in an otherwise bureaucratized school. In this case, *individual* rights are used to trump the pragmatic needs of school bureaucracies to efficiently organize children into the predictable and calculable units that can be controlled from above. For example, advocates for children with autism frame the requirements in the language of individual rights to a public education, and without reference to cost:

> The Individualized Education Plan (IEP) is a written document that outlines a child's education. As the name implies, the educational program should be tailored to the individual student to provide maximum educational benefit. The key word is individual. A program that is appropriate for one child with autism may not be appropriate for another.
>
> The IEP is the cornerstone for the education of a child with a disability. It should identify the services a child needs so that he/she may grow and learn during the school year. It is also a legal document that outlines:
>
> - The child's special education plan by defining goals for the school year
> - Services needed to help the child meet those goals
> - A method of evaluating the student's progress
>
> **The objectives, goals and selected services are not just a collection of ideas on how the school may educate a child; the school district must educate your child in accordance with the IEP.** (Emphasis added; See http://www.autism-society.org/site/PageServer?pagename=life_edu_IEP)

But advocates for autistic children do not have a monopoly on the use of the language of individualism. IEPs, in which individuals put demands on the state, are not the only expression of America's individualistic *habitus* in education. The homeschool movement is also a powerful assertion of individual parental rights as well, albeit in the opposite direction. In effect, it is an individual assertion that the government has no right to intrude into the affairs of the individual family unit. Indeed, advocates for homeschoolers are among the most articulate in asserting parental rights over the education of their children, and are focused on requiring governments, colleges, and other bureaucratic institutions to evaluate homeschooling on a case-by-case basis. They too have mastered the habitual language of American individual rights:

> One of the most important applications of this right of private [parental] judgment, at least to the homeschooling community, is the right of parents to decide how their children should be educated. Parents should have a prior right to make such decisions that is superior to any claim of government. (Michael P. Farris, *The Home School Court Report*, 2006, http://www. hslda.org/parentalrights/courtreport22_6.asp)

Homeschool advocates typically argue that the United States Constitution so took such "parental rights" for granted, that they did not even mention them in the Bill of Rights:

> Moreover, it was unimaginable that a socialistic state which purported to care for children over and against fit and willing parents would ever result from the state and national governments being created in the wake of our separation from Britain. No one would ever envision a form of government that pitted fit parents against the state over the right to make decisions concerning their children.
>
> Thus, it was some time before a constitutional clash occurred between parents and the government over the right to raise children. It happened in Oregon in the 1920s, when the anti-Catholic bigotry of the era manifested itself in a law which banned all private education and demanded that children must be educated only in government schools. ("Parental Rights in Black and White" in *The Home School Court Report*, March/April 2006, http://www.hslda.org/parentalrights/default.asp)

The Supreme Court has not recognized the validity of this argument, although in each state since the 1980s, there is a powerful acknowledgment that there is such a thing as parental rights established by state legislatures, which have sanctioned homeschooling. This reflects a unique *habitus* of the United States, with its skepticism about the rights of the state. As will be discussed in the next chapter, this is not the case in many other open democratic countries, like Korea or Japan, which have a fundamentally different *habitus* with respect to the relationships between school, society, and child. At extremes, this is present in the uneasy tension between the school's right to act *in loco parentis* and the capacity of parents to demand IEPs. At its most basic, of course, is the tension present at every parent-teacher meeting where rights are negotiated, and there is inevitably a conflict of interest between the bureaucratic needs of the teacher to categorize the student relative to others, and the emotional act of parenting.

This *habitus* of individuality in the public school systems in the United States is most apparent in comparisons to other countries. But it is also apparent in the unusually wide range of K–12 institutions that have emerged in the United States. Besides homeschooling, there are of course charter schools, elite private academies, and other institutions that other countries do not have. The emphasis is even embedded in the structures of public high schools, which emphasize that students have individual schedules and go to a teacher's classroom rather than establishing a group of students as a "class" and then sending teachers to a classroom "owned" by the group of students. A further side-product of the *habitus* of individualism is the dispersal of authority in the United States through the multitude of elected districts, states, and political appointees. This gives at least a nod to the idea that it is the parents, or at least the voters, who are in charge of schooling. But again, this is only one of the three *habitus* of American schooling—along with equality (discussed above) and utilitarianism (discussed below). Individual parental and student rights cannot—and do not—always trump egalitarianism or utilitarianism. Thus, we have individual rights, at the same time desegregation orders apply to people of one race or status group. And of course, curricula is always simplified in the name of utilitarian efficiency relative to bureaucratic goals.

Utilitarian Business Models

As de Tocqueville pointed out, this odd blend of egalitarianism and individualism exists in the context of utilitarian habits that often equate the pursuit of happiness with the accumulation of wealth. Such utilitarianism is the cultural touchstone to which political discussion inevitably returns. Is the new policy cost-efficient? Does it result in future productivity gains? Are standards aligned with goals, and is there a way to see if these goals are met? Many such programs are tied to the assumed advantages of markets, i.e., the institution business people are most likely to understand.

Frederick Hess is one such advocate of utilitarian market models, and writes as if it is the only thing that matters:

> . . . accountability seeks to compel students and teachers to cooperate . . . seeks to harness the self-interest of students and educators to refocus schools and redefine the expectations of teachers and learners . . . . Today district and school leaders spend their time leading with their subordinates to cooperate because they can imagine no other ways to drive change. They are mistaken. We can drive change by requiring educators to meet clear performance goals and attaching rewards to success and consequence to failure. (Hess 2006, 78, 80)

Ravitch (2010, 149–160) has described this impulse toward accountability as an old one in urban American schools, where the goals of schooling are closely tied to performance in the capitalist job market where the incentives are not simply diplomas, but job security and salaries. Thus the ultimate measure of success for school administrators is not simply test scores, but the job market—student success in the job market is the gold standard for any American degree, be it a high school diploma, graduation certificate from vocational education, Bachelor's degree, or even a doctorate.

Hess's (2006, 78) dream is a bureaucratic structure that assumes that workers can be managed by distant administrators with a mix of incentives and sanctions, i. e., "rewards to success and consequences to failure" to do whatever it is to comply with pre-existing expectations, presumably those established by the business interests who control politics and generate demands for the workforce. Like the gods on Olympus, it is assumed that a system of manufactured adults can be created, which is rooted not in "fond wishes and good intentions," but the data of the hard-nosed businessperson poring over spreadsheets.

The irony, is that this impulse toward efficiency and utility is still an awkward fit; "tough love" policies avoid most obviously "the blueberry problem" of what to do with *individual* children who do not meet "clear performance goals," despite the rewards for success or consequences for failure, and regardless of good intentions. For that matter, unaddressed also are the problems associated with that other value deep in the American *habitus*: equality of opportunity. The calculus of utilitarianism, with its green eyeshades of clear measurable accountability, unfortunately does not fit well with those other forms of American cultural *habitus*, including egalitarianism and individualism.

So like a game of rock, paper, scissors, the emotionalized tension goes back and forth between parents, teachers, and ultimately children. No side ever actually wins, but the game goes on across time, as the uneasy dance continues in the context of a bureaucratic order.

The School Bureaucracy as a Philosophical *Habitus* for American Schools

The sum of the game of rock, paper, scissors of course is a *habitus* of cognitive dissonance, as the ideals of utilitarian bureaucratic administration and a society seeking equality of opportunity while rewarding individual achievement uneasily coexist. Political lines are drawn and redrawn between the paradoxes such tension creates, even as the nature of the dissonance limits reform. These are ultimately the limits to the *habitus* of American schooling, and for this reason, the same paradoxes and conundrums emerge and reemerge as the logical limits of each are reached.

But, whatever the lines of the political battles, highlighted are the emotions of the parents involved first not in the interests of the larger group seeking to educate a workforce, citizenry, or other larger moral community *in loco parentis*, but in that of *their* child. This is the most basic conundrum, as any high school teacher, who has say, 160 students, and must nevertheless deal with each as an individual who has two parents. The teacher may or may not be able to tell one child from another, but the parent, invested in their one child, surely can.

To cope with this paradox the teacher must have a bureaucratic mind, one that "sees like the state." In this mind, each child is necessarily viewed by the teacher as only a pre-existing unit, i.e. a "learner" which must be fitted into the template of a pre-existing curriculum; after all there is no other way to organize 160 data points. But again there is a tension in this game of *rochambo*; each one of those data points in fact has a parent who is aware of, and emotionally involved in, their individual child, and sees the teacher as a *personal* extension of their authority as indeed under the doctrine of *in loco parentis* they are. But this is of course really only a convenient fiction. But it is indeed convenient.

The end results are the lurches every few decades between doctrines of egalitarianism, individualism, and utilitarianism as questions of fairness, individual preferences, and efficiency push up against each other. Much of this lurching is unique to the American cultural system. But still, the United States while it may be at one extreme in terms of these goals, is still only one of many which has sought to institutionalized and bureaucratized education in the public sphere. Other countries value these qualities, but not necessarily in the same way, or with the same logic. And they too have habits, justifications, and cultural assumptions emerging out of *their* systems, which are not easily brought to other locations.

Plausible Alternatives? American *Habitus* and International Comparisons

American *Habitus* and Greener Grass

For a society like the United States grounded in utilitarianism, the assumption is that one more program will be identified that can then create a desired result. Internally, this emerges as models like Dewey's at the University of Chicago in 1900, or today's charter schools are pointed to as examples. The wish is that if only you could replicate what is done elsewhere, things will be ever more perfect. Or, perhaps an international model can be found, by assuming that an education is just an education, and a standardized test score an accurate measure of overall effectiveness. But of course they are not, because ultimately what tests measure is what is important to a *particular* society; even if what is important to a particular society is always changing.

Searching for Solutions: From Testing Regimes to International Comparisons

Testing is basic to the nature of the modern bureaucratized society as described in chapter 8. For this reason, elaborate testing regimes are created to regulate virtually every education system in the world. This is done as ostensibly an "objective process," but in fact is, as in every school system, is implicitly embedded in preexisting values and a system of dominance. This is a bureaucratically normal process that involves "gaming the measuring rod," as described in chapter 8. Indeed, as the overall system adapts to measure and ultimately reproduce itself, any type of internal validity is frustrated.

The testing regimes, and the "gaming" that occurs internally, was the subject of chapter 8. Chapter 10 takes this paradox one step further, and asks what it means to compare schooling regimes between countries. As Bourdieu wrote, each system has its own *habitus* of dominance. What this means is that the internal values and contradictions between systems will be different and respond to testing instruments differently. This does not mean that countries do not make cross-national comparisons. Indeed, they do so in often uncritical ways that reflect idealistic wishes for their own children. This is why the California State Board of Education adopted South Korean math standards in the 1990s in an attempt to become "more competitive" internationally. This happened even though the *habitus* of the two societies were very different. California's experiment has of course failed to meet its lofty goal of producing South Korean math whizzes in the farms of California's Central Valley.

Still, a great deal can be learned by comparing dissimilar systems. Each has its own contradictions, and as a result its own unique game of *rochambo*. The point of examining such cases is not so much what it tells about international comparisons, but what is revealed about the more general nature of education in society.

Chapter 10

The Modern World and Mass Public Education: Bureaucratized Schools around the World

Tests Scores, Mission Statements, and Institutionalized Angst

I have lived, worked, or studied in Germany, Tanzania, Thailand, and the United States. Each of these countries has a system of mass public education, which the government and people believe is the basis for the future that will come, just like Durkheim wrote. But in each there is also dissatisfaction with the existing system, and a frustration with today's youth for ostensibly being lazier, dumber, softer, and less focused than previous generations. Common coffee table talk from people in whichever country is that:

a) Our country's moral fiber is threatened because the public schools are not adequate.

b) I need to get my own child into a schooling situation that avoids the pitfall of my country.

c) Another country's education is better because either "everyone knows it," or "the international test scores show it."

d) The schools are far too bureaucratic, unfair, and don't enforce behavior rules.

e) In the past schools were much better; the better days were usually when "I" went to school.

f) And finally, that if only X were tried (pick your silver bullet), things would magically be better.

What is interesting is not so much the actual comparisons that people make around the coffee table, but that it is a similar tale of insecurity about the national self. As wrote in chapter 1, anxiety about "our" schools is a constant in every country—and for that matter at every time—as is befitting an enterprise that takes a nation most "precious resource" and forms them into adults.

Such anxiety is the result of the "self-serving fallacy" written about by social psychologists, except in reverse. Meaning, just as individuals give themselves the benefit of the doubt, they tend to be more critical of their own institutions, i.e. those that they have a personal emotional attachment to, than of institutions that they are less familiar with and not attached to.

But if this is true, so is implicit praise for "the other guys'" schools too. I have told Germans about how explicit tracking in comprehensive California schools is avoided until after the 12th grade, and there is a lament that "why can't we be that good . . ." But when I tell Californians about the advantages of tracking in German schools, including the emphasis on trades for many 16-year-olds and academic achievement in the upper tracks of the stratified system, there is the same comment: "Why can't we be that good?" They are envious of each other at the same time.

Central to this complaint about our own schools, is also a rarely recognized triumph, which is that every country (including the United States, Germany, Tanzania, and Thailand) assume that *all* children should be educated, that schooling is necessary for national revitalization, and that more or better education provides a context for solving whatever problems a country has. Notably, no one in any of these countries has ever told me that schools should be eliminated, that education is unnecessary, or that the government should not play the major role in making sure that children can read, write, and participate as citizens in creating society. Everyone believes that *not* teaching a child to read and write is tantamount to child neglect. Likewise, everyone assumes that the best way for this to happen is for *their own* seven-year-old child to continue onto study at the university. As far as I can tell, such values are virtually universally held (OK, I have never been to rural Afghanistan to verify). In each example, as is discussed below, there is always a strong demand for schooling, even in refugee camps, where the modern state is absent.

Nevertheless, mass public education is still a new phenomenon. This dominance of the modern ethos of education has within the last 200 years supplanted older values, rooted in family, farm, and tradition.[1] After all, even in the United States only one hundred years or so ago, children were routinely pulled out of class to tend to farm chores, marry, and raise a family. The faith in universal mass public education is a new international expectation and *habitus*. And while such values make sense in the context of particular political, social, and ecological conditions, there are dissonances. Just like American education is embedded in the dissonance between equality, individualism, and utilitarianism, other countries wrestle with contradictions created by their own need for both values and bureaucratic order. This chapter quickly (and briefly) first explores the nature of these dissonances in Germany, where a very different system has emerged that reflects enduring German values. The final part of the chapter is an even briefer review about the *habitus* found in the mission statements of the more advanced school systems in countries like Singapore, Korea, Canada, and Finland. In doing this, I do not undertake a comprehensive comparison of each country's education system. Rather my goal is to establish that all countries everywhere embed a unique *habitus* into the education system. This *habitus* is always bureaucratized.

In each country, it is observed that the self-conceptions of what is important as expressed is in fact different from both the United States and each other. Each presumably is tied into its own peculiar game of *rochambo*.

Building German *Bildung*, and other Habitual Conundrums

As a reminder, the *habitus* underlying the American school system is embedded in deeply held beliefs about egalitarianism, individualism, and utilitarianism. This is the strength as was discussed in Chapter 9; and an American *habitus* celebrates those values and ignore the tensions and dissonances.

But these are *American* values and *American habitus,* meaning they are not universal values. This is apparent though only in the context of an understanding of other countries' *habitus*. An example of this is in Germany, which like the United States has an old education system and strong traditions of literacy; by 1885, there were 7.5 million children attending school out of a total population of 47 million, typically for eight years (Ringer 1969, 30, 39). Nevertheless, the German system is rooted in different assumptions about what education is for, and how it reproduces modern society. Just one important element of this is what is known in German as *Bildung*, which generally is translated as "cultivation" or "education for its own sake" in part because there is no precise English translation (see e.g., Perry 2004).[2]

The value placed on a *habitus* of *Bildung* is seen in how reward structures are created in the German schooling system. This is particularly apparent in how the German bureaucracy organizes students into different streams based on ability after the fourth year of school (i. e., age 10), and has been doing so for over one hundred years. This is because, as Ringer (1968, 30) notes, *Bildung* in the late nineteenth century was not for everyone, and in fact reflected the German social stratification system,[3] as much as educational values, and meaning that it in fact had

> more to do with German social stratification than any other factor . . . [Children in the lower level schools, had were] taught reading, writing, arithmetic, and religion under a regime of the most rigorous discipline. They were destined to be useful as producers, as soldiers, and as docile subjects.

Meanwhile the boys (and just a few girls) were selected on the basis of examinations and teacher recommendations for an academic *Gymnasium* track where academies were emphasized. Reflecting the stratification system, most of these students came from the bourgeois and petty nobility.

Equality and Inequality in the German Education System

German educational traditions at the secondary level are among the oldest, with strong roots in the middle classes who received formal learning and training in order to become servants for the aristocracy and church (Ringer 1969, 15–28). By the end of the nineteenth century, Germany was industrializing quickly, as did business interests in the United States. The ruling nobility/business interests naturally looked to older systems of education when developing the new mass institutions. But the old institutions in Germany were different, and notably did not include a strong tradition of independent rural school districts as were found in the United States. Rather schools were tied to the church and nobility.

In this context Germany's stratified education system was adapted to the demands of industrialists and society for specific types of skilled laborers, while also protecting the preexisting prerogatives of the elite. A stratified school system, similar to that recommended in the United States by the Committee of Ten in the 1890s, emerged particularly in Prussia. In this system, students pursued the humanities and sciences under the tutelage of teachers who had scholarly credentials from universities. In the late nineteenth century, only a small percentage of able boys were to be sent to these schools after the four years of primary school, while the masses were educated only to that "useful" level of literacy. Not surprisingly, those admitted were often the sons of nobles and the new entrepreneurial elite, which created the system in the first place; the assumption was that this stream would be trained in the classics, and then go onto the university, and eventually staff the higher levels of German business and government. The class emerging from this educational system with its heavy emphasis on qualifying examinations, came to rule the German nation in the early twentieth century.

As for the German masses they were educated in new schools in the rural areas and cities. As in the case of the United States, those who did not make the testing cut were tracked into different functional tracks—it just happened at about 10 years old, rather than 18 years old. Those tracked into lower-level schools ended study at about age 15, after which there were apprenticeships in farming, trade, and the so-called practical trades, which today are called an *Ausbildung* (outside *Bildung*) i. e., a learned skill that does not require the *Bildung*-style cultivation found at the *Gymnasia* and universities. Many of these apprenticeships were negotiated with the German business interests. Government education ministries took charge of the new system.

The development of the German system was disrupted by World Wars I and II, but resumed afterwards with the same stratified structure in both West and East Germany, despite the destruction of the older Prussian order. During the 1960s and 1970s, the proportion of students entering the *Gymnasium* stream expanded rapidly as the social democracy of West Germany, and after 1991, a United Germany created new opportunities. Today approximately 40 percent of all German students attend *Gymnasium*. But, today still 60 percent of German children are enrolled in lower-level schools, which have since been split into two streams, including the *Hauptschule*, which ideally leads to apprenticeships after ninth grade (15–16 years old), and the *Realschule*, which leads to apprenticeships after tenth grade (16–17 years old). *Gymnasium* continued to have 13 grades until the early 2000s when reforms to reduce the total number to 12 years were introduced.

From a comparative perspective, what is interesting is that this strong segregation in the schooling did not translate into sharp socioeconomic stratification coming out of the more utilitarian tradition in the United States. Despite the stratification in the school system, Germany today has more equal distribution of income and access to social-welfare benefits including health care benefits, education, and other social-welfare programs than the United States. Measures of the Gini coefficients of income inequality, Human Development Indexes, health condition, etc., all indicate that overall Germany is a modern egalitarian social democracy, despite the strong stratification in the education system.

Thus, while education is not as strongly associated with income and social welfare as in the United States, in Germany segregation emerged in both social class and ethnicity. In the higher-level *Gymnasia*, the children of factory workers, immigrants, and hand workers were less likely to be found than the children of the German-born bourgeois. Indeed, an important predictor for success in *Gymanisum* in the early 2000s was whether a parent or parents had attended such a school themselves, and particularly whether they had an "immigrant background," meaning whether typically they or their parents were born in Turkey (see Spiegel 2009).

International Comparisons and What They Really Mean

The Finnish Miracle in the World's Imagination

Unlike any other country, the Finnish success in education captured the imaginations of educational policymakers worldwide in the early 2000s and became the envy of the various publics. Finland in the 1970s and 1980s reformed its bureaucratic-schools system and created a system that emphasized equity, public financing, and life-long learning. Ninety-nine percent of Finnish students complete the compulsory program in comprehensive schools, which brings students to age 16, and includes, one year of preschool and nine years of comprehensive school. Ninety percent complete the upper-level secondary school system, which includes both a vocational track and a separate academic track potentially leading to the university. These institutions take the student to age 18 or 19. About 25 percent of the population completes university-level tertiary programs, a rate similar to that or perhaps a little lower than that in the United States. Consistent with Scandinavian norms, all education is free of significant tuition cost to the student (see Darling Hammond 2010, 165).

Finland's school reform of the late twentieth century instituted longer periods of instruction, reorganized classes, and freed teachers' time to develop autonomy in curricular and classroom development. Linda Darling-Hammond (2010, 164–176) describes how Finland eliminated their achievement gap between the 1970s and 1990s through a series of specific policies adjustments that were sustained across decades. Those who have studied the Finnish system typically point to the high requirements for teacher training and the high level of autonomy afforded teachers in structuring classroom activity.

> The aim [of Finnish education policy] is a coherent policy geared to educational equity and a high level of education among the population as a whole. The principle of lifelong learning entails that everyone has sufficient learning skills and opportunities to develop their knowledge and skills in different learning environments throughout their life span. (Quoted in Darling-Hammond 2010, 163)

Judging from this statement, the *habitus* of Finnish schools is different again from that of the German *Bildung* or the American emphasis on utility. In Finland there is a stronger emphasis on equality and less academic stratification than in Germany, even though both countries have more overall social equality than the United States. There is also an explicit focus on "life-long learning" not necessarily found elsewhere. For an American ear, what is left out of this description of Finnish school is any mention of education as having an economic function, or that it is needed for workforce preparation.

The Finnish schools themselves are relatively small (about 300 children), and class sizes also smaller, usually 20+. Schooling is tied to the benefits of the Finnish social democracy, which provides ready access for students to meals, health care, and so forth. There are no centralized national tests in Finland, but there is monitoring of student achievement via sampling, with the result that the worst excesses of "teaching to the test" predicted by Campbell's Law are avoided, or as Darling Hammond (2010, 168) illustrates with a quote from Sahlberg:

> Finnish education policies are a result of four decades of systematic, mostly international development that has created a culture of diversity, trust, and respect within Finnish society, in general, and within its education system in particular . . . Education sector development has been grounded on equal opportunities for all, equitable distribution of resources rather than competition, intensive early interventions for prevention, and building gradual trust among education practitioners, especially teachers.

The irony of course is that praise for the success of Finnish schools is rooted in the consistently high test scores on PISA exams that Finnish students achieve relative to other countries (see Table 10.1). Despite the weak basis for making such international comparisons on the basis of such limited test scores (how do you effectively compare literacy in Finnish to Korean?), correlations between this success and favored policies are routinely identified, and in particular, pointed to by other countries as being exemplary.

Equity, Educational Policies, and Mission Statements Around the World: Singapore, Japan, Korea, and Ontario

Finland's emphasis on a "high level of education among the population as a whole," and "lifelong learning" throughout the life span, are very different goals than those found in the mission statements of American schools (see chapter 3). Other countries, of course, have yet other educational *habitus*. For example, the much admired Singapore's system, a small city-state with four official ethnic groups/languages, emphasizes the importance

Table 10.1 International Test Scores for the PISA Exam, OECD Countries—Compiled by Wikipedia.

2000		2003		2006	
Reading literacy		**Mathematics**		**Science**	
1. Finland	546	1. Finland	544	1. Finland	563
2. Canada	534	2. South Korea	542	2. Canada	534
3. New Zealand	529	3. Netherlands	538	3. Japan	531
4. Australia	528	4. Japan	534	4. New Zealand	530
5. Ireland	527	5. Canada	532	5. Australia	527
6. South Korea	525	6. Belgium	529	6. Netherlands	525
7. United Kingdom	523	7. Switzerland	527	7. South Korea	522
8. Japan	522	8. Australia	524	8. Germany	516
9. Sweden	516	9. New Zealand	523	9. United Kingdom	515
10. Austria	507	10. Czech Republic	516	10. Czech Republic	513
11. Belgium	507	11. Iceland	515	11. Switzerland	512
12. Iceland	507	12. Denmark	514	12. Austria	511
13. Norway	505	13. France	511	13. Belgium	510
14. France	505	14. Sweden	503	14. Ireland	508
15. United States	504	15. Austria	506	15. Hungary	504
16. Denmark	497	16. Germany	503	16. Sweden	503
17. Switzerland	494	17. Ireland	503	17. Poland	498
18. Spain	493	18. Slovakia	498	18. Denmark	496
19. Czech Republic	492	19. Norway	495	19. France	495
20. Italy	487	20. Luxembourg	493	20. Iceland	491
21. Germany	484	21. Poland	490	21. United States	489
22. Hungary	480	22. Hungary	490	22. Slovakia	488
23. Poland	479	23. Spain	485	23. Spain	488
24. Greece	474	24. United States	483	24. Norway	487
25. Portugal	470	25. Italy	466	25. Luxembourg	486
26. Luxembourg	441	26. Portugal	466	26. Italy	475
27. Mexico	422	27. Greece	445	27. Portugal	474
		28. Turkey	423	28. Greece	473
		29. Mexico	385	29. Turkey	424
				30. Mexico	410

of a "moral compass" in the context of developing a "zest for life" and a group-focused society, explicitly emphasizing morality and responsibility to family, community, and nation. Left out are the goals found in Western societies for achieving individual potential:

> The person who is schooled in the Singapore Education system embodies the Desired Outcomes of Education. He has a good sense of self-awareness, a sound moral compass, and the necessary skills and knowledge to take on challenges of the future. He is responsible to his family, community and nation. He appreciates the beauty of the world around him, possesses a healthy mind and body, and has a zest for life. In sum, he is
>
> • a **confident person** who has a strong sense of right and wrong, is adaptable and resilient, knows himself, is discerning in judgment, thinks independently and critically, and communicates effectively;
> • a **self-directed learner** who takes responsibility for his own learning, who questions, reflects and perseveres in the pursuit of learning;
> • an **active contributor** who is able to work effectively in teams, exercises initiative, takes calculated risks, is innovative and strives for excellence; and,
> • a **concerned citizen** who is rooted to Singapore, has a strong civic consciousness, is informed, and takes an active role in bettering the lives of others around him.
> (Source: http://www.moe.gov.sg/education/desired-outcomes/)

The South Korean system is also admired for its capacity for generating sky-high math scores (Table 10.1) is the product of a system, which, like the United States, is focused explicitly on the development of workers; indeed, in the South Korean government, education is included under the purview of the Minister for Education, Science, and Technology. In effect, the ministry views the national goal of "building a first-class country" to be the result of a unification between education, science, and technology by, among other things, making what they hope will be "happy schools."

Such goals are structured into the planning for the subject areas described in Figure 10.1.

Ironically, this table indicates that the Korean school day is dominated not by the science and mathematics for which they are envied (due to the PISA scores), but by Korean and English language instruction. Music and Fine Arts instruction is also sustained through the first ten years of education in ways it is not in the United States.

Korea's successes are all the more impressive when it is realized that this success occurred following a rapid expansion of middle and high school systems. As recently as 1980, only about half all South Korean students attended high school, and only about 75 percent went to middle school.

Subjects	School Grades	1	2	3	4	5	6	7	8	9	10	11	12
		Elementary School						Middle School			High School		
S U B J E C T A R E A S	Korean Language	Korean Language 210 328		238	204	204	204	170	136	136	136	*Korean History 68*	
	Moral Education	Mathemati-cs 120 136		34	34	34	34	68	68	34	34		
	Social Studies			102	102	102	102	102	102	136	170		
	Mathematics	Disciplined Life 60 68		136	136	136	136	136	136	102	136		
	Science			102	102	102	102	102	136	136	102		
	Practical Arts	Intelligent Life 90 102		·	·	68	68	Technology Home Economics 68 102 102			102	Elective Courses	
	Physical Education			102	102	102	102	102	102	68	68		
	Music	Pleasant Life 180 204		68	68	68	68	68	34	34	34		
	Fine Arts			68	68	68	68	34	34	68	34		
	Foreign Languages (English)	We art the first graders 80 ·		34	34	68	68	102	102	136	136		
Optional Activities		60	68	68	68	68	68	136	136	136	204		
Extra curricular Activities		30	34	34	68	68	68	68	68	68	68	8 units	
Grand Total		830	850	986	986	1,088	1,088	1,156	1,156	1,156	1,224	144 units	

Figure 10.1 Korean Education System.

Source: Korean Institute for Curriculum and Evaluation, 2008, in Darling Hammond 2010, 176.

Japan's emphasis on educational reform has a similar approach to Korea, in that the emphasis is on building human resources, as well as "friendly rivalry" in order to foster a "spiritually rich and strong Japanese people."

> Human resources are the foundation of the nation and society and the major developed countries are putting their national destiny on the line and pouring their efforts into educational reform. In order to further develop Japan into a truly rich and cultured nation that can overcome the various issues it faces as times and society change, it is necessary to open up a new era through friendly rivalry and aim to foster spiritually rich and strong Japanese people, and, as a national strategy, to further promote educational reform in all fields of education in order to develop human resources. (http://www.mext.go.jp/english/reform/index.htm)

Canada does not have a centralized ministry of education, but does have provincial ministries. The mission statement of high-scoring Ontario is as follows:

Ontario students will receive the best publicly funded education in the world, measured by high levels of achievement and engagement for all students. Successful learning outcomes will give all students the skills, knowledge and opportunities to attain their potential, to pursue lifelong learning, and to contribute to a prosperous, cohesive society.

This statement is made in the context of a comprehensive schooling system, which, like the United States, lasts 12 years. Ontario's statement itself is different again, sharing elements with the United States' emphasis on personal potential, and Finland's emphasis on lifelong learning. Emphasized is the centrality of a curriculum that can be "measured by high levels of achievement and engagement," implying the importance of testing. In addition there is a focus on public finance, since the students will receive "the best publically funded education in the world." Lifelong learning (as with the Finns) is there as well, as is an explicit connection to the economy and, like Singapore, a need to contribute to a "prosperous, cohesive society." Missing are Singapore's, South Korea's and Japan's emphasis on national identity; the Ontario statement does not indicate that reinforcement of Canadian (or Ontario) identity is central to the mission of the schools.

Such mission statements are important because of what they tell us about the way a country thinks about education—its meaning and purpose in their *habitus*. What these selected countries have in common is that they are high scoring on international comparison tests and the educational systems are the envy of other countries, although in each of these countries there is dissatisfaction and anxiety with what the schools do—and do not do—for their children. For example, both South Korean and Japanese are critical of their own school systems for creating the exam pressures, which lead to higher suicide rates and bullying.

Contrast these views to President Obama's assertion that economic capital is the primary, if not only reasons, for pursing an education:

President Barack Obama said in a speech at the University of Texas this afternoon that education "is the economic issue of our time."

Addressing a friendly and appreciative audience in Gregory Gym, the president sought to underscore the link between long-term economic prosperity and a better-educated population.

"It's an economic issue when the unemployment rate for folks who've never gone to college is almost double what it is for those who have gone to college," he said. "Education is an economic issue when nearly eight in 10 new jobs will require workforce training or a higher education by the end of this decade. Education is an economic issue when we know beyond a shadow of a doubt that countries that out-educate us today will out-compete us tomorrow." (August 9, 2010, http://www.statesman.com/blogs/content/shared-gen/blogs/austin/politics/entries/2010/08/09/education_the_economic_issue_o.html)

Conclusion: So What Do International Comparisons Really Say?

Test scores on the PISA exams are summarized in Table 10.1. The PISA scores are one of two international exams (the other is the TIMMS), and they focus on reading literacy (in whatever the national language is). Mathematics and science are presumably defined relative to international standards, rather than national standards, although both mathematical and scientific reasoning also require some type of language facility. As the table below indicates, Finland, Canada, and Korea are often near the top of these rankings. In 2010, the most recent data, schools in Shanghai, China were at the top.

The collection of reference articles that Wikipedia used as citations to these comparative rankings is illustrative of the anxieties that such scores produce, irrespective of how problematic such statistics are for validity and reliability in measuring the variable "relative international education quality":

• "La France, élève moyen de la classe OCDE" (France, average student of the OECD class) *Le Monde*, December 5, 2001
• "Miserable Noten für deutsche Schüler" (Abysmal marks for German students) *Frankfurter Allgemeine Zeitung*, December 4, 2001
• "Are we not such dunces after all?" *The Times*, United Kingdom, December 6, 2001
• "Economic Time Bomb: U. S. Teens Are Among Worst at Math" *Wall Street Journal*, December 7, 2004
• "Preocupe-se. Seu filho é mal educado." (Be worried. Your child is badly educated.) *Veja*, November 7, 2007
• "La educación española retrocede" (Spanish education moving backwards) *El País*, December 5, 2007
• "Finnish teens score high marks in latest PISA study" *Helsingin Sanomat*, November 30, 2007

Still perhaps such statistics do tell something about the overall nature of school administration, and the development of consistent plans. Linda Darling-Hammond (2010, 192) summarized what high-scoring schools from the PISA and TIMMS tests in Finland, South Korea, and Singapore had in common. As she noted, all three countries rehabilitated their school systems with sustained reform efforts lasting a period of 30 years. This sustained effort has not only put them on the top for TIMMS and PISA scores but they also graduate over 90 percent from secondary school and the majority of students go on to college. In the case of Korea, this has also translated into the highest rates of tertiary education completion (roughly the Bachelor's level) in the world. South Korea graduated 63 percent of its 25–34 year olds the Bachelor's level in 2009.[4]

Darling-Hammond (2010, 192–193) summarizes six points that all such "high performing" as defined by test-scores, countries have undertaken in order to get these results:

– They have funded schools adequately and equitably. In Finland the school system is almost entirely public, while in Korea and Singapore, the government has moved the elite private schools founded by missionaries and colonial powers under the public umbrella. Regardless of whether education funding is private or public, it is valued.
– The relationship between high international test scores and high stakes national testing systems emphasizing test-taking skills is spurious. In Korea and Finland, external (i. e., national) examination systems were eliminated. The only exams in these two countries are voluntary college entrance exams. In Singapore, there are external exams at grade 6, which require students to make extensive written responses, i. e., they are not focused on multiple choice and machine grading.
– National standards and curricula are focused on encouraging teachers to teach higher-order thinking, inquiry, and innovation. This is typically done with an emphasis on the use and design of technology and technical problems.
– All three countries built strong teacher-training programs with salaries comparable to professions like engineering.
– Teachers are provided with 15–25 hours per week for preparation, learning, student assessment, and other activities outside the classroom. They are encouraged to engage in action research and collaboration with other schools, and universities.
– Each country established goals focused on equity, improvement, and other activities to improve schools, and these goals were sustained regardless of political winds of the day.

Darling-Hammond created this list as an action plan for reforming the United States' school system; she is probably right that if policies were adopted they would focus American schools on equity, sustained funding, critical thinking, and the promotion of teaching as a well-paid and honored profession. Presumably after 20–30 years high school–graduation rates would rise, as would in-class learning.

Nevertheless, this laundry list of reforms I think begs a question, which is: Are such reforms possible in the context of an American *habitus* rooted not only in equity, but also in individualism and utilitarianism? For example, given the demand of the American *habitus* for utility, can a system that values higher-order thinking for its own sake (e. g., German *Bildung* or arts in Korea) be promoted? This may give high scores on the PISA and TIMMS exams, but how would it match the demands of the AP, SAT, and state-testing regimes for pragmatic fact-specific knowledge? Or how do you sustain policies across 20 years in a society that both values parental rights, and permits political bodies ranging from Congress all the way down to the 13,506 school boards, each to set policy and supervise teachers?

All this of course is besides the inherent flaws involved with comparing something like "reading literacy," which implies that a multitude of languages and writing systems can be compared using one exam. In addition there is the methodological question of whether there is any logical significance to the averages obtained. What does it mean to say that the United States (#15) has a 504 in math literacy, and France (#14) has a 505? Are these really distinctions that should be used to drive education policy about a particular country or pedagogical decisions?

Nevertheless, there is an anxiety around the world about how countries measure up on international comparisons. Whether the differences are real, significant, valid, or reliable is almost besides the point when evaluating a test like PISA or TIMMS. This is not surprising perhaps in a modern world embedded in bureaucracies, which habitually and necessarily compare and measure themselves from 30,000 feet because that is what they know best how to do. Measurement is indeed necessary for any such large-scale bureaucratic endeavor, but often it becomes the endeavor itself.

What they do tell us is that very different countries, like Korea, Finland, Singapore, and Canada have an unusual mastery of what TIMMS measures in terms of the mathematics, science, and language, which make up the international comparisons. It also tells us that when such very different countries do well on such a test, that there is a consensus emerging about what comprises the core of these three subjects.

But ultimately, the PISA and TIMMS comparisons are limited, as the discussion of testing in chapter 8 indicates. They do not measure anything except the international consensus about what comprises math, science, and language, which is a very limited slice of what education is in any country much less the broader world. If such national tests assist administrators like a state from 30,000 feet within the United States, the view of the worldwide comparison must be from 50,000 or 60,000 feet, which is something like using a telescope on the moon to study class room dynamics. In the process more and more detail about the *habitus* of the individual student, teacher, and classroom is lost. This is in addition to what is *not* tested for; history, many kinds of science, music, arts, foreign languages, culture, social science, sports, and so forth are obscured and devalued.

Ultimately, this reflects the fact that different school systems are expressions of shared *habitus*. While they do share some subject matter, which perhaps the TIMMS tests measures, comparative education is a far more complicated phenomenon (see appendix 10.1). Perhaps the TIMMS tests reflect an international *habitus* that does exist with respect to education in any one country. But perhaps not.

The international comparisons also do not tell us much about the role between children, parents, and society. Or, for that matter, whether they share the consequences of values with the United States rooted in individualism, equality, and utilitarianism. But if the mission statements are any indication of such issues, it would seem that the schools of other countries see themselves differently, particularly with respect to the economy. Certainly it is different from President Obama's utilitarian assertion that "education is the economic issue of our time." Germany defines education in terms of the elusive *Bildung*—which may not be easy, and Singapore sees schooling as a moral institution needed to reproduce family, society, and nation.

Appendix

Schooling without *Habitus*: Refugee Camps

Refugee camps provide a context for understanding how connected any school curriculum is to national identity. Waters and LeBlanc (2005) did not use the term *habitus* in their description of refugee camp schools, but they did demonstrate, that the absence of a state means that there is little consensus around which shared curricula, and a shared vision of the future, can emerge. Following Ramirez (1997), they write that the "myth of childhood" explains how in a refugee camp childhood socialization is connected to a plausible future is missing.

[Ramirez] notes that mass education is the institution for disseminating the five myths that legitimize a political order: (*a*) the myth of the individual, (*b*) the myth of the nation as an aggregation of individuals, (*c*) the myth of childhood socialization and continuity over the life course, (*d*) the myth of progress, and (*e*) the myth of the state as the guardian of the nation.

In each of the refugee situations they studied (Afghans in Pakistan, Mozambicans in Malawi, Indochinese in Thailand, and Burundians in Tanzania), they found that the school systems established under the auspices of the United Nations and the host country, did not anchor refugee children to a plausible future, which, due to the inherently flawed political situation refugees live in, is missing. Lacking is what Durkheim described as the "society" that needs to be reproduced. This is because in the case of modern refugees, there are three separate entities that could provide the anchor that is a national *habitus*: The home country (which is by definition is absent from the refugee camp), the host country, and the United Nations High Commissioner for Refugees, who in fact creates the schools in the first place. The result is a difficult dance between the three.

> Limitations on the development of education systems in refugee camps are reflected in the conflicting curricula that have emerged from the refugee situations . . . For example, in camps for Afghan refugees, education was seen as being a means for asserting male dominance in Pakistani camps, gender equality by the refugee relief regime, repatriation by the UNHCR, and different versions of history by refugee leaders. Whether there was a strong host state (e. g., Thailand) or a weak one (e. g., Somalia), a plethora of programs emerged as interested parties sought to satisfy a wide variety of competing constituencies.

Waters and LeBlanc (2005) go on to describe the problems associated with creating school systems under the tutelage of the United Nations. Taking the grounding of an effective "who are we?" story out schooling does not work in refugee camps because it removes the roots of what is done in the classroom from any type of cultural *habitus*. Lacking clear roots in a national identity, such schools often search in vain for a core curriculum. Decisions must be made about what language will be taught, style of numeracy curriculum, and even style of music. Potentially most controversial is the history curriculum, which ultimately rests on how the collective future is viewed. This goes back to what can be thought of as "the myth of childhood," which is really about lifelong socialization:

> Educators also are challenged by the "myth of childhood socialization and continuity over the life course." Indeed, the emptiness of this myth

is palpable from the very nature of refugee persecution and flight. Finally, by definition, refugees cannot assert that their state is the guardian of a national identity, given that the refugee is no longer part of that nation. Nevertheless, in such a context, children are still socialized. Still, despite such dissonance, a "myth" that there will be continuity through the children is necessarily sought. School systems necessarily search for such an anchor, even when it is not available or is implausible. (Waters and LeBlanc 2005, 144).

Chapter 11

Why School Reform Will Always Be with Us: Emotion and Rationalization

Introduction

The modernist dream of a perfectible society and ever more perfect union is still strong in the United States. Americans continue to believe that if we have more information, more money, more confidence, and more political will, even our children will become more perfect. Or to borrow the words of James Scott's definition of "high-modernist ideology"

> [the ideology of the modern world] is best conceived as a strong, one might even say muscle-bound, version of the self-confidence about scientific and technical progress, the expansion of production, the growing satisfaction of human needs, the mastery of nature (including human nature), and above all, the rational design of social order commensurate with the scientific under-standing of natural laws. It originated, of course, in the West, as a by-product of unprecedented progress in science and industry. (Scott 1999, 4).

But the dream is also one born of a culture, morals, and values, not just abstract and disembodied science and technical mastery of natural elements and human nature. This culture in turn is created and recreated in the modern school, which shares this faith in scientific and technical progress. This is the case in the United States despite the fact that, as de Tocqueville pointed out in the 1830s, American utilitarianism is an ideology, not a disembodied scientific force. A "can do" ideology pushed its people toward, as the US Constitution asserts, toward an ever more perfect union.

But such pragmatism does not, as de Tocqueville also noted, lend itself to deep philosophical ponderings of whether, for example, a project is possible in the first place, what the long-term unintended consequences might be, or what the underlying assumptions are about the nature of childhood. In the case of schools that product is 18-year-old adults which is in fact delivered much later; often decades later. The result is that those students, who themselves were the product of the schools, are bound to be disappointed by the elaborate promises implied by such optimistic planning.

The problem is that as de Tocqueville wrote the Americans were always attracted to the new and novel, even though in the end they were likely to be disappointed. In other words, the underside of this utilitarian people is a restless search for that ever more perfect system. This is reflected in the two- to four-year-long elections cycles to which politicians are held accountable, and hold school administrators accountable. Such a short attention span does not lend itself to the types of long-term planning Linda Darling-Hammond praised in Finland and Korea.

Philosophers know that any society exists in the context of broader assumptions. This is why perhaps de Tocqueville emphasized in the case of the Americans, that they valued individualism and egalitarianism more so than other countries. What he saw of the American character in the 1830s, of course, was a persistent *habitus,* which still endures. Again, that such values are not always reconcilable with each other, much less utilitarianism, is not a surprise. But, as in de Tocqueville's day, Americans optimistically ignore the inconsistencies, seeking not only to create that more perfect union promised in the Constitution but also a more perfect parent, teacher, child, and school system.

So despite the fact that the United States' twenty-first-century system of mass schooling, employing as it does 2–3 million teachers, and educating over 50 million children, is larger and more massive than what de Tocqueville might have imagined, I don't think that he would be too surprised about the underlying tensions. This is because the strengths and contradictions emerge out of the same *habitus* de Tocqueville observed. As in the 1830s, Americans still seek to perfect a practical system promises that they believe has practical goals, while preserving equally important for guaranteeing equal opportunity and individual rights. The relationships that students, teachers, parents, and taxpayers have with each other still emerges out of the dissonances coming from such *habitus.* But here is where the limits of American pragmatism are reached. The limits are set in the context of two irreconcilable forces in modern society: persistent parental love, in the context of all-dominating bureaucratic routines. The *habitus* of the bureaucracy ultimately, of course, wins out over the demands of parental love, but it takes 13 long years of both the parents' and child's lives to do so.

The Limits of Parental Love in Raising Modern Children

Parental attachment and love is a highly individualistic phenomenon. It occurs between a specific parent and specific child and cannot be traded, bought, or sold to another child or parents, much less to a bureaucratic school, or even the teacher hired by the school districts' Human Resources department. The parent is focused on only *their* child, and the child on *their* parent. In a society as individualistically focused as the United States, this relationship is celebrated. Parents have individual rights and responsibilities, as do children. For that matter, the state has a responsibility to not infringe on those rights, even though ultimately, schooling does just that by using a predetermined bureaucratic formula to simplify the process of creating an adult.

Ideology to the contrary, teachers hired in the labor force do not have the same emotional attachments that parents do, as I assume even third grade teacher Phillip Done would acknowledge. But the parent also cannot transmit the full range of knowledge, skills, emotions, and attachments, which create the future mass society. In the wealthy modern world, only the state can do this via a standardized and bureaucratic school systems; there are in fact limitations to what parental love can provide in a modern society. And as homeschool mothers know, parental love by itself cannot both efficiently provide routine instruction in literacy and numeracy, while also permitting them to participate in the modern differentiated work force. This is why so many parents willingly, and even enthusiastically surrender control over their child to public bureaucracies.

This is the context in which compromises emerge in the United States to accommodate the persistent commitment to individualism. Parents make demands on the school system to serve their child and meet the unique circumstances created by their values, whether these emerge out of personal religious conviction, or the accommodation of individual learning styles. "Individualized Educational Plans," which at least pretend to deliver the semblance of what the parents believe *their* child deserves, are created, even though it is not possible for a passionless bureaucracy to ever recreate what the parent provides. All it can do is view children as the abstractions of a bureaucratic state.

So children are raised both in reference to their emotionally tied parents, and the broader bureaucratized society. Some such issues are practical, focused by the demands adults believe the economy will need in the future. Others are cultural, as Durkheim and Bourdieu wrote, and are the basis for the reproduction of values, hierarchical relationships, cultural taken-for-granteds, and cultural capital. The problem is that what today's adults believe is important is often not a great predictor of what the society or its labor market will demand 30, 40, or 50 years in the future.

The Limits of Bureaucratic Efficiency in Raising Modern Children

Jamie Vollmer's "blueberry ice cream problem" reveals yet another paradox about the nature of the bureaucratically focused childhood. For there to be norms, rules, and behaviors, some people who do not match expectations must be discarded. Emotionally committed parents cannot of course generally discard their children as Viviana Zellizer (1994) argues—they stick with their offspring whatever the quality of the blueberry might be; in fact they do not even take them back for a trade-in on a better model. For the parent, *their* child is indeed priceless, and of incalculable worth. But for the bureaucratic school, funded with tax money, the child is not of incalculable worth; rather the child is a number in the budget, and a test score. And at the end of the day, or at least the end of the year, the teacher will cash their paycheck, and return to their own priceless children. During the day, they may claim that they do not and cannot discard imperfect blueberries—and in many ways they do not. But the analogy only goes so far, and in the end it is really just another one of the paradoxes that mean that schools will always be a source of anxiety and dissatisfaction. Bureaucratic efficiency has limits in its capacity to raise children that parents do not. Teachers and schools necessarily must see with the simplified vision of a state, while parents do not; the result is a struggle over what is "priceless." The problem is that in a world in which the schools are *us*, rationalization cannot trump emotion, or vice versa.

Rationalization and Emotion

The Strength of Rationalization in Mass Modern Societies

Modern society is a rationalized and bureaucratized one. As Max Weber long ago pointed out, modern society is an iron cage where there is no emotion, passion, or humanity. It is a society in which we ourselves become servants and products of what we created, locked in that iron cage. As Weber wrote, we become "narrow specialists without minds, pleasure-seekers without heart . . ." even while this "nothingness imagines has climbed to a level of humanity never before attained." This is the morality that our bureaucratic schools reproduce (Weber 2002, 158).

But having acknowledged this gloomy destiny, Weber of course went on to recognize that this happens because ever more complex institutions create an ever more wealthy economy in which all those very productive "narrow specialists" must find yet another set of specialists to help raise and educate their children, who in turn go forward and re-create that iron cage. Whether you like or dislike this prospect is a moral judgment I leave to the reader, since as Weber (2002, 158) writes

> we have fallen into the realm of value-judgments, with which this purely historical analysis should not be burdened. Nor should it be burdened by judgments rooted in faith.

The fact of the matter is that bureaucratic organization is the only way to organize a complex task like a public education system. Indeed, the public school system in many ways *is* modern society, since it is there that the habits and routines needed of adults are, as Durkheim wrote, recreated. Notably, they are not re-created in the spirit of individual parents, but of a more general "society," which in its own happenstance way expresses its values through public policy. In doing this, society inevitably puts a price on the priceless child.

The Limitations of Rationalization in Mass Modern Societies

There are though still inherent limitations to public schools, the most important of which is that it will never, ever, bureaucratize the emotion of parental love or reproduce the connections of the family. This is because, as Goldstein et al (1994, 8–9) enumerated, children are fundamentally different than the rational adults for whom such bureaucratic institutions designed. To wit:

> Unlike adults, children change developmentally frequently and rapidly;
> Unlike adults, children do not measure the passage of time by the passage of the clock, but "by the urgency of their instinctual and emotional needs.";
> Unlike adults children experience events "as happening solely with reference to their own persons";
> Unlike adults, "children are governed in much of their functioning by the irrational part of their minds";

And at least in the early years, children also do not separate the private (family) from the public (school) sphere.

Or in summary, children entering school at the age of five years old do not have a conception of the broader world; indeed it is the job of the school to create in this, a sense of institutional *habitus*—a *habitus* rooted in the very DNA of bureaucracy, and its twin behaviorism.

The Centrality of the Sacralized Child

Central to this rationalized adult world is the fact that for a significant portion of their lifetime, child and parent do indeed exist in a neither world, which is both emotional and rational at the same time. In this world, as Vivian Zelizer (1985/1994) writes it becomes necessary to "price the priceless child," and ultimately turn the child over to the outside world to be reared in the likeness of the larger society. In the context of modern society, there is really no way to avoid such a paradox.

But the sacralized child, raised in the rationalized school, ultimately creates the limitations of what can be done, as parent and institution struggle over the child. Viviana Zelizer writes of the peculiar relationship between childhood, the market, and schooling that emerged with mass public schooling in the twentieth century:

> Children were to be kept off the market, useless but loving, and off the streets, protected and supervised . . . Child work and child money became defined primarily in educational not instrumental terms . . . A profound paradox was created. The twentieth century family was defined as a sentimental institution, "the antithesis of a market economy's concept of human relations, "as Carl Degler aptly puts it. Yet even the family seemed to capitulate to the dominant cash nexus, as the value of its most precious member, the sacred child, was now routinely converted into its monetary equivalent. (Zelizer 1985/1994, 210–211)

In understanding these paradoxes, what emerges are the practical limits of what the American school can do in the American culture.

The Limitations of American Schools

The limitations of American schools are embedded in the tension between what we demand of them and what they can be; what they are, and what they are not. They are bureaucratized education systems capable of only imperfectly transmitting older values. They are not a tool for planning the future, replacing parents, or reifying a glorious past. At the same time, schools are a mass producer of adults, a competitor with parents, and employer of teachers. And ultimately they are the repository of the dreams of parents and society alike.

American schools, because they are embedded in the contradictory cultural *habitus* of egalitarianism, individualism, and utilitarianism will always come up short on each, despite having made promises to the contrary. The disappointments will be chronic as parents, teachers, and taxpayers maneuver for position and assert that what they view as theirs be restored. What is more, as Mancur Olson (1982) writes that as the society ages, and distributional coalitions form, the capacity to seek reform declines and rigidifies.

In other words, there are limitations to what schools can and cannot do for children, despite what political interests may assert. They cannot be a parent, guarantor of equality, and just employer of teachers all at the same time. And certainly they do not love a child as a parent does. By the same token, it is extraordinarily difficult for the parent to be the teacher—there just are not the economies of scale gained by having a bureaucratic institution.

Dealing with Children for What They Are—and Aren't

As for children, they are not rational calculating adults that bureaucratic action assumes, wallowing in its behavioristic assumptions about incentives and sanctions. Children are impulsive, emotional, and messy individuals, who are only in the process of becoming adults. They are unlikely to be responsive to a complex rationalized rulebook and respond only imperfectly to the incentives and sanctions proposed there. No matter how much schools or juvenile institutions assume that children are rational calculating little versions of themselves, embedded in the Pavlovian responses to economic calculation. They aren't; just ask the teacher Francesca, Philip Done, or Jaime Escalante. And as a result, they are not responsive to adult institutions like the marketplace.

What children are is curious, excitable, interesting, emotional, leaky, and sacralized. They are not just the hope for the future; they are the future. They will create society, and even take care of their parents when they grow old. But they will do these things via the clunky institutions created by the state because these indeed, are more efficient than doing it than children are as individuals.

Dealing with Parents for What they Are—and Aren't

Parents on the other hand, are (typically) adults and responsive to adult institutions. Usually, anyway. Usually because they are not likely to be responsive when it comes to their own children. They view the school through their own child's eyes, and are concerned not with the school as an institution, but for its relationship to their individual child. Their own child is always central to their view of the school, and institutions emerge to pander to this interest, whether it is access to charter schools, special programs, favoritism in sports, or elsewhere. Or as teachers are fond of saying, "squeaky wheels get the grease." In this emotion-ridden context, parents continue to be involved in schooling, and called on by teachers to assist in the bureaucratic tasks of teaching, testing, and creating adults. This works perhaps to the extent parents are indeed part of the broader society—but there are limitations. Most notably, parents are not generally teachers, and by themselves, cannot create an adult able to function in the broader world.

Dealing with Teachers for What They Are—and Aren't

The teacher is a bureaucrat hired in the labor market to raise and care for someone else's child. They are part of a guild that seeks, like other guilds, to monopolize a task, regulate entry, and exclude those whom they deem ineligible or a threat. This is an inherently paradoxical and risky position, and unlikely to be taken up by anyone without the elaborate employment guarantees extended in virtually every modern school system.

Teachers are also academically qualified in the status symbols of society—typically more so than the parents of the children they teach. In the case of the United States, this means that teachers have a college degree—a status distinction shared with only about 30 percent of adults—and specialized postgraduate training, a distinction shared with even fewer. This places teachers ahead of most parents in the social hierarchy.

What teachers are not, pretentions and professional assertions to the contrary, are parents who have a long-term commitment to one child and who can act, as the legal doctrine asserts, *in loco parentis*. Unlike teachers parents are not bureaucratic creatures, and no bureaucracy can replace them, no matter how carefully they dissect the task in university-based schools of education. Rather the commitment of teachers is to masses of children for defined periods of time—and typically for only the nine or ten months per year for which they are paid.

Dealing with Modern Schools for What They Are—and Aren't

Schools create a future society that is rationalized and bureaucratized. This society has a complex division of labor, in which we will each take on specialized tasks in a complex economy.

One of these complex roles will not be parents, even though parenting has not and will not be bureaucratized. As the example of foster care and juvenile institutions demonstrate, bureaucracies are not effective parents. And while schools at least give the illusion of being loving particularly in lower grades, not even the best teacher loves the hundreds (or thousands) of children passing through their classroom as a parent might. Teachers are perceived to have a great deal of power by both parents and children. Their words are scrutinized for meaning, and dissected for what it means in terms of hierarchy. This is formalized in later years with a system in which teachers award grades, which are for a few short years, a key source of social status in an unequal society.

Inequality and the American *Habitus*

America, like every country, has a system of social inequality, which schooling reproduces via economic, social, and cultural capital. In the United States, this system of inequality is closely related to the capacity of people and groups to succeed in a competitive capitalist market system. As discussed in the text, this is also one reason why behaviorist logic works so well in the *habitus* of the schools; it is the same logic used to describe success in the marketplace. It is also the logic which says that the product of schools is value-added for the labor market and views schooling as a financial investment for the future. But, as Robert Frank pointed out, such levels of inequality lead to competitive arms races, which cause increasing levels of debt for family and nation, as masses move into educational institutions, but without displacing demands to preserve advantages for elites which use schooling to define hierarchical-status distinctions.

There are two direct legacies resulting from the demands that public schools both sort by social status, and sustain meritocratic standards. First, is the persistent emphasis on workforce preparedness as being the mission of the schools. More so than other countries, American schools are viewed as having a responsibility to the business community, which finances them via tax money. Second, is the right of individual American family to purchase preexisting advantage in the school system via "concerted cultivation" for their children, which will perpetuate advantages via the meritocracy. To a large extent, this reflects what Bourdieu described as the need to reproduce the dominance of the established hierarchy. The net result is that the quality of education in American schools is highly dependent on the wealth of parents and neighbors, in the context of a insisting on an ideologically pure meritocracy. This of course leads to an irony, because this inequality happens in the context of an ideological commitment to equal opportunity. That there is a persistent inequality of opportunity in the United States is undoubted. It permits the hierarchy of education from Harvard Law School, which Justice Scalia claimed was the very best, all the way down to the poorest kindergarten in the Bronx or in a rural backwater. Study after study shows that this inequality is important, has lifelong consequences, and reproduces existing patterns of inequality. In the case of American society, this is no more apparent than when seen through the lens of race despite the expressed commitment to end this type of discrimination.

Jonathan Kozol in particular writes about the consequences of persistent inequalities that emerge in American schools. He writes eloquently about how this manifests itself in terms of both poverty and race. Indeed, as he emphasizes, after decades of neglecting the problem of racial segregation, American schools in the early 2000s are even more segregated than they were at the heyday of integration in the 1970s. Meaning that an African American or Latino child is more likely to be in a school that was *de facto* segregated today than in the 1970s. This is the case in places like Los Angeles, and the cities of the north. Given the persistence of the problem and despite strong efforts to the contrary, it is likely that the problem will continue well into the twenty-first century.

The reason why this is likely to persist is that while the United States is not the only country with a racial problem, it is a country with a racial problem that also has a strong belief in equal *individual* opportunity without reference to ethnicity, or other inherited group identities. And this belief, since at least 1954, dominates education policy, irrespective of the fact that it flies in the face of data that indicate opportunity continues to be shaped by wealth, social class, and race. Indeed, countries that have a weaker emphasis on individual opportunity are more successful at wrestling with their racial issues by either accepting segregation and recognizing group rights (bilingual Canada comes to mind), or emphasizing the importance of shared national identity and multilingualism, which is perhaps why Singapore is more focused on issues of "zest for life," and a "moral compass" rather than the need for racial integration as the United States is. Insisting that group identity is relevant, requires acknowledging that language and ethnicity are important distinctions which need to be preserved, as indeed other countries like Canada does for its French-speaking minority, and others. Ultimately it comes back to what Durkheim, and later Bourdieu, wrote about the nature of education systems being first and foremost an expression of the culture itself and the need of that culture to reproduce itself.

Why The United States Will Never Have *Bildung*, Happy Schools, Zesty Schools, or Lifelong Learners

Jonathan Kozol and many other Americans often wish that American schools would be more like the schools of other countries. But I believe this reflects American anxieties about their own intrinsic values, rather than specific flaws in policy or the implementation of policy. For example, Americans often wish their schools were more academic (like Singapore, Germany, and Korea), better focused on the job market requirements (like Finland and Germany), have better math students (like Finland and Korea), less income inequality (like Germany, Finland, and Canada), or better integrated (like Singapore). Each of these conditions can be found elsewhere if a search is undertaken. But such qualities are the product of a cultural system/*habitus* in which they are embedded, just as the contradictions in the American system are unique to that system.

As a result programs and systems are difficult to just borrow and inject into the DNA of American *habitus*, no matter how much political will may be exerted to say, adopt the Korean math curriculum in California. Americans have perhaps the longest experience trying to inject the academic values of German *Bildung* along with an elite emphasis on German *Gymnasium*-style academics into American schools; indeed such a goal was explicit when the American university system first emerged in the nineteenth century. German ideals were exploited explicitly by the Committee of Ten and others from elite eastern universities in the 1890s, but quickly ran into the buzz-saw of American pragmatism and egalitarianism, which saw public schools as being an engine of economic growth and individual opportunity rather than an institution for the cultivation of elite German *Bildung*.

Nevertheless, American schools still seek to adopt disembodied techniques, methods, and approaches in the utilitarian hope that input *A* will produce desired result *B*, as typically expressed in a calculable series of test scores. In this context, math programs have been imported from Korea, teaching techniques from Finland, and more math programs from Singapore. But the importation hasn't improved test scores, as promised, if for no other reason than that they are disembodied from the systemic *habitus*, culture, and practices of Korea, Finland, and Singapore.

Habitus, Education, and Pedagogy

Ultimately underneath the programs, curricula, and test scores is the conservative nature of education systems, each seeking to preserve itself, and the values of its past in a game of *rochambo*. Just as the American educational *habitus* from the 1910s still echoes in America as it replays the tensions between utilitarianism, equality, individualism, so do Germany, Singapore, Korea, and Finland struggle with their own frustrations. Except that the *habitus* is different and rooted in different values, be it the demand for *Bildung* in Germany, zest in Singapore, happy-school experiences in Korea, or lifelong learning in Finland. All this of course sounds good from the outside, but looking closely at the schooling battles in any one of these countries inevitably reveals that they suffer from the same disease: assuming that the schools elsewhere are better, and the other kids are somehow smarter. In particular, there are predictions of the imminent demise of society as it is known in their own remembered childhood, as their own unique version of *rochambo* plays itself out, which in Asia often means that America is envied for its emphases on individualistic "critical thinking," while in Germany there is an envy of the pragmatism found in the American curriculum and a vast university-system, where opportunities are available to the poor, and ethnic minorities.

Dreams of the Other: Why Other Peoples' Kids Are Always Smarter

This is of course relates to what Robert Frank wrote about perceptions of inequality, albeit writ larger, and internationally. Because parents love their children, and want the best for them—as measured against others— the failures of your own children are measured by the successes of others. In this context, every child—and every country—comes to measure itself against the achievements of others, and inevitably comes up wanting. Someone else's kid is always smarter, a better runner, a better test taker, and more clever. By the same token, another country is always doing better at what you think is important.

The irony of course is that the other children—and other countries— are performing the same mental exercise. Ultimately when it comes to their own children, comparisons often trump the cultural exceptionalism assumed in other spheres. Thus in the same way that Korea is triumphal in describing its economic gains, they wring their hands over a test-driven teen-suicide rate, even as Korea is topping international test rankings.

Why School Reform Is Always with Us

The net result of this is that given the nature of school and society, there will always be demands for reform. And this means that there will be continuing demands to use the tools of bureaucracies to reform. These tools will include demands for more precise calculation, prediction, efficiency, and centralized control. Currently, this pressure is in the form of business interests, but in the future it may again be from social work, education schools, or other bureaucratic players. What is clear is that given the nature of the task, the tug-of-war between parents and bureaucracy will never quite be resolved.

Because such a situation is ultimately not resolvable, centralized education ministries will demand more control or decentralize, depending how soon or quickly the contradictions appear. In this process there will be routine but improbable goals for "assessment" of an unassessable *habitus*.

The Improbable Goals of Assessing *Habitus*

Despite the assumptions of an "ever more perfect union" highlighted in the US Constitution, perfection cannot be achieved in a system with such contradictions. But while it is never possible to achieve perfection, it is possible to strive for it. Indeed, many of the strengths of the American system emerged out of this striving, as the system sought to educate every child and achieve a more perfect standards for equality, efficiency, and individual liberty. The mass education underlying American society today emerged from this improbable search. In particular, the unusual insistence that no child be left behind before twelfth grade—an unusually high standard in the world—provides an entrance point for immigrants, the children of the poor, and others who elsewhere are likely to be explicitly tracked out of the mainstream as 10- to 12-year-olds in many countries.

This though has come at a cost, as large numbers of youth are sustained in a school system that is not particularly challenging to large numbers, and the development of weak "non-academic" tracks for teenagers. Perhaps most importantly, it inevitably leads to a strain between parents, youth, teachers, and the public school bureaucracy, each of which is often working out its own anxieties at counter-purposes.

In this context it is perhaps not so surprising that dissatisfaction with the American public school system is a constant. Running a mass public bureaucracy that educates all children while preserving standards of utility, individualism, and equality is not possible in the short or the long term. Still there is honor in the trying. Drives to make schooling more relevant to the workforce are important for ensuring that there is an integration with cultural values of utility deeply held by the broader society. Courses in applied mathematics, communication, and focused internship resonate better than older (and obsolete) traditions that focused on Latin, Greek, or oratory, i. e., *Bildung*.

Cultural demands in the United States for racial equality have led to a broadening of opportunity for millions of children who get "second chances" not found in other educational systems. This in turn is related to issues of individualism and the belief that every child is unique and deserving—despite the practical capacity of a bureaucratic institution to deliver on such promises. In this context, there are calls for reform—typically framed in terms of utilitarianism (make the schools more productive, especially for business); individualism (No Child Left Behind, Individual Education Plans, and equalization of funding); or to make opportunity more equal (*Brown v. Board of Education*, various anti-poverty programs).

Faced with the dissonance of the situation, interests groups flee to the familiar, preferring the comfortable arrangements of the past. Teachers retreat to their unions, businesses to their school boards and legislatures, and students who knows where. What Mancur Olson (1982, 38–40) called "distributional coalitions" seek to preserve what advantages they have, while seeking yet more. The consequences are the crises schools continue to respond as political realizations emerge about the practical incapacity to achieve all tasks at the same time. But instead of giving up goals for unachievable accountability, simply new methods are tried, tests re-designed, and the incalculable calculated.

This brings me to the improbable goals of assessment. Assessment is part of the utilitarian modernist dream described by James Scott. The idea is that if a test, methods, and incentives can be identified, articulated, and administered, the future needs of a glorious new planned society can be engineered. This was the dream of the early twentieth-century hereditarians who focused on creating the talented 10 percent, along with the content and docile 90 percent. It is the dream of more sophisticated thinkers today who equate administrative and curricular design with a carefully planned and engineered future.

Thus the twentieth century is littered with administrative innovations intended to articulate activity in the schools with a desired future. The range of attributes assessed in individuals is impressive: IQ, physical fitness, patriotism, critical thinking, math facts, mathematical reasoning, spelling, reading, science facts, problem solving, bussing, school lunch programs, antipoverty programs, racial integration, critical thinking, drinking rates, smoking rates, and rates of sex, etc. Others tried to assess the preparation of the teachers, qualities of the school, actions of the parents, and so forth.

The problem with all this of course is that the children tested today are inherently assessed on yesterday's goals and objectives. But the world that they will create in the future will not be that of the past. They will instead use the *habitus* and knowledge acquired in schools to create something that was not planned for—in this context the assessment standards will be irrelevant. This relates back to the very nature of schooling and the product of its bureaucracies: future adults. In chapter 1, I wrote that this production bureaucracy is like no other because it is "self-reflective," in the sense that it is producing the adults that will in turn produce the next society. The adults produced will always seek to understand who they are and how their own schooling shaped the world they created.

But despite the fact that the products of school bureaucracy will always be of unknown quality, school bureaucracies are still just that: bureaucracies. As bureaucracies, they seek to manage themselves in a fashion that is efficient, predictable, calculable, and controlled. To do this, they seek to be accountable. The question is to whom will they be accountable for the quantity or quality of adults produced? The answer to this rhetorical question is not straightforward. At the time that the bureaucracy is established, they are accountable to the state, parents, voters, and taxpayers. Generating this accountability is the stuff of exams, and other short-term assessments with which students, teachers, parents, and citizens bludgeon each other and their politicians in the present tense. But this still says little about the future that these self-reflective adults create 30, 40, 50, or even 70 years after they began school at five years old.

Why Do Schools Continue to Calculate the Incalculable? Bureaucratic Control, Behavior, and the Ironic Irrationality of Childhood

So, ultimately, bureaucratized schools insist upon calculation of the incalculable, and control of the uncontrollable, i. e., the adults of decades hence. This need to calculate and control is the *habitus* of the any bureaucratized society, not a particular characteristic of schooling per se. But in the schools it takes on a dynamic that highlights the anxieties humans have about their children and the future. Assessment protocols have a way of assuaging these anxieties. They satisfy the bureaucratic demand for control, which somehow permits the overall system to go forward toward its unseeable and unachievable goal.

But this still leaves out the raw material. If bureaucracies behave in a predictable rationalized fashion, so do the irrational children, regardless of attempts to simplify them for the bureaucratic boxes. And so schools move forward seeking out the capacities for bureaucratic action, even while insisting that every child is precious. And while deep down every teacher does know that children are indeed precious, they still push forward with the only assumption that they can in their profession, which is that every child must always fit into the preexisting simplified box created by the bureaucracy they serve.

All that is lacking is an answer to what might be thought of as the "blueberry question." What happens to the children who do not fit the preexisting boxes, despite the skill and apparatus of control? The blueberry problem, because it is so central to the nature of modern American schools, gets a chapter of its own.

Chapter 12

From Spoiled Blueberries to Classical Social Theory

One might almost speak of a crisis of education. There are particular problems for each country, for each civilization, just as there are particular problems for each parent; but there is also a problem for the whole civilized world, and for the uncivilized so far as it is being taught by its civilized superiors; a problem which may be as acute in Japan, in China or in India as in Britain or Europe or America. The progress (I do not mean the extension) of education for several centuries has been from one aspect a drift, from another aspect a push; for it has tended to be dominated by the idea of getting on. The individual wants more education, not as an aide to the acquisition of wisdom but in order to get on; the nation wants more in order to get the better of other nations, the class wants it to get the better of other classes, or at least hold its own against them. Education is associated therefore with technical efficiency on the one hand, and with rising in society on the other. Education becomes something to which everybody has a "right," even irrespective of his capacity; and when everybody gets it-by that time, of course, in a diluted and adulterated form-then we naturally discover that education is no longer an infallible means of getting on, and people turn to another fallacy: that of "education for leisure"-without having revised their notions of "leisure." As soon as this precious motive of snobbery evaporates, the zest has gone out of education; if it is not going to mean more money, or more power over others, or a better social position, or at least a steady and respectable job, few people are going to take the trouble to acquire education. For deteriorate it as you may, education is still going to demand a good deal of drudgery. (Eliot 1932/1950, 452–453)

Eliot, T.S. (1950)

A *Habitus* of Control: Blueberry Ice Cream

In this final chapter it is appropriate to return to the blueberry ice cream story by Jamie Vollmer. For in this story is encapsulated the limits to how schools are used to reform society in a country that values utilitarianism, equality, and individualism all at the same time. More so than other stories told here, the blueberry ice cream story tells us what the limits are to what mass public education can do. It also tells us why there are likely to be as many battles about school reform in the coming century, as there have been in the last.

The Limits to Public Education of an Unequal Utilitarian Society

In essence what underlies the continuing attempts at school reform is a "*habitus* of bureaucratic control" in which politicians and administrators seek to measure and shape that which is difficult to control and measure and has only vaguely worded goals—but they are still held responsible for "results." Jamie Vollmer may travel the country telling his blueberry story about a factory that can discard imperfect inputs, i. e., blueberries, and get a surprised recognition each time. But the only reason that the surprise is elicited is that the bureaucracies have conditioned everyone to think in a particular fashion about how human affairs are organized. The *habitus* is to think of any organization—including schools—as being a production bureaucracy that controls both its inputs and has a precisely defined product; it is not about "coping," or simply getting on. Schools, as should be apparent by now, cannot do this. They are not making blueberry ice cream; rather as Durkheim wrote, they are making a future society. This is done as T. S. Eliot wrote (see Preface p. 4) in a way that "as only the Catholic and communist know, *all* education must ultimately be religious education . . . The problem turns out to be a religious problem," which again, as Max Weber (2002, 158) wrote unavoidably means that the problem is not one of historical analysis but the value-judgments that both sociologists and education scientists try so assiduously to pretend do not exist.

Control and Seeing Children Like a State Does

But even if schools are not a production bureaucracy, they still do shape lives and create ways of thinking that shape future society itself. They do this in a fashion that seeks to control their product—the children that will become the adults. The fact that logically, this control will never be absolute does not matter; a culture or *habitus* that emerges out of the attempts to control, and shape the lives, society, and even personalities of all concerned. Because, not only do institutions and bureaucracies have *habitus,* which simplifies children, so do the individuals who are shaped by those institutions, including not only children, but teachers, parents, and administrators as well.

High- and Low-Quality Blueberries

At the heart of this is the blueberry problem. Bureaucracies created to process anything, be they widgets, tires, blueberry ice cream, or adults must deal with the exceptions. In most types of bureaucracies it is possible, and even necessary, to discard the wastage. But this is not possible with children. This is the phenomenon the bureaucratic school will never completely be able to cope with; and so reform efforts will never go away. They didn't during the last one hundred years, so why should they go away in the next one hundred years? They are in fact a constant in the educational bureaucracy of the United States and every other country. They are rooted in a *habitus* of that country, the emotions invested in children, and the unique, but paradoxical cultural *habitus* that every country reproduces.

A Century of Battles over School Reform

The high modernist term "reform" implies that there is a solution to a problem—that changes or programs will make a former problem go away. Many scientific and engineering marvels have permitted this. Famine has almost disappeared (and been replaced by obesity epidemics) because the food supply is better managed. The problem of rapid transport from the eastern United States to the western United States was solved with the establishment of predictable mass air service. Pickpockets have been banished from many cities through improved policing and social-work programs. President Kennedy in 1961 set a goal of placing a man on the moon by the end of the decade, and it worked. The list of formerly bad things that have been improved and reformed could go on much longer. But the point is that once a particular reform is adopted, the idea is that the problem goes away.

But school reform of course does not work that way. No matter how vigorous the reformers are, the institutions for socializing children by the normative scripts of adults remain imperfect and a source of frustration for parents, teachers, and school administrators. Children, the focus of so much attention, are probably the most frustrated of all as they struggle to cope with the regimentation implied by the age-graded curricula. The goal itself, the creation of good productive adults, with no blueberries discarded, remains a utopian one, no matter what reform advocates may assert.

School reform is nothing new in the United States, nor in other countries. In fact, it is a constant. Americans, as well as many others have a faith that education can solve social problems and perfect society. Education and its school rooms have been, and continue to be, seen as the basis for society itself as President George H. W. Bush noted in 1990 (see page 11–12 above), and others have noted since. But, such abstract faith inevitably leads to overpromising—and in the case of the United States, this often comes in the form of utopian promises to perfect children, and by extension, society. This belief in perfectibility underlies much of school history, as reformers seek to achieve goals established by utilitarian businesses models that promise better workers, child psychologists seeking to free children from the oppressiveness of society, or the goals of immigrants, African Americans, women, and others for equal access to opportunity.

Each of these goals is in fact contradictory. But as Tyack and Cuban (1995, 3) note, "Faith in the power of education has had both positive and negative consequences [because] it has helped to persuade citizens to create the most comprehensive system of public schooling in the world . . . and install a sense of the common good." But overpromising is a problem. And it is this overpromising, i. e., the continued faith in the capacity of educational reform, that is both its strength and downfall.

Educational *Habitus* and Why School Reform is So Difficult

To understand the limitations and inherent conservativeness of school reform, a thought experiment is useful. Imagine again what someone born in the midst of America's school reforms of the 1930s experienced the twentieth century. They began school about 1935 in the midst of the Great Depression. Their teacher would have been born about 1885–1890 and been educated just before the "whole child" movement began; she undoubtedly continued to assert the importance of rote learning, avoided the new-fangled phonetics books, at least during the primary school years, and knew where the "board of education" was kept. Nevertheless, education reformers in 1935 were already attempting to create schools that would recreate the boom times they remembered, i. e., in the 1910s and 1920s.

The introduction of a high school curriculum with intelligence testing utilizing testing regimens that tracked students into future occupations was in full swing by the 1940s, when our hypothetical child was a teenager. John Dewey (1859–1952) and other reformers finally succeeded in creating a new school system in which rote learning was no longer central, and the child came to be understood as a psychological creature.

A majority of the children born in 1930 finished high school about 1948, itself a new phenomenon; fewer than 40 percent in the 1930s had completed such a level. For the first time, many would find their way into college on the coattails of the great expansion of higher education paid for by the GI Bill—indeed some 20–25 percent of the children born in 1930 would have a Bachelor's degree by the time they turned 30 in 1960.

But what of the 75–80 percent who did not complete college and did not take advantage of the GI Bill? Because the money of business interests was still needed to expand the schools, the focus in their education was on the applied skills needed in the labor market of the 1940s and 1950s. Thus after high school graduation, the bulk of the 1930 birth cohort was tracked into an industrial labor force in which factory workers, clerical workers, construction workers, managers, mechanics, housewives, and a whole range of other occupations were required. Tracking into these streams was by gender, race, and social class, among other factors.

But the industrial country that the cohort born in 1930 found themselves in during the 1950s was different than that of the pre-Depression world of the scientific planners of the 1930s. After all, our fictional cohort found themselves watching World War II as children and then schemed to become part of the great consumer economy of the 1950s. Unlike earlier generations, they bought cars and suburban houses. Jobs were still often in factories, but they made products like aircraft, plastics, automobiles, and computers, which their teachers had never dreamed of in the 1930s. They also created a new world of music and entertainment using the technology of the phonograph, radio, and television. Many of the men were drafted into the Cold War military, and some fought in Korea. The generation born in 1930 at first grudgingly and, eventually, enthusiastically asserted the importance of the Civil Rights movement, with its emphasis on racial equality, in particular, and the expansion of equal opportunity in the segregated world where African Americans lived.

The children born in 1930 felt the rush of American triumph in the 1950s and 1960s, before the tragedy of the Vietnam War. Their younger siblings, and the oldest of the 3.7 children they bore during the baby boom of 1946–1964 perhaps fought the Vietnam War and maybe demonstrated against it. Our cohort acquiesced to the demands of the women's movement and came to recognize the importance of egalitarianism in a labor market, where all had the same opportunity to seek gainful employment. More and more people previously excluded from economic opportunity found themselves working and creating wealth.

The 1930 cohort then found their way into the 1970s, as their own children grew up and graduated from high school. Their investments and pension funds financed the next technological revolutions, involving computing, mass air transport, and so forth. Our 1930 cohort became 50 in 1980 and probably was no longer working in the factory, which was beginning to disappear as the "rust belt" was created in the American Midwest, and as car manufacturing shifted overseas. Others soon found a computer on their desk. Retiring after 1990, they found chances to travel to places the teachers who taught them in elementary and high school between 1935 and 1948 never dreamed of: a peaceful Europe, China, India, and beyond. After 2000, many moved to retirement villages that catered to the "active senior," who on average could expect to live another 15 years. The survivors of the cohort of 1930 were 80 years old in 2010. A little over 50 percent have died, but many of the survivors continue to be active socially and politically. A few are still serving in political office and government advisory positions where they make policy for today's youth.

However, the original question was, what did this have to do with the educational program that the cohort born in 1930 and educated in 1935 and 1948? How much of this wonderful world actually emerged from the school houses of 1935–1948, or for that matter, the faculty meetings of the 1930s reformers? It is clear that, despite the best attempts of the scientific educators of the early twentieth century, we do not have the pre-Depression world they used as their templates. Indeed, all we have really inherited from these schools is a society still embedded in a *habitus* of utilitarianism, individualism, and egalitarianism. In effect they gave us the same insecurities and conundrums that they too inherited: in particular the tensions between bureaucratic order, business sense, and the need to develop a "whole child." It is just that the insecurities are framed differently. The old issues are now framed as a Nation at Risk Report (1982) and the No Child Left Behind Law (2002). But the question and frustrations are similar. There are a question about the relationships between children, parents, the state, and that blueberry problem. And still no one knows what to do about the bad blueberry problem.

The Persistence of the Bureaucracy

Bureaucracy, invented by the Pharaohs of Egypt, Chinese Emperors, and others remains the most efficient way to organize human tasks. Its highest form of course has been achieved in the last two hundred years with the Industrial Revolution and the creation of the modern world. But for over three thousand years, bureaucracy as a form of human organization has been becoming stronger and more pervasive, not less. And unless something extraordinary happens, bureaucracy with its dependence on rulebooks, hierarchy, efficiency, predictability, calculability, and control will dominate twenty-first-century schools. Certainly reforms will be tried, and successes achieved, but the broader social system will still seek to simplify the nature of learning, education, childhood, as James Scott wrote about in *Seeing Like a State,* and James Q. Wilson wrote in *Bureaucracy.* And as it does this, schools will re-create creatures who will turn around and complain about the process that created them. They will still create their own children, and their grandchildren and great-grandchildren, who will do things we cannot predict today, except perhaps knowing that they will complain about whatever education system they create for their progeny.

The irony of all this, is that despite our ambitions to plan and control, we will not. Lest we forget, our society in the early 2000s is deeply influenced by leaders who were born in the 1930s and 1940s and educated at a time when racial segregation was seen as normative and typing done in female-dominated secretarial pools rather than on personal computers. Encyclopedias for them were books purchased on installment plans, and not a few clicks on a computer keyboard. Lest we forget this generation also went to the moon, financed the computer revolution, ended The Cold War, and presided over the election of an African American president in 2008. And just as surely as they were taught obsolete skills in their childhood, so are we today teaching skills that will be obsolete. That the bureaucracy continues to pretend this is not the case perhaps gives it a goal and reason to exist. But it is kidding itself when it asserts that one policy or another will create a better or more efficient human being than another.

Education, Pedagogy, and *Habitus* in the American Schools

To understand how and why this faith in educational reform is so persistent, it is useful to return to the question of what exactly a national school system is, not just in the United States, but in other countries as well. As Durkheim and Bourdieu wrote, education systems are the means by which societies pass on the cultural, moral, and political capital—the *habitus*—of the older generations to the new. Schools are the means by which older generations both justify the status quo and communicate to the young what they think a moral, plausible, and good future might be. Schools do this by developing a pedagogy that expresses values in a fashion that reaffirms what they believe is good and habitually disregards the ideas—and people—who are discredited. One result is that society is never reproduced as they intend. And just as the people who created the schools of the 1930s did not train for desktop computers, those who create the schools of the 2010s cannot create the world of 2060. But they will try. And in spite of it all, the reproduction of society occurs in the context of their trying.

This brings me back to the issue of school reform. School reform in the United States has long implied that a problem can be identified, a solution developed, and the problem then solved. But solving a problem means throwing out the rejects—those are the blueberries—who do not meet the new paradigm, and as a result, the *habitus* of egalitarianism pushes back with laws that have titles like "No Child Left Behind."

In the case of schools, though, this has not happened. For at least the last one hundred years, there have been battles over school reform, many of them revolving around the same issues of accessibility, meritocracy, economic development, and fairness. That these problems have not been solved as promised is not necessarily a cause for surprise and lament but one for *analysis*. In particular it is the basis for asking questions about what roles that schools can and should play in society, and what they cannot. This analysis will not tell us how schools can become the magic tool for social development that reformers imagined. Rather such an analysis tells us what the limitations of proposed reforms are.

Most importantly, it separates the ideology of reform from the practical capacity of human institutions to change. Dreams and means are different in bureaucratic institutions, particularly ones rooted in emotions such as the schools.

The Distinction between Pedagogy and Education

Thus, my ultimate conclusion is a frustrating one: Schools will never be perfected as advocates would wish and promise. There will never be a perfectly picked-through bunch of blueberries. There will continue to be tensions, as people embedded in society argue about which pedagogy will satisfy their ideals. The only really sad thing is that the bureaucratic forms that these tasks must take, remove from consideration the more interesting questions that Durkheim raised about the nature of schools so many decades ago. As I conclude this chapter about a metaphor borrowed from a blueberry ice cream factory, it is perhaps important to return to Durkheim's most basic definition of education:

> Education is the influence exercised by adult generations on those that are
> not yet ready for social life. Its object is to arouse and to develop in the child

a certain number of [specific] physical, intellectual and moral states which are demanded of him by both the political society as a whole and the special milieu for which he is specifically destined. (Durkheim 1973, 71)

In other words, as T. S. Eliot wrote, the education system is ultimately a key religious institution, binding a people together.

Such a definition of course does not help a beginning teacher or education student solve problems of classroom management that will confront them. It does not even help them see like a state, as indeed they must; rather it only tells them that they must do so—a frustrating conclusion perhaps for the more idealistic among us. But I hope that this book does provide the context in which the problem will be addressed. And ultimately, that is the purpose of a book like this, which directs the reader back to the most basic questions of why we have schools and education.

Notes

INTRODUCTION

1. I am so focused on classical sociology that I even helped translate one of them into English (see Waters T., and D. Waters 2010; Weber 2010). For more of the emphasis on including classical theory in sociology, have a look at three of my previous books: *Bureaucratizing the Good Samaritan, The Persistence of Subsistence Agriculture*, and *When Killing is a Crime*. In different ways, these books have liberal doses of the classics of Karl Marx, Emile Durkheim, Karl Polanyi, Adam Smith, Thomas Hobbes, and especially Max Weber.
2. For a sociological exceptions to this, see Bills 2004. Bills systematically develops classical sociological understandings when describing the relationships between work and education. Sociologists Francisco Ramirez, John Meyer, and their colleagues (see e.g. Meyer, Ramirez and Soysal 1990; Meyer, et al (1992) have also been active for many years writing about the connection between world society and formal education.

2 AMERICAN MASS PUBLIC EDUCATION AND THE MODERN WORLD

1. Or as Mancur Olson (1982) describes them, "distributional coalitions," which come together to seek advantage in the establishment and maintenance of government programs.
2. The result at an extreme is that the system can be described as one valedictorian in 2010 cynically described it, by quoting H. L. Mencken:

   The aim of public education is not to spread enlightenment at all; it is simply to reduce as many individuals as possible to the same safe level, to breed and train a standardized citizenry, to down dissent and originality. That is its aim in the United States, whatever pretensions of politicians, pedagogues other such mountebanks, and that is its aim everywhere else. http://www.youtube.com/watch?v=LD17aDBVhX8

3. There is a long debate in education circles about what the purpose of schooling is, e.g. preparation for the labor force and college, or preparation for citizenship. Current (2010) testing programs assume that the primary purpose of schooling in the United States is preparation for economic activity. Indeed, this is reflected in speeches by President Obama emphasizing the role of schooling for college

and workforce preparedness. In contrast, scholars like Diane Ravitch (2010) and Desivala Meiers (1995) emphasize that the school system is preparation for a more general concept of citizenship that includes work-force prepardness but also goes beyond preparation for the narrow demands of the economy. They (and others) emphasize that schooling is also about instilling democratic values, equality, and so forth.

4. The United States was long a literate society. Evidence from seventeenth- and eighteenth-century New England indicate that literacy was widespread—indeed in the eighteenth century North American colonies were among the largest per capita consumers of English books. Literacy though was focused on reading, not writing; with the goal being to read *The Bible*, as well as an emerging popular literature, which included almanacs, newspapers, and for children "chapbooks"—moral stories designed to instruct (see Monaghan 2005).

 Learning itself was focused by a Protestant insistence that all societies fund schools, typically via the church. Monaghan (2005) writes that in the eighteenth and nineteenth centuries, "Alphabetic" instruction emphasizing reading for sounds, typically was a three-year course of instruction to gain fluency in reading the Bible out loud. Instruction in writing followed after this course was completed, though was not as universal. Emphasis was on elegance of script as much as content or composition. For the very small number of seventeenth century children who studied further, there was instruction in the numeracy needed to keep account books

5. See e.g. Becker 2008.

6. Only about one-third of the African American population in 1890 attended school (Ravitch 2000, 38). The vast majority of this population was in the South where facilities for schooling remained poor for rural whites and especially weak for rural blacks.

7. Oddly enough, W. E. B. DuBois (1903b) endorsed this position in his essay "The Talented Tenth."

8. The philosopher John Dewey (1859–1952) helped align these two interests in a "pragmatist" school of educational philosophy and was particularly active in fusing educational policies, understandings of child development, and American democracy and economy. Out of this odd alliance of business interests and "whole child" advocates emerged a pragmatic utilitarian consensus, which dominated American education at least until 1954 and *Brown v. the Board of Education*, when the Supreme Court reminded America that equality of opportunity was also a critical element of public schooling.

9. Assumptions about school curriculum have long echoes. In 1972 at age 15, I was taken to visit Washington DC for the first time by my grandmother. This was a major trip for a California boy, and many relatives began to chip in. One relative who sent me $10 to buy books about Washington DC was Aunt Lola, who was a retired teacher in Hutchinson, Kansas. She was born in 1895 and retired from teaching about 1960. She must have received her teaching certificate from the County Superintendent of Schools about 1915.

 Aunt Lola was a great admirer of Lincoln, and urged me to visit the Lincoln Memorial, Ford's Theater, and so forth. What sticks in my mind 38 years later is that in her note to me, she wrote that I must have memorized the Gettysburg Address, I assume because she had for the 35 or 45 years of her teaching career insisted that her students do so. I remember feeling very inadequate when responding to her with a thank you letter. In retrospect, I probably should not have felt so bad. My own teachers were one or two generations of education schools beyond this type of rote memorization (I only had to memorize the states and their capitals), and I had never memorized the Gettysburg Address as her students apparently did. Nevertheless, this anecdote does illustrate why and how classroom instruction is inherently resistant to change. For what it is worth, I think too, that my powers of intellectual reasoning and sense of the English language would have been better developed by memorizing the Gettysburg Address rather than the capital of North Dakota!

10. *Brown v. Board of Education* was explicitly aimed at the racially segregated system of schools found mainly in the south and rooted in the history of white racism. But the underlying legal principles it identified was that public schools must provide equal access to all and that any segregation, no matter what the reason, created inequality and was soon used as precedent by other groups. Among the inequalities identified were those rooted in gender, language abilities, and poverty, issues that at times coincided with race, but often did not.

Such issues could still be identified with the underlying principles of *Brown v. Board of Education,* which emphasized equal protection in the provision of schooling irrespective of the conditions over which a child had no control, whether it was lack of exposure to English, poverty, child abuse, or a host of other conditions. Thus, besides outlawing overt discrimination, the principles established by Brown and other decisions were to be used to justify the use of schools to remedy social and economic inequality across a range of conditions.

3   Bureaucratized Childhood and the Persistence of Schooling Systems: Irrationality in Rationality

1. Notably older forms of both production and political administration were not necessarily bureaucratic and often relied on the personality of a charismatic leader; such administration was by force of personality rather than a reliance on impersonal calculation, efficiency, predictability, hierarchy, and reliance on written rules.

4   Behaviorism, Developmentalism, and Bureaucracy: Leaky First Graders, Defiant Teenagers, Jocks, Nerds, and the Business Model

1. And perhaps most imperceptibly, but no less important, the American population changed physiologically during the last century, as ages for puberty declined as a result of nutritional, physiological, and social changes. The ages of physiological

maturity also declined into the years when "children" are of school age and confronted laws, rules, and norms, which in many ways reflected earlier *habitus*.

2. In this respect the docile adult reflects the product the schools create, irrespective of the ideologies regarding individualism. As in all human institutions, what Durkheim calls the sacred and profane are often mirror images of each other.

5 THE SORTING FUNCTION OF SCHOOLS: INSTITUTIONALIZED PRIVILEGE AND WHY HARVARD IS A SOCIAL PROBLEM FOR BOTH THE MIDDLE CLASS AND PUBLIC SCHOOL 65 IN THE BRONX

1. Criminologists call this "strain theory" because it means that there is always a strain between the capacity of people to acquire status markers and their capacity to purchase them.
2. In addition to this, by 2010, every Supreme Court Justice had been a student at Harvard or Yale Law Schools.
3. More wealthy make it into such places by filling particular spots on sports teams like sailing, lacrosse, golf, and so forth, filling "legacy slots," faculty and celebrity preferences, and so forth. Golden (2006:6–7) indeed estimates that such forms of elite "affirmative action" for the wealthy and privileged account for 33–60 percent of the admissions slots at elite universities and liberal arts colleges. It may be meritocratic, but the competition is ultimately restricted to those prequalified by reason of pedigree. In the process, the *habitus* of past elites is re-created, rewarded, and conserved.
4. Ironically, Lemann's critique of the system helped get him a position as Dean of Journalism at the elite Columbia School of Journalism in 2003. Lemann is also a 1976 graduate of Harvard University where he was President of the Harvard *Crimson* newspaper.
5. See G. Becker http://www.econlib.org/library/Enc/HumanCapital.html
6. The consequences of the American educational dystopia have been further explored by Michael Golden who investigated how America's elite systematically creates a meritocracy that rewards children who acquire the habits and practices of the upper class. To a large extent, he writes, the SAT, and other scorekeepers in the meritocracy measure the capacity of a student to comply with the demands of the preexisting power system. Such a point is further developed by Jerome Karabel (2005) who investigated the "hidden history" of admissions policies at Princeton, Harvard, and Yale. He too found that there were mechanisms and preferences in place that permitted the upper classes to be admitted and succeed at these institutions at higher rates than the poor, regardless of a presumed "level playing field." As a result of alumni and faculty preferences, special action admissions for music, elite sports, and the children of celebrities, politicians, and major donors are routine.
7. Statistics published for 2008–2009 indicated that P. S. 65 was 69 percent Hispanic/Latino; 28 percent Black, non-Hispanic; and 1 percent white. The school

continued to have a disproportionately large number of uncredentialed teachers as well. See http://www.greatschools.org/cgi-bin/ny/other/2241#students

8. Ironies abounded in schools like P. S. 65, including the fact that many of the resegregated schools were renamed for Civil Rights leaders like Martin Luther King Jr. and Thurgood Marshall were largely attended by black and Hispanic children, a situation that makes them in the argot of the school's "diverse." Indeed, P. S. 65 itself was renamed for Mother Hale, an African American hero who established a home for unwanted children of the drug-addicted.

9. Douthat (2005) described one of the initiation rituals into the rarified precincts of conservative icon William F. Buckley's salon: Midnight skinny-dipping off of Buckley's yacht.

6   Teachers, Parents, and the Teaching Profession: The Miracle of Bureaucratized Love

1. For critiques of Ravitch's position, see Wolfe in the New York Times (http://www.nytimes.com/2010/05/16/books/review/Wolfe-t.html), Salam in the National Review (http://www.nationalreview.com/agenda/255330/diane-ravitch-making-number-interesting-claims-reihan-salam), and Anderson in the Washington Post (http://www.washingtonpost.com/wp-dyn/content/article/2010/02/25/AR2010022505543.html).

7   The Child Savers

1. During recent decades, enrollments in Catholic institutions have declined. However, this has occured at the same time that enrolments in evangelical institutions have increased.

2. See http://www.acf.hhs.gov/programs/cb/stats_research/afcars/tar/report16.pdf.

8   Seeing Like a State: Efficiency, Calculability, Predictivity, Control, Testing Regimes, and School Administration

1. Similar examples could have been developed with the nationalization of school curriculum following World War I, the emergence of the SAT to evaluate university applicants (and the subsequent invention of prep schools to game that measuring stick), federal efforts to desegregate schools following the *Brown v. Board of Education* decision in 1954 (and the insistence on racial categories to do so), and the policies adopted following America's "Sputnik Moment" in 1957 (with the resultant shaping of schools to deliver science and math education at the expense of other subjects). What all these examples share in common is that a national solution was designed to address what traditionally

were local issues, and it happened in a fashion that satisfied the needs of the central bureaucracy to monitor process and national goals, as much as achieve the more general (and vague) goals of education. In doing this, each eventually foundered on the tensions between parents, children, and bureaucracy, which are embedded in the nature of modern schooling.

2. Ironically, in simplifying the product of the schools in a fashion to measure progress on testing averages, some of the most complicated algorithms imaginable were developed. Alas, they are not so complicated that they cannot be gamed!

3. *The Mismeasure of Man* is widely cited in books dealing with the study of race and ethnicity in the United States. It is rarely though discussed in the literature generated by the education establishment. I have looked for citations to the book in the many books and readings I have used for this book, and such citations are exceedingly rare.

4. It should be acknowledged that the modern educational systems did not invent the principles of promotion by examination. The Chinese "Mandarins," i.e., the civil servants selected to serve the Emperor on the basis of tests in ancient Chinese calligraphy, art, and literature is the classic manifestation of this phenomenon. This situation was replicated in the German Empire under Bismarck, and many other places.

5. Campbell's Law also extends to the companies that administer and score the tests that the school districts purchase. For an excellent critique, see Farley (2009).

10 The Modern World and Mass Public Education: Bureaucratized Schools around the World

1. Indeed, only became possible with the publication of mass market books, mass literary, and the establishment of national identities this made possible (see Anderson 1983).

2. *Bildung* as a quality has been addressed in a variety of contexts. See e.g., Ringer (1969), Habermas (1971). When I taught at Zeppelin University in Germany in 2007–2008 the concept was part of the marketing plan for the University. One of the marketing campaigns used a English/German play on words to highlight that students who came to the university were "Building *Bildung*."

3. Philosopher Jurgen Habermas in his 1971 book *Toward a Rational Society: Student Protest, Science, and Politics,* by emphasizing that in German, such gerunds always connotes an process of change and development:
   a. *Bildung* literally means "formation," but also "education" and (cultural) "cultivation." In German these narrower meanings always connote an overall developmental process. [For example] *Willensbildung,* literally "formation of the will" has been translated [poorly] as "decision making." Given the meaning of *Bildung, Willensbildung* emphasizes the process (of deliberation and discourse) through which a decision was "formed," not the moment at which it was "made."

4. http://english.yonhapnews.co.kr/national/2011/09/14/0302000000AEN201 10914006800315.HTML

Bibliography

Adler, Patricia, and Peter Adler. 2003. "Pre Adolescent Cliques, Friendships, and Identity." In *Inside Social Life*, 4th ed. Edited by Spencer Cahill. 252–272. Oxford: Oxford University Books.

Anderson, Benedict. 1983[2006]. *Imagined Communities, New Edition*. New York: Verso Books.

Becker, Howard. 2008. "Human Capital" in the Library of Economics and Liberty. http://www.econlib.org/library/Enc/HumanCapital.html

Bennett, William, Chester Finn, and John Cribb, Jr. 1999. *The Educated Child: A Parent's Guide from Preschool through Eighth Grade*. New York: The Free Press.

Bills, David. 2004. *The Sociology of Education and Work*. New York: Blackwell Publishing.

Bourdieu, Pierre, and Jean Claude Passeron. 1977[1990]. *Reproduction in Education, Society, and Culture, Second Edition*. Thousand Oaks, CA: Sage.

———. 2009. *In Sociological Theory in the Classical Era: Text and Readings*. 2nd ed. Edited by Laura Desfor Edles and Scott Appelrouth. Boston: Pine Forge Press.

Bowen, William G., Matthew M. Chingos, and Michael S. McPherson. 2009. *Crossing the Finish Line: Completing College at America's Public Universities*. Princeton, NJ: Princeton University Press.

Bronfenbrenner, Uri (1979). *The Ecology of Human Devleopment*. Cambridge: Harvard Univeristy Press.

Brooks, David. 2001. *Bobos in Paradise*. New York: Simon and Schuster.

———. 2005. "Karl's New Manifesto" in *New York Times*, May 29, 2005.

Brubaker, Rogers. 1984. The Limits of Rationality: An Essay on the Social and Moral Thought of Max Weber. New York: George Allen, and Unwin.

Campbell, Donald T. (1976). "Assessing the Impact of Planned Social Change," *Occasional Paper Series*, Paper #8, The Public Affairs Center, Dartmouth College.

Coleman, James. 1966. "Equality of Educational Opportunity" The Coleman Report Washington, DC: US Government Printing Office.

Collins, Randall. 1971. Functional and Conflict Theories of Educational Stratification. *American Sociological Review* 36:1002–1019.

———. 1979. *The Credential Society: An Historical Sociology of Education and Stratification*. New York: Academic Press.

Cuban, Larry. 1993. How Teachers Taught, Constancy and Change in American Classrooms, 1880–1990. 2nd ed. New York, Teachers College Press.

———. 2005. The Blackboard and the Bottom Line. Boston: Harvard University Press.

Currie, Elliott. 2004. The Road to Whatever. New York: Picador Press.

Darling-Hammond, Linda 2010. The Flat World and Education: How America's Commitment to Euity will Detemrine our Future. New York: Teacher College Press.

Darling-Hammond, Linda, and B. Arnett Berry. 1988. Evolution of Teacher Policy. Santa Monica, CA: Rand.

de Tocqueville, Alexis. 1836[1990]. Democracy in America, Volume 2. New York: Vintage.

Domhoff, G. William. 1998. Who Rules America in the Year 2000? Mountain View, CA: Mayfield Publishing Company.

Done, Phillip. 2005. 32 Third Graders and One Class Bunny. New York: Center Street Books.

———. 2009. Close Encounters of the Third-grade Kind. New York: Center Street Books.

Douthat, Ross Gregory. 2005. Privilege: Harvard and the Education of the Ruling Class. New York: Hyperion Books.

Douthat, Ross 2010. "The Roots of White Anxisty." New York Times, July 18, 2010.

DuBois, W. E. B. 1903a[1999]. The Souls of Black Folk. Edited by Henry Louis Gates, Jr. and Terri Hume Oliver. New York: Norton Critical Edition.

———. 1903b." The Talented Tenth." At TeachingAmercanHistory.org http://teachingamericanhistory.org/library/index.asp?document=174

Durkheim, Emile 1956. Education and Sociology. Glencoe, Ill.: Free Press.

Durkheim, Emile. 1973. On Morality and Society. Edited and Translated by Robert Bellah. Chicago: University of Chicago Press.

Eliot, T.S. 1932/1950. Selected Essays. New York: Harcourt, Brace, and Company.

Erikson, Erik 1950/1963. Childhood and Society., 2nd ed. New York: Norton.

Espenshade, Thomas J., and Alexandria Walton Radford. 2009. No longer Separate Not Yet Equal: Race and Class in Elite College Admission and Campus Life. Princeton, NJ: Princeton University Press.

Farley, Todd. 2009. Making the Grades: My Misadventures in the Standardized Testing Industry. Sausalito, CA: Polipoint Press.

Frank, Robert H. 2007. Falling Behind. Berkeley: University of California Press.

Freire, Paulo. 1968/1970. Pedagogy of the Oppressed. New York: Herdar and Herdar.

Freedman, Samuel G. 2007. "Where Teachers Await Their Fates" New York Times, October 10, 2007.

Fuller, Bruce. 2007. Standardized Childhood: The Political and Cultural Struggle over Early Education. Stanford, CA: Stanford University Press.

Gaither, Milton. 2008. Homeschool: An American History. New York: Palgrave MacMillan.

Golden, Daniel. 2006. *The Price of Admission: How America's Ruling Class Buys Its Way into Elite Colleges and Who Gets Left Outside the Gates.* New York: Three Rivers Press.

Goldin, Claudia, and Lawrence F. Katz. 2010. *The Race Between Education and Technology.* Boston: Harvard University Press.

Goldstein, Joseph, Albert J. Solnit, Sonja Goldsteing, and Anna Freud. 1996. *The Best Interests of the Child.* New York: Free Press.

Gould, Stephen Jay. 1996. *The Mismeasure of Man, Revised and Expanded Edition.* New York: Norton.

Grenfell, Michael, and David James, eds. 1998. *Bourdieu and Education: Acts of Personal Theory.* New York: Routledge.

Habermas, Juergen. 1971. *Toward a Rational Society: Student Protest, Science, and Politics.* Boston: Beacon Press.

Hall, Edward T. 1976. *Beyond Culture.* New York: Anchor Books.

Hanuschek, Eric A., John F. Kain, Daniel M. O'Brien, Steven J. Rivkin. 2005. "The Market for Teacher Quality." *NBER Working Paper 11154.*

Hayes, William. 2004. *Are We Still a Nation at Risk Twenty Years Later?* Lanham, MD: Scarecrow Press.

Hess, Frederick M. 2006. *Tough Love for Schools: Essays on Competition, Accountability, and Excellence.* Washington: American Enterprise Institute.

Hine, Thomas. 2000. *The Rise and Fall of the American Teenager.* New York: Harper Perennial

Hochschild, Arlie Russell. 1983. *The Managed Heart.* Berkeley: University of California Press.

HSLDA (Home School Legal Defense Association). 2010. "Home School Works!" http://www.hslda.org/docs/study/rudner1999/Rudner2.asp.

Ilich, Ivan. 1971. *Deschooling Society. New York: Harper and Row.*

Jones-Gore, Sherry. 2009. "What's the Hurry? A Retrospective of Former Foster Care Youth". MA Thesis, Social Science Program." CSU Chico.

Karabel, Jerome. 2005. *The Chosen: The Hidden History of Admission and Exclusion at Harvard, Yale, and Princeton.* Boston: Mariner Books.

Kett, Joseph F. 1978. *Rites of Passage: Adolescence in America 1790 to the Present.* New York: Basic Books.

Klein, Malcolm. 1995. *The American Street Gang: It's Nature, Prevalence, and Control.* New York: Oxford University Press.

Koretz, Daniel. 2009. *Measuring Up: What Educational Testing Really Tells Us.* Cambridge, MA: Harvard University Press.

Kozol, Jonathan. 2007. *Letters to a Young Teacher.* New York: Crown Publishers

Kunzman, Robert 2009. *Write These Laws on Your Children: Inside the World of Conservative Christian Homeschooling.* Boston: Beacon Press.

Lareau, Annette. 2003. *Unequal Childhoods: Class, Race, and Family Life.* Berkeley: University of California Press.

Lemann, Nicholas. 2000. *The Big Test: The Secret History of the American Meritocracy.* New York: Farrar, Straus, and Giroux.

Mathews, Jay. 1989. *Escalante: The Best Teacher in America.* New York: Harry Holt and Company.

Mathews, Jay. 2009a. *Work Hard, Be Nice: How Two Inspired Teachers Created the Most Promising Schools in America.* Chapel Hill, NC: Algonquin Books.

———. 2009b Three Smart Rules for Home School Regulation. *Washington Post* August 21, 2009.

Meiers, Deborah. 1995. *The Power of their Ideas.* Boston: Beacon Press.

Meyer, J. W., F. O. Ramirez, and N. Soysal 1992. The World Expansion of Mass Edcuation, 1870–1980. *Sociology of Education* 65:128–149.

Meyer, J. W., F. O. Ramirez, R. Robinson, and John Bell-Bennett 1977. "The World Education Revolution, 1950–1970", *Sociology of Education* 50: 242–258.

Monaghan, E. Jennifer. 2005. *Learning to Read and Write in Colonial America.* Amherst: University of Massachusetts Press.

National Council on Excellence in Education Reform (NCER) 1983. *Nation at Risk: the importance for Education Reform.*

Nieto, Sonia. 2003. *What Keeps Teachers Going?* New York: Teachers College, Columbia University.

Olson, Mancur. 1982 *The Rice and Decline of Nations: Economic Growth, Stagflation, and Social Rigidities.* New Haven, CT: Yale University Press.

O'Neill, Barry. 1994. "The Invention of the School Discipline List," *School Administrator,* December 1994.

Orfield, Gary and Chungmei Lee. 2004. "Brown at 50: King's Dream, or Plessy's Nightmare?" Harvard Civil Rights Project.

Pentasuglia-Filipek. 2008. *The Status of Violence Prevention in West Viginia Elementary Schools: A Case Study.* Marshall University. A Dissertation in partical fulfillment of the requirements for the degree of Doctor of Education in Educational Leadership.

Perry, Myers. 2004. *The Cult of Bildung: Its Downfall and Reconstitution in Fin-de-siecle Germany Rudolf Steiner and Max Weber.* New York: Oxford.

Piaget, Jean. 1970. *Science of Education and the Psychology of the Child.* Translated by Derek Coltman. New York: Orion Press.

Posnick-Goodwin. 2010. "The Blame Game." *California Teacher* 152: October 2010.

Ramirez, Francisco (1997) "The Nation State, Citizenship, and Global Change: Institutionalism and Globalization," in *International Handbook of Education and Development: Preparing Schools, Students and Nations for the Twenty-first Century,* ed. William Cummings and Noel F. McGinn (London: Elsevier), 47–62.

Ravitch, Diane. 1974. *The Great School Wars: New York City, 1805–1973.* New York: Basic Books.

———. 2000. *Left Back: A Century of Battles Over School Reform.* New York: Touchstone.

———. 2010. *The Death and Life of the Great American School System: How Testing and Choice Are Undermining Education.* New York: Basic Books.

Ravitch, Diane, and Chester Finn. 1987. *What Do Our 17-Year Olds Know: A Report on the First National Assessment of History and Literature.* New York: Harper and Rowe.

Rimm, Sylvia. 1995. *Why Bright Kids Get Poor Grades*. New York: Three Rivers Press.

Ringer, Fritz K. 1969. *The Decline of the German Mandarins: The German Academic Community 1890–1893*. Cambridge: Harvard University Press.

Ritzer, George. 2008. *The McDonaldization of Society 5*. Boston: Pine Forge.

Rudner, L. M. 1999. "Scholastic Achievement and Demographic Characteristics of Home School Students in 1998." *Education Policy Analysis Archive*.

Scott, James. 1999. *Seeing Like a State: How Certain Schemes to Improve the Human Condition Have Failed*. New Haven, CT: Yale University Press.

Sergiovanni, Thomas, J. 2009. *The Principalship: A Reflective Practice Perspective*. New York: Allyn and Bacon.

Siemsen, Cynthia. 2004. *Emotional Trials: The Moral Dilemmas of Women Criminal Defense Attorneys*. Boston: Northeastern University Press.

Sizer, Theodore. 1984. *Horace's Compromise: The Dilemma of the American High School*. Boston: Houghton Mifflin.

———. 1996. *Horace's Hope: What Works for The American High School*. New York: Houghton Mifflin.

———. 2004a. *Horace's Compromise: The Dilemma of the American High School*. Boston: Mariner Books.

———. 2004b. *The Red Pencil*. New Haven, CT: Yale University Press.

Smith, Adam 1776. *The Wealth of Nations* at http://www.econlib.org/library/Smith/smWN.html

Spiegel Magazine. 2009. "How Blunt Can One Be About Immigration?" Oct. 14, 2009. http://www.spiegel.de/international/germany/0,1518,654921,00.html.

Sprenger, Marilee. 2008 *The Developing Brain: Birth to Age Eight*. Thousand Oaks, CA: Corwin Books.

Stiglitz, Joseph Amartya Sen and Jean-Paul Fitoussi 2010. *Mismeasuring our Lives. Why GDP Does not Add Up*. New York: The New Press.

Sullivan, Dolores, P. 1994. *William Holmes McGuffey: Schoolmaster to the Nation*. Rutherford, NJ: Fairleigh Dickinson University Press.

Tyack, David, and Larry Cuban. 1995. *Tinkering Toward Utopia: A Century of Public School Reform*. Boston: Harvard University Press.

Verstegen, Deborah 1991. "Funding Rural, Smaller Schools: Strategies at the Statehouse" *Eric Digest*. www.ericdigests.org/pre9221/rural.htm

Volmer, Jamie. 2002. "The Blueberry Story". http://www.jamievollmer.com/blueberries.html.

Volokh, A., and Snell, L. 1998. "Strategies to Keep Schools Safe." The Reason Foundation. Policy Study 234.

Waller, Willard. 1932. *The Sociology of Teaching*. New York: John Wiley and Sons.

Waters, Tony. 1999. *Crime and Immigrant Youth*. Thousand Oaks, CA: Sage.

———. 2001. *Bureaucratizing the Good Samaritan: The Limits of Humanitarian Relief Operations*. Boulder, CO: Perseus Books.

———. 2005. "Why Students Think That There are Two Kinds of American History Taught. *The History Teacher*.

————. 2007. "The Sacred and the Profane in the US History Curriculum." *The Social Studies.*

————. 2007. *The Persistence of Subsistence Agriculture: Life Beneath the Level of the Marketplace.* Lanham, MD: Lexington Books.

Waters, Tony, and Kim LeBlanc. 2005. "Refugees and Education: Mass Public Schooling without a Nation-State." *Comparative Education Review* 49:129–147.

Waters, Tony, and Dagmar Waters 2010. The new Zeppelin University translation of Weber's 'Class, Status, Party' *Journal of Classical Sociology* 10(2):153-158.

Weber, Max. 1947. *From Max Weber.* Edited by H. H. Gerth and C. Wright Mills. New York: Free Press.

————. 2002. *The Protestant Ethic and the Spirit of Capitalism.* Tr. By Stephen Kalberg. Roxbury Publishing Company.

————. 2010. "The Distribution of Power within the Community: Cases, Staende, Parties." Translated by Dagmar Waters, Tony Waters, et al. *Journal of Classical Sociology* 102:137–152.

Wilder, Laura Ingalls. 1941. *Little House on the Prairie.* Harper Brothers: New York.

————. 1943 *These Happy Golden Years.* New York: Harper Brothers.

Wilson, James Q. 1991. *Bureaucracy: What Government Agencies Do and Why They Do It.* New York: Basic Books.

Wineburg, Sam. 2001. *Historical Thinking and Other Unnatural Acts.* Philadelphia, PA: Temple University Press.

Wiseman, Rosalind. 2002. *Queen Bees and Wannabes.* New York: Three Rivers Press.

Wooden, Wayne and Randy Blazak 2000. *Renegade Kids, Suburban Outlaws: From Youth Culture to Delinquency.*, 2nd ed. New York: Wadsorth.

Wollstonecraft, Mary. 1792. *A Vindication of the Rights of Women.* http://oregonstate.edu/instruct/phl302/texts/wollstonecraft/woman-contents.html

Young, Michael. 1958. *The Rise of the Meritocracy, 1870–2033: An Essay on Education and Equality.* New York: Penguin Books.

Zelizer, Viviana A. 1985. *Pricing the Priceless Child: The Changing Social Value of Children.* New York: Basic Books.

Zimmerman, Jonathan. 2009. *Small Wonder: The Little Red Schoolhouse in History and Memory.* New Haven, CT: Yale University Press.

Index